Union Relative Wage Effects

H. Gregg Lewis

Union Relative Wage Effects

A Survey

The University of Chicago Press

Chicago and London

H. GREGG LEWIS is professor emeritus of economics at Duke University and the author of *Unionism and Relative Wages in the United States: An Empirical Inquiry,* also published by the University of Chicago Press.

The University of Chicago Press, Chicago 60637
The University of Chicago Press, Ltd., London

Printed in the United States of America
95 94 93 92 91 90 89 88 87 86   5 4 3 2 1

An earlier version of Chapter 3 appeared in the *Journal of Labor Economics* 1 (January 1983): 1–27, as "Union Relative Wage Effects: A Survey of Macro Estimates."

Library of Congress Cataloging in Publication Data

Lewis, H. Gregg.
Union relative wage effects.

Includes bibliographical references and index.
1. Wages—United States—History. 2. Trade-unions—United States—History. I. Title.
HD4975.L468 1986 331.2′973 85-8663
ISBN 0-226-47721-5

In memory of my friend

Wesley S. Mellow

who gave me extraordinary help in

the preparation of this book.

Contents

List of Tables

Acknowledgments

This book is a survey of almost 200 empirical studies containing information on the relative wage effects of labor unionism in the United States. I am deeply indebted to the many authors who supplied information to me about their studies. In this connection I owe a special debt to Richard B. Freeman, James L. Medoff, and Wesley S. Mellow.

I have also benefited from discussions of portions of the book manuscript in workshops at Duke University, Appalachian State University, University of California at Los Angeles, University of Chicago, National Bureau of Economic Research at Cambridge, University of North Carolina at Chapel Hill, North Carolina State University, University of Pennsylvania, Princeton University, University of South Carolina, and Virginia Polytechnical Institute and State University.

My research and writing of the book was supported financially by the Earhart Foundation, the National Science Foundation, and the Sloan Foundation.

Portions of several of the studies were written in the language of econometrics. My colleague, George Tauchen, translated them for me, but he should not be blamed for my statistical failings. John Lew Silver and Stanley Paskoff conversed with the computer for me on numerous occasions. Martha Rappaport and Constance Rayborn typed the book manuscript.

H. G. L.

December 1984

1 A Quick Trip through the Book

1. Scope of the Survey

This book is mainly a survey of empirical studies of the union/nonunion relative wage differential or wage gap in the United States since 1963. It is an extension of my earlier survey [121] of similar studies before 1963.

That survey, which was an exhaustive one, covered 20 studies that appeared in the period 1945–61. It contains detailed reviews of each of the 20 studies. Data reported in the studies were checked back to their sources for transcription and arithmetic errors, and statistical procedures were replicated. For several of the studies in which the statistical work was not carried to the point of providing numerical estimates of the wage gap, I made the additional calculations required to reach the numerical estimates. And in several instances I made additional or alternative estimates that were prompted by disagreement with the statistical procedures used or by the availability of superior or more recent data.

The chief result of the survey was a set of estimates, by period, of the mean union/nonunion wage gap in the United States. In particular, I estimated that in 1957–58 the mean gap was 10–15 percent.

The present survey, which is certainly not an exhaustive one, covers almost 200 studies, the first of which appeared in 1966 (see References). This large number precludes study-by-study reviews. Indeed, most of the studies are identified in the text and tables only by the number attached to the study in the reference list. Moreover, most of the wage gap estimates that I have retrieved from these studies are based on wage equations fitted by computer to data stored on magnetic tape covering large numbers of individual workers or establishments. Authors seldom described in detail in their papers the instructions they gave the computer to produce the numbers they reported. Thus systematic checking of these numbers against the data tape is quite impractical. Nevertheless, I looked for signs of error and sometimes found errors. However, I will not make the outlandish claim that no errors, including my own, have gone undetected.

The list of surveyed studies, though long, does not exhaust all of the pertinent studies that have appeared since 1963. Although the list of references includes a few Ph.D. dissertations, I have not tried to assemble all of the pertinent dissertations listed annually in the *American Economic Review*. I have assembled, but not covered in this book, a considerable number of papers containing wage gap estimates for narrow groups of workers such as nurses, fire fighters, and college professors. However, a few such papers contained special features that warranted their inclusion. I have also excluded several otherwise relevant papers that reported empirical findings in too little detail to permit me to calculate wage gap estimates comparable to those discussed in later chapters or whose findings I could not interpret.

2. Wage Gaps, Wage Gains, and Wage Inequality

Chapter 2, with the above title, first defines the concept of the union/nonunion wage gap which is central to the empirical work presented in this volume. For an individual worker this wage gap is the excess of his wage if unionized (covered by a collective bargaining agreement) over his wage if nonunion (not so covered) at a given specification of his working conditions. The chief task of this book is to estimate the average wage gap for the whole U.S. work force in recent years and variations in the gap across work force sectors.

The idea behind the wage gap concept is a simple one. At any given date and set of working conditions, there is for each worker a *pair* of wage figures, one for unionized status and the other for nonunion status. Unfortunately, only one wage figure is observable, namely, that which corresponds to the worker's actual union status at the date. The other wage figure must be estimated, and the estimation task is formidable.

In most of the studies surveyed in this book, the wage gap has been estimated by fitting wage equations by ordinary least squares (OLS) to cross-section (CS) data for individual workers on wages, union status (unionized or nonunion), and other variables supposedly controlling for differences among workers in productiveness and in characteristics of their employments. I term these as Micro, OLS, CS wage equations. Chapter 2 explains how wage gap estimates may be calculated from such equations.

The wage *gain* concept defined next in Chapter 2 is quite different from that of the wage *gap*. In the gap concept the contrast is by union status in the presence of the existing unionism. Thus in this book all gap concepts involve union versus nonunion contrasts, it being understood, of course, that unionism is present. The wage gain for a worker, however, is the excess of his wage in the presence of the existing unionism, given his union status, over his wage in the absence of monopoly unionism—i.e., the absence of unions with power to affect wages. In the gain concept the contrast is a presence versus absence contrast at given union status. Thus estimation of union-induced wage gains requires estimation of wages in the hypothetical U.S. economy in which monopoly unions are absent. In Chapter 2 I argue that such wages cannot be inferred from wage equations (and related data) fitted to recent U.S. data.

For a long time students of unionism have speculated about the impact of unionism on wage inequality or wage dispersion, and in recent years several empirical papers on this subject have appeared. (These studies are reviewed in Chapter 10.) Here, too, it is important to distinguish sharply between gap contrasts (union versus nonunion in the presence of unionism) and gain contrasts (presence of existing unionism versus absence of monopoly unionism). The last section of Chapter 2 deals with these conceptual issues.

3. Estimates from Macro Equations: The Problem of Interpretation

In estimating union/nonunion wage gaps from cross-section wage equations fitted to individual-worker data, it is critical that the right-hand side of the equation include a variable classifying each worker by his union status (unionized or nonunion). The equation may include other "unionism" variables such as the fraction of workers unionized in the worker's industry or occupation or locality, but the key variable is that for union status.

Unfortunately, until the late 1960s there were no large surveys of workers containing the needed information on wages and wage-explanatory control variables that also classified the workers by their union status. Thus in the early post-1963 studies and in several later studies modeled after them two alternative procedures were used to estimate "relative wage effects" of unionism. In the first procedure, the wage equation is fitted to individual-worker data on wages and right-hand control variables, but the union status variable is replaced by an extent of unionism variable measuring the fraction of workers unionized in the worker's industry (or occupation, etc.). In the second procedure, the wage equation for individual workers is aggregated by industry (or occupation, etc.), and the resulting equation is fitted to data on the industry aggregates. The effect of the aggregation is to replace the union status variable by an extent of unionism variable. I term the wage equations yielded by these two procedures as macro equations. Chapter 3 reports "relative wage effect" estimates that I have drawn from 42 studies containing such macro equations.

In calculating these "relative wage effect" estimates from the macro equations and related data, I interpreted the extent of unionism variable as though it were a union status variable. Question: Are these "relative wage effect" estimates also *wage gap* estimates? In Chapter 3 I prove that they are not. Instead they are exactly or approximately estimates of the sum of the union/nonunion wage gap and a separate extent of unionism effect. I also show that estimates of this extent of unionism effect are very sensitive to the choice of the particular extent of unionism variable used and to the specification of the set of wage-explanatory control variables included in the equation. As a consequence, the sum of the estimates of the wage gap and the extent of unionism effect cannot be decomposed with useful precision into its two components.

4. Simultaneous Equations Estimates: The Problem of Robustness

Chapter 4, with the above title, is the first of six chapters dealing with one or another aspect of wage gap estimates drawn from wage equations fitted to individual-worker data on wages, union status, and control variables. Most of these equations were fitted to cross-section (CS) data by ordinary least squares (OLS); they are what I term Micro, OLS, CS equations. All of these Micro, OLS, CS equations fail to explain much—typically one-half or more—of the variance of wages among workers covered in the fitting of the equations. Thus we know that important control variables were omitted from the equations, and this imperfect control may lead to biased wage gap estimates. Of course, if the union status selection process were random, given the included control variables, the omission of some control variables would not be a problem. Union status selection, however, surely is not random.

One intuitively appealing way of dealing with this problem is to treat the explanation of wages and of union status selection simultaneously. This is what the 28 studies surveyed in Chapter 4 have tried to do. These simultaneous equations (SE) studies postulate a system of equations consisting of at least the wage equation or equations and one or more equations explaining union status. The equation system then is fitted to the cross-section (CS) data using techniques purportedly designed to produce unbiased wage gap estimates.

For most of the simultaneous equations (SE) estimates there are matching ordinary least squares (OLS) estimates. The SE estimates are very much more dispersed than the OLS estimates. They are not systematically smaller than the OLS figures or consistently larger. Furthermore, the SE figures display considerable sensitivity to the set of variables included in the wage and union status equations, the fitting techniques used, the assumptions made about the error terms in the equations, and the set of data to which the equations were fitted. The dispersion around zero of the differences between the OLS wage gap estimates and their matching and supposedly unbiased SE counterparts is so large that not even the sign of the omitted-variable or selectivity bias in the OLS figures is clear.

5. Estimates from Panel Data: The Problem of Measurement Error

Chapter 5 continues the search for evidence on the direction and size of the omitted-variable or selectivity bias in wage gap estimates derived from Micro, OLS, CS wage equations. The chapter covers gap estimates drawn from 17 studies using panel or longitudinal data.

The central notion underlying the methods used in the panel studies is that a worker's relative wage position, though subject to life cycle and transitory changes, tends to persist over time and that a substantial part of this persistent or fixed component of his relative wage may remain unobserved to the econometrician. This component, fixed for each worker but varying across workers, may be correlated with worker union status. However, the fixed component may be eliminated by comparing the relative wage of each worker at one date with *his* relative wage at another date. These time series wage comparisons are the key ingredient of the panel studies.

From most of the 17 panel studies I was able to draw both panel and corresponding cross-section (CS) wage gap estimates. With few exceptions the panel estimates were smaller than the CS estimates. The average ratio of panel to CS gap estimate was close to one-half. Thus these studies suggest that Micro, OLS, CS wage gap estimates may be upward biased by a factor as large as two.

However, I am reluctant to accept this suggestion. In the first place, the dispersion in the ratio of panel to CS wage gap estimates was large. The ratios varied from close to zero to close to unity, making it difficult to estimate with precision the amount of bias in the CS estimates if, indeed, it is the CS estimates that are biased. But, second and more important, I fear that the *panel* estimates are seriously downward biased by union status measurement errors. All of the panel studies rely heavily on accurate distinction in the panel data between workers who changed their union status and those who did not. Unfortunately, data from the panel studies suggest that appreciable fractions of those *reported* as changing status probably experienced no status change. Such inaccuracy in the status change data is very likely to lead to downward bias in the ratio of panel to cross-section wage gap estimates.

I present empirical evidence in Chapter 5 that misclassification of workers by union status may account for all of the average difference between panel and CS gap estimates and, in addition, for part of the dispersion in the ratio of the two estimates. Thus after surveying both simultaneous equations and panel wage gap estimates, I have come up empty-handed in my search for the sign and numerical size of the omitted-variable or selectivity bias in Micro, OLS, CS gap estimates.

6. Micro, OLS, CS Estimates: Data Problems

Most of the available estimates of union/nonunion wage gaps come from Micro, OLS, CS wage equations. These estimates, I have argued, may suffer from omitted-variable or selectivity bias. But this is not the only source of error in these (and other) wage gap estimates. In Chapter 6, with the above title, I examine estimate errors arising from four types of imperfections in the data other than failure to observe unobservables: (a) the omission of fringe benefits in the dependent wage variable, (b) the use of an annual or weekly wage instead of an hourly wage, (c) misclassification of workers by union status, and (d) nonrandomness by design in some of the commonly used micro-data sets.

In the most commonly used household surveys the wage measures that may be calculated from the data exclude employer expenditures for fringe benefits that are not paid directly to workers and hence do not show up promptly in worker pay envelopes. I have derived estimates of the effects on wage gap estimates of these omitted employer expenditures from 23 studies surveyed in Chapter 6. From these studies I estimate that inclusion of the fringe benefit expenditures would raise mean wage gap estimates for the U.S. work force as a whole by two or three percentage points depending on the underlying wage measure used.

In a substantial fraction of the studies from which I have drawn wage gap estimates the dependent variable was annual or weekly earnings rather than an hourly earnings or wage figure. If unionism produces a union/nonunion differential or gap in hours worked, wage gaps estimated from annual or weekly earnings will differ from those estimated from hourly wage figures. I have calculated hours gap estimates from 16 different studies surveyed in Chapter 6. Among the studies with at least moderately broad worker coverage, the hours *per year* gap was about minus 3 percentage points and the hours *per week* gap was about minus 1.8 percentage points. That is, wage gap estimates based on annual earnings tend to be about 3 percentage points lower and those based on weekly earnings about 1.8 percentage points lower than corresponding estimates based on hourly earnings.

The union status questions in the commonly used large sample surveys are simple ones. There is good reason, therefore, for expecting that in these surveys only a small fraction of workers were misclassified by union status. The evidence we have on the extent of misclassification is consistent with this expectation (see Chapters 5 and 6). Although even a small fraction of misclassified workers may lead to large bias in wage gap estimates obtained by panel methods, the corresponding bias in Micro, OLS,

CS gap estimates is likely to be small and of uncertain sign. At present we have too little empirical evidence—I am able to cite only two studies in Chapter 6—to estimate the size of the bias in Micro, OLS, CS gap estimates.

The *National Longitudinal Surveys* (NLS) and a portion (the so-called nonrandom half) of the *Survey of Economic Opportunity* (SEO) and of each of the surveys of the *Panel Study of Income Dynamics* (PSID) were not random samples of the U.S. population. In particular, in all of these surveys the relative frequency of black workers was much higher than in the corresponding U.S. population. This nonrandomness probably leads to a negligible problem of bias in Micro, OLS, CS wage gap estimates if the underlying wage equations are fitted separately by color to the data. Then the only problem is to use the appropriate population weights in averaging the black and white gap estimates, which I have uniformly attempted to do.

However, Micro, OLS, CS wage equations often were fitted to the combined data for both black and white workers. Then the resulting wage gap estimate is an average of underlying separate gap estimates by color, in which the black gap estimate is heavily overweighted unless in fitting the wage equation each observation is weighted by the reciprocal of its sampling probability. Such weighting, however, seldom was done. In Chapter 8 I estimate that the (upward) bias from overweighting of blacks was about 1.2 percentage points in the PSID and SEO, about 2.4 percentage points for the NLS Older Men, and about minus 0.9 percentage points for the NLS Young Men.

Chapter 6 also briefly discusses biases produced by the use of a money rather than real wage, a union membership rather than a collective bargaining concept of union status, and by the nonrandomness caused by excluding workers with missing data.

7. Micro, OLS, CS Estimates: Variations in the Wage Gap across the Labor Force

Chapter 7 is the first of three chapters that survey the wage gap estimates derived from Micro, OLS, CS wage equations provided by the large number of empirical studies that have appeared since 1963. This chapter, for example, cites 91 studies. The focus of Chapter 7 is on the question: Does the union/nonunion wage gap vary across the U.S. work force by characteristics of workers and their workplaces and, if so, by how much?

Wage gap differences are estimated for each of the following worker and workplace characteristics: sex, color, marital status, major industry, major occupation, region, city size, years of schooling completed, age, years of labor market experience, years of seniority with current employer, extent of unionism (in the industry, occupation, etc.), private versus government employment, establishment or firm size, industry or locality unemployment rate, industry concentration ratio, workplace hazards, worker health status, and worker military veteran status.

On the basis of the evidence presented in Chapter 7, the wage gap is certainly not a constant across the U.S. work force, though the gap differences by sex, veteran status, extent of unionism, and perhaps industry concentration ratio appear to be small or of uncertain sign. The gap is greater for black workers than for white (though here one of the chief data sources indicates no color difference), for nonmanufacturing than for manufacturing, for construction than for other nonmanufacturing, for blue-collar than for white-collar workers, for laborers than for operatives, for operatives than for craftsmen, for the South than for the Northeast region, for small cities than for large, for private than for government employees, for workers reporting poor health than for workers reporting good health, for hazardous than for other work, for other marital status than for the married. The wage gap falls as years of schooling, establishment or firm size, and industry unemployment rates rise. For age, years of experience, and years of seniority the gap at first and for some time falls and then rises.

These union/nonunion gap differences reflect differences by union status in the U.S. relative wage structure. The structure of relative wages for unionized status is not the same as that for nonunion status. For example, in both structures wages rise as schooling completed rises, but the gap between them falls. Thus, since the gap is positive, except perhaps at very high schooling, there is less dispersion or inequality by schooling in the unionized than in the nonunion wage structure. Is what is true of schooling true in general? The answer in both Chapters 7 and 10 is negative.

8. Micro, OLS, CS Estimates: Calculating and Adjusting Mean Wage Gap Estimates

The focus in Chapters 8 and 9 is on the average union/nonunion wage gap in the U.S. work force in recent years. The basic estimation inputs are fitted Micro, OLS, CS wage equations and related numbers reported in (or obtained by correspondence with the authors of) recent studies of wage differentials in the United States. Since the focus in these chapters is on the overall mean wage gap, I have ignored studies in which the worker coverage was narrow—nurses, police, fire fighters, and even sectors as large as that of contract construction.

In Chapter 9 I first calculated for each broad coverage Micro, OLS, CS wage equation the unadjusted estimate of the mean wage gap. I then adjusted these estimates for nonrandomness in the underlying data files, differences in the left-hand wage variable, incomplete worker coverage, and incompleteness in the set of right-hand wage-explanatory control variables as follows: (1) overweighting of blacks, (2) omission of fringe benefit expenditures, (3) use of an annual or weekly wage rather than hourly wage, (4) use of an arithmetic rather than logarithmic dependent wage variable, (5) omission of black workers, (6) omission of workers employed in nonmanufacturing, (7) omission of white-collar workers, (8) omission of blue-collar workers, (9) omission of workers employed outside of Standard Metropolitan Statistical Areas, (10) age adjustment for estimates drawn from the *National Longitudinal Survey of Young Men*, (11) omission of workers less than 25 years of age, (12) omission of government workers, (13) omission of occupation as a control variable, (14) omission of industry as a control variable, and (15) omission of extent of unionism as a control variable. These adjustments are spelled out in Chapter 8. The purpose of these adjustments was to bring the unadjusted estimates more nearly into equality by accounting for some of the factors that I thought had produced dispersion among them. Although the adjustments were not perfect, they did reduce the dispersion considerably.

9. The Adjusted Micro, OLS, CS Gap Estimates

Chapter 9 presents unadjusted and adjusted estimates of the U.S. overall mean wage gap drawn from Micro, OLS, CS wage equations reported in 117 different studies. For each study I selected what I regarded as the best unadjusted estimate—that requiring the least adjustment. These best estimates were sorted by year or period, and for each year or period again I selected the best estimates. The upshot of this survey is a set of wage gap estimates (%), one for each year in the period 1967–79 as follows:

1967 = 12%, 1968 = 12%, 1969 = 12%, 1970 = 13%,
1971 = 16%, 1972 = 13%, 1973 = 16%, 1974 = 15%,
1975 = 17%, 1976 = 20%, 1977 = 19%, 1978 = 19%,
1979 = 14%, mean 1967–79 = 15%.

(The estimates for 1967–70 are within the estimate range, 10%–15%, that I made for 1957–58 in my 1963 survey.) I have much more confidence, of course, in the mean estimate, 15 percent for 1967–79, than in the individual yearly figures which range from 12 to 20 percent and show an upward trend.

I describe these estimates of the U.S. mean wage gap, all derived from Micro, OLS, CS wage equations, as "upper bounds" because I believe that in general such estimates suffer from upward bias resulting from the omission of control variables correlated with the union status variable. I do not rule out the possibility that during 1967–79 the U.S. mean wage gap averaged as high as 15 percent, but I suspect that the average was lower.

10. Unions and Relative Wage Inequality

In Chapter 10 the focus shifts to questions about the effects of unionism on wage inequality. Has unionism raised the relative wage position of black workers? Of female workers? What has been the effect of unionism on the overall dispersion of relative wages among individual workers? As they stand, these questions are ambiguous because it is unclear whether the unionism effect is a *gap* effect in which the contrast is by union status in the presence of unionism or a *gain* effect in which the contrast is between the existing unionism and its "absence." In Chapter 2 I argue that *gap* effects may be estimated, though probably with some error, from Micro, OLS, CS wage equations but that *gain* effects cannot be estimated from these equations.

Yet three recent studies reviewed in Chapter 10 purport to estimate black/white or female/male differences in union-induced relative wage gains. I show there that the "gain" estimates consist only of a gap component that can be estimated and omit a gain component of unknown sign and size. In Chapter 7 I estimate that the union/nonunion gap in the female/male wage differential was small. I also estimate there that the corresponding gap for the black/white differential was perhaps 5–10 percent.

Chapter 10 also reviews 10 recent papers that report numbers described as estimates in the gain sense of the impact of unionism on relative wage dispersion among individual workers. In two of the studies there are strong suggestions that for blue-collar workers in manufacturing unionism has made wage dispersion smaller for unionized status than for nonunion status. This is a *gap* effect. However, none of the studies has provided estimates of the union/nonunion *gap* in wage dispersion for the whole U.S. work force, although two studies hint that this gap is close to zero. And none of the studies has estimated the effects of unionism in the gain ("presence versus absence") sense on the overall wage inequality in the U.S. work force or in any of its parts.

2 Wage Gaps, Wage Gains, and Wage Inequality

1. The Union/Nonunion Relative Wage Gap

This book is mainly a survey of estimates of union/nonunion relative wage differentials or *gaps* provided by a large number of post–1963 studies of wage differentials in the United States. For an individual worker the wage gap is the excess of his wage if unionized (covered by a collective bargaining agreement) over his wage if nonunion (not so covered) at a given specification of his working conditions.

We know far too little about wage determination in all of its fine detail to estimate the wage gap worker by worker. However, the task of estimating the mean wage gap for the whole U.S. labor force and even for some of its large segments is not, I think, so formidable. This is the central task of this book.

In recent years the wage gap, so understood, usually has been estimated by fitting wage equations to cross-section (CS), individual-worker (micro) data on wages, union status (union or nonunion), and other variables supposedly controlling for differences among workers in working conditions and worker quality. Most of these equations are encompassed in their form by equation (2.1):

$$W = a_n + a_{nx}x + a_{ny}y + U[(a_u - a_n) + (a_{ux} - a_{nx})x + (a_{uy} - a_{ny})y] + e, \tag{2.1}$$

where W is the natural logarithm of a worker's wage, x is a set of variables specifying the working conditions and quality of the worker, y is the fraction of workers who are unionized in the industry (or geographic area, or occupation, etc.) in which the worker is employed, U is the union status of the worker (equal to unity if unionized and zero if nonunion), e is a residual reflecting left-out variables, and the a's are the estimated coefficients of the equation. I term y an *extent of unionism* variable. (In the empirical wage equations covered in this survey extent of unionism variables y more often than not were omitted.) Equation (2.1) may be rewritten and sometimes has been fitted as two separate equations:

$$W_i = a_i + a_{ix}x + a_{iy}y + e_i; \; i = u \text{ if } U = 1; \; i = n \text{ if } U = 0. \tag{2.2}$$

Frequently the wage equations contained few or no cross-product or interaction terms Ux or Uy between union status U and other right-hand variables x or y. When there are no such cross-product terms, equation (2.1) becomes

$$W = a_n + a_x x + a_y y + (a_u - a_n)U + e, \tag{2.3}$$

and equations (2.2) become

$$W_i = a_i + a_x x + a_y y + e_i; \; i = u \text{ if } U = 1; \; i = n \text{ if } U = 0. \tag{2.4}$$

Measurement errors in the dependent wage W variable or in the classification of workers by union status U and nonrandom sampling in the underlying data set of course may lead to biased estimates of the wage equation (2.1) (see Chapter 6). Furthermore, since residual variance is by no means usually negligible and selection of workers by union status U is surely not random, the left-out variables (e's) also may lead to bias, a fact that econometricians not only have noticed but have tried to overcome (see Chapters 4 and 5).

Assume, however, that equation (2.1) has been estimated without bias. Then an unbiased estimate of the wage gap M, conditional on or given x and y, is

$$M \equiv E(W_u - W_n | x, y) = a_u - a_n + (a_{ux} - a_{nx})x + (a_{uy} - a_{ny})y. \tag{2.5}$$

(To avoid cumbersome notation, I use the symbol M both for the concept of the wage gap and for its estimate. The text will make the distinction between concept and estimate wherever confusion otherwise might arise.) Of course if the wage equation contains no cross-product terms Ux or Uy, as in (2.3), $M = a_u - a_n$, the coefficient of U in (2.3). Define $\hat{W}$ as $E(W|x, y, U)$, the expected value of W in (2.1) conditional on x, y, and U. Then the wage gap M is the partial derivative of $\hat{W}$ with respect to union status U. Thus the presence of the union status variable U on the right-hand side of the wage equation, either explicitly as in (2.1) and (2.3) or implicitly as in (2.2) and (2.4), is critical for estimating the wage gap. In this connection notice that the critical variable is *union status U*, not *extent of unionism y*. Serious problems of interpretation of the unionism content of the wage equation arise when extent of unionism y is used instead of union status U (see Chapter 3).

In the specification of the wage equation (2.1) the dependent variable W is measured in natural logarithmic units. Therefore, the wage gap M also is measured in these log units, and throughout the rest of this book the reported estimates will be in these units. To translate the gap M so measured into a percentage difference, simply perform this calculation: $100(e^M - 1)$.

Equation (2.5) allows for the possibility that the wage gap M depends on the characteristics x and y of workers and their employments. Indeed, if the gap is not generally zero, we would expect to find that it varies somewhat systematically across the labor force. Chapter 7 presents evidence on this variation.

2. The Mean Wage Gap

Let $\bar{x}$ and $\bar{y}$ denote the means of the right-hand variables x and y among workers included in the fitting of the wage equations (2.1). Then, from (2.5), the estimate of the mean wage gap among included workers is

$$\overline{M} = a_u - a_n + (a_{ux} - a_{nx})\bar{x} + (a_{uy} - a_{ny})\bar{y}. \quad (2.6)$$

If the fitted wage equation contains no interaction terms Ux or Uy of union status with other right-hand variables, as in equation (2.3), then the estimated mean wage gap is simply $a_u - a_n$, the coefficient of union status U in the wage equation. Of course, when the interactions are absent, the equation contains no information on variations in the gap among the included workers.

On the other hand, when union status interactions are present, calculation of the mean gap requires not only the fitted wage equation but also the means of the variables interacted with union status. Several studies in fact reported the calculated value of the mean gap $\overline{M}$. Several others reported somewhat similar numbers from which $\overline{M}$ easily could be calculated as follows. Let x^u and y^u be the means of x and y among unionized workers and x^n and y^n the corresponding means for nonunion workers. The reported numbers, M^u and M^n, were

$$M^i = a_u - a_n + (a_{ux} - a_{nx})x^i + (a_{uy} - a_{ny})y^i, \; i = u,n. \quad (2.7)$$

But then the mean gap $\overline{M}$ is

$$\overline{M} = \overline{U}M^u + (1 - \overline{U})M^n, \quad (2.8)$$

where $\overline{U}$, the mean of U, is the fraction of included workers who were unionized. However, for most of the surveyed wage equations with union status interactions, the calculation of $\overline{M}$ from the wage equations and associated means was done by me rather than the authors.

Clearly M^u and M^n must bracket $\overline{M}$, but the sign of $M^u - M^n$ in general is ambiguous. The wage gap literature has not adopted a standard practice with respect to which of the summary numbers M^u, M^n, and $\overline{M}$ is calculated and reported. Some authors reported one or both of M^u and M^n, others $\overline{M}$, and most of them none of these. In this book I present only estimates of $\overline{M}$, in part to save time but mainly because estimates of $\overline{M}$ from wage equations (2.1) with union status interactions tend to be closer (than estimates of M^u or M^n) to corresponding wage gap estimates $a_u - a_n$ from similar equations (2.3) without the union status interactions.

Frequently the variables interacted with union status included dummy variables for such worker characteristics as sex, race, marital status, region of residence, occupation, and industry in which employed. For example, let x be a dummy variable for sex, equal to unity if male and zero if female. Then it is quite straightforward to calculate the implied mean gap separately by sex or, alternatively, the deviations of the sex means from the overall (both sexes) mean gap $\overline{M}$. Thus the deviation for males is $(a_{ux} - a_{nx})(1 - \bar{x})$ and for females is $-(a_{ux} - a_{nx})\bar{x}$. Wherever possible, I have calculated these deviations of category mean gaps from overall mean gaps, and they comprise much of the evidence on variations in the wage gap across the labor force discussed in Chapter 7. In addition, for continuous variables I have recorded their slope coefficients which are also discussed in Chapter 7. For example, if x is years of school completed, entered linearly as a continuous variable in the wage equation, its wage gap slope coefficient is $(a_{ux} - a_{nx})$.

In a few studies e^W rather than W was the left-hand variable in equations otherwise the same as (2.1). For such equations I first calculated a wage gap estimate—call it b_U—measured in the natural units of the wage and then divided b_U by the mean of e^W among workers covered in fitting each such equation.

For those studies in which equation (2.1) was fitted separately for each of several mutually exclusive worker groups, I first calculated the estimated mean wage gap $\overline{M}_k$ for each of the groups by the procedures set out above and then calculated the all-group mean: $\overline{M} = \Sigma N_k \overline{M}_k / \Sigma N_k$, where N_k is the number of workers in the k-th group.

3. The Distinction between Wage Gaps and Wage Gains

I turn now from the concept of a union-induced wage *gap* to that of a union-induced wage *gain*. There is, of course, an obvious sense in which the wage gap for a worker measures a wage gain: if for him the wage gap is greater than zero, the expected value of his wage would be higher if he were unionized than if he were nonunion. In what follows, however, the wage *gain* concept is quite different from that of a wage *gap*.

Imagine a hypothetical U.S. economy differing from the existing one in its laws regarding unions and collective bargaining. In particular, in this hypothetical economy "antitrust" laws long have made unions powerless to affect wages. Such an economy might have unions and collective bargaining, but they would be compatible with competition in the labor market. I think that it is this contrast between competitive and monopoly unions that I and numerous others have had in mind when we referred to the contrast between the "absence" of unionism and its "presence." In this hypothetical economy a worker paid a wage W in the presence of the existing unionism would be paid a wage V where V like W is measured in logarithmic units. His unionism-induced *absolute* wage *gain* A is the expected value of the excess of his wage W in the "presence" of unionism over his wage V in the "absence" of unionism:

$$A_i \equiv E(W_i - V|x, y); i = u \text{ if } U = 1; i = n \text{ if } U = 0. \qquad (2.9)$$

Notice that for each worker there is a pair of absolute gains, one of which is actual and the other potential. For example, if the worker is nonunion, his actual absolute gain is A_n and his potential absolute gain is A_u. Notice also that his wage gap M is the same as the excess $A_u - A_n$ of his potential absolute gain over his actual absolute gain. Thus knowing absolute gain pairs implies knowing wage gaps M and more.

There is also a *relative* wage *gain* concept. I denote by the superscript a the all-worker (both union and nonunion) mean of the actual values of a variable. Thus A^a is such a mean of the absolute gains A. The *relative* wage *gain* R of the worker then is

$$R_i \equiv A_i - A^a; i = u \text{ if } U = 1; i = n \text{ if } U = 0. \qquad (2.10)$$

For *relative* gains as for *absolute* there is a pair of gains, one actual and one potential. For a nonunion worker his actual relative gain is R_n, his potential relative gain is R_u, and his wage gap M is the excess $R_u - R_n$ of his potential gain over his actual gain. Notice that if we knew the absolute gain pairs A_u and A_n and the mean A^a, we would also know not only the wage gaps M but also the relative gain pairs R_u and R_n.

Thus the wage *gap* for a worker is the excess of $\hat{W}_u$ over $\hat{W}_n$ or of A_u over A_n or of R_u over R_n. The wage *gain* for a worker, on the other hand, is the excess of his expected wage (absolute or relative, actual or potential) in the presence of unionism over its counterpart (absolute or relative) in the absence of unionism. The wage gap therefore is similar to the wedge produced by a payroll tax between the before-tax wage and the after-tax wage, while the wage gain is similar to the difference between either the before-tax wage or the after-tax wage, given the tax, and the wage that would be paid in the absence of the tax.

4. Mean Wage Gains

I denote the mean of a variable among unionized workers by a superscript u and the corresponding mean among nonunion workers by a superscript n. Then

$$A^a = U^a A^u_u + (1 - U^a)A^n_n = A^n_n + U^a\Delta = A^u_u - (1 - U^a)\Delta,$$
$$\Delta \equiv A^u_u - A^n_n = R^u_u - R^n_n, \quad (2.11)$$

and

$$0 = R^a = U^a R^u_u + (1 - U^a)R^n_n = R^n_n + U^a\Delta = R^u_u - (1 - U^a)\Delta; \quad (2.12)$$

where U^a (or equivalently $\overline{U}$), the mean of union status U, is the fraction of workers who are unionized. The means A^i_i and R^i_i for $i = u, n$ are means of actual rather than potential gains. The mean R^a of actual *relative* wage gains of course must be zero, but the same is not necessarily true of the *absolute* gains.

Let M^a (or $\overline{M}$) be the economy-wide, all-worker mean wage gap. In Lewis [121, pp. 27–45] I assumed (after a bit of what I thought was supporting argument) that the economy-wide Δ was approximately equal to M^a. Thus with estimates of M^a in hand, I approximated R^u_u and R^n_n for the whole economy with the help of (2.12) as follows: $R^n_n \simeq -U^a M^a$, $R^u_u \simeq (1 - U^a)M^a$. (However, I strongly resisted the temptation to set A^a equal to zero and do the same approximation for A^n_n and A^u_u.) Since the wage gap for a worker is $A_u - A_n = R_u - R_n$, it follows that the mean gap $M^a (= \overline{M})$ is

$$\begin{aligned} M^a &= U^a(A^u_u - A^u_n) + (1 - U^a)(A^n_u - A^n_n) \\ &= A^u_u - A^n_n - [U^a(A^u_n - A^n_n) + (1 - U^a)(A^u_u - A^n_u)] \quad (2.13) \\ &= \Delta - [U^a b_{A_nU} + (1 - U^a)b_{A_uU}], \end{aligned}$$

where $b_{A_iU} = A^u_i - A^n_i = R^u_i - R^n_i$ $(i = u, n)$ is the simple regression coefficient of A_i or R_i on union status U across all workers. The magnitudes of these coefficients are not by any means obvious to me. Hence I no longer assume that in the economy as a whole $R^n_n \simeq -U^a M^a$ and $R^u_u \simeq (1 - U^a)M^a$.

5. Can Wage Gains Be Estimated from Empirical Wage Equations and Related Data?

We now have a large stock of empirical wage equations (2.1) fitted to data for recent years and thus in the presence of unionism. From these equations and related data we can calculate wage gaps (2.5). Can we also calculate from these same equations and the related data absolute or relative wage gains?

Write the counterpart of (2.1) in the absence of unionism as

$$V = b + b_x x + e_v. \tag{2.14}$$

This equation cannot be fitted to recent data because V cannot be observed in the presence of unionism. The coefficients of (2.14) in that sense are unknown. But if wage *gains* are to be calculated from (2.1), the coefficients of (2.14) must be inferred, somehow or other, from those of (2.1).

In most of the studies reporting fitted wage equations (2.1), no extent of unionism variables y appear on the right-hand side. Moreover, in these studies whenever "wage effects of unionism" are reported, the concept is that of the wage gap, although sometimes the descriptive language suggests some confusion between the gap and gain concepts. However, recently several studies have appeared with wage equations that include both union status U and extent of unionism (fraction unionized) y variables. Some of these studies (Chambers [37], Gay [73], Holzer [94], Killingsworth [111], McLaughlin [129], Mishel [138], and Podgursky [160]) present estimates that are (1) clearly not estimates of the wage gap and (2) are described unmistakably, I think, as estimates of wage gains.

How did the authors of these recent papers infer the coefficients of (2.14) from those of (2.1)? Chambers, Gay, Killingsworth, McLaughlin, and Podgursky have little to say on this question, and I suspect that the reason for their silence is that they thought the answer was obvious: in the "absence" of unionism both U and y would be zero for all workers. Therefore set $U = y = 0$ and then $W = V$ in (2.1) to obtain

$$V = a_n + a_{nx} x + e. \tag{2.15}$$

But then it follows from (2.1), (2.5), (2.9), and (2.15) that

$$A_i = a_{ny} y + UM; i = u \text{ if } U = 1; i = n \text{ if } U = 0; \tag{2.16}$$

where M is the wage gap (2.5). Mishel [138] also used equations (2.16) but expressed some misgivings about the validity of (2.15).

In his table 6 Holzer [94] presented estimates, separately for black and white young males, of what he called "overall" wage effects of unionism. It is helpful in interpreting his numbers to write equation (2.16) as follows:

$$\begin{aligned} &A_i = a_{ny} y + UM; M = a_u - a_n + (a_{uy} - a_{ny})y; \\ &i = u, \text{ if } U = 1; i = n \text{ if } U = 0. \end{aligned} \tag{2.17}$$

For the group of workers involved let $\bar{y}$ be the mean of y, $\overline{U}$ the mean of U, y^u the mean of y and M^u the mean of M among workers for whom $U = 1$, and A^a is the mean of the A_i calculated at actual values of U. Then

$$A^a = a_{ny}\bar{y} + (a_u - a_n)\overline{U} + (a_{uy} - a_{ny})\overline{U}y^u. \tag{2.18}$$

Differentiate (2.18) totally with respect to $\bar{y}$ to obtain

$$\frac{dA^a}{d\bar{y}} = a_{ny} + M^u \frac{d\overline{U}}{d\bar{y}} + (a_{uy} - a_{ny})\overline{U} \frac{dy^u}{d\bar{y}} . \quad (2.19)$$

I suspect that what he wanted to estimate was $dA^a/d\bar{y}$ in (2.19). However, instead of using the infinitesimal calculus he used the calculus of finite differences and in the process made an error. When (2.18) is differenced by the calculus of finite differences, the result is:

$$\frac{\Delta A^a}{\Delta\bar{y}} = a_{ny} + M^u \frac{\Delta\overline{U}}{\Delta\bar{y}} + (a_{uy} - a_{ny})(\overline{U} + \Delta\overline{U}) \frac{\Delta y^U}{\Delta\bar{y}} . \quad (2.20)$$

But Holzer wrote $\overline{U} + \Delta\overline{U}$ in the last term of (2.20) as $\overline{U} + \Delta\overline{U}/\Delta\bar{y}$ and implicitly assumed that $\Delta y^u/\Delta\bar{y} = 1$.

The above procedure for inferring the coefficients of (2.14) from those of (2.1) by setting $U = y = 0$ is simple, but incorrect. First it assumes that the estimated coefficient a_{ny} of the extent of unionism variable y for nonunion workers does not depend upon which of many possible extent of unionism variables is used, or alternatively, that the y variable used is the correct one. Should y be measured by industry, and in what detail? Occupation? Geographic area? Some combination of these and, perhaps, other variables? None of the authors really addresses these questions. Furthermore, the estimates of the coefficient a_{ny} are by no means invariant to the choice of the y variable (see Chapters 3 and 7).

Second, the procedure also assumes that (1) the wage gains of *nonunion workers in nonunion* ($y = 0$) *sectors* are always zero, independent of the extent of unionism U^a ($= \overline{U}$) in the economy as a whole and of the way union workers are distributed by worker characteristics x, and (2) that in the "absence" of unionism and conditional on x all workers would be paid the wages paid in the presence of unionism to nonunion workers in nonunion sectors. Surely in the general equilibrium of the economy in the presence of unionism the wage gains (or losses) of nonunion workers do depend upon whether the working force is 5 percent, 20 percent, or 50 percent unionized, on which categories of workers are unionized, as well as on the effectiveness of labor unions in achieving wage gains for their workers. Essentially what I am arguing here is that the coefficients (the a's) in the fitted cross-section wage equation (2.1) depend on the extent of unionism in the economy as a whole and by categories of workers and on the effectiveness of unions. If these latter are nonnegligibly changed, the coefficients in (2.1) will change, making it impossible to infer (2.14) from (2.1) and, therefore, making it impossible to estimate wage gains from (2.1).

6. Unions and Wage Inequality

What have been the effects of unionism on wage differences by color, sex, schooling, experience, region, industry, and the like? On the economy-wide inequality of wages among individual workers? In Lewis [121, pp. 7–9 and chapters 8 and 9] I attempted to say something about several of these questions, and they are the focus of several post–1963 studies reviewed in Chapter 10.

a) Unionism and Wage Differences by Color (Sex, etc.)

Consider first wage differences by color (or the similar differences by sex, etc.) I use subscripts 1 and 2 to distinguish black (subscript 1) workers from white (subscript 2) workers. Let $\hat{W}_{ij}$ be the expected value of W, conditional on worker and employment characteristics x and y, for a worker in union status $i = u,n$ and color status $j = 1,2$. Then $M_j \equiv \hat{W}_{uj} - \hat{W}_{nj}$ for $j = 1,2$ is the union/nonunion wage gap for color status j. Similarly, the black/white or color wage gap for union status $i = u,n$ is $C_i = \hat{W}_{i1} - \hat{W}_{i2}$. The excess, call it D, of C_u over C_n is the union/nonunion difference in the color wage gap:

$$\begin{aligned} D \equiv C_u - C_n &= (\hat{W}_{u1} - \hat{W}_{u2}) - (\hat{W}_{n1} - \hat{W}_{n2}) \\ &= (\hat{W}_{u1} - \hat{W}_{n1}) - (\hat{W}_{u2} - \hat{W}_{n2}) \\ &= M_1 - M_2. \end{aligned} \tag{2.21}$$

Thus the union/nonunion difference in the color wage gap is the same as the black/white difference in the union/nonunion wage gap. Estimates of such union/nonunion gap differences (by sex, color, etc.) are the subject of Chapter 7.

D $\equiv C_u - C_n = M_1 - M_2$ is measured in the presence of the existing unionism and compares the color gap C_u for unionized status with the corresponding color gap C_n for nonunion status. However, what most economists have in mind, I think, when they refer to the "effect of unionism on the black/white wage differential" is a comparison of the color gap in the presence of the existing unionism with the corresponding color gap in the absence of monopoly unionism. Let W_j^a be the mean of W among workers who are actually $j = 1,2$ workers, V_j^a the corresponding mean of wages V in the "absence" of unionism, and $A_j^a = W_j^a - V_j^a$ the corresponding mean absolute wage *gain* of j workers. Then the effect, call it F, of unionism in the *gain* sense on the black/white wage differential is

$$F \equiv (W_1^a - W_2^a) - (V_1^a - V_2^a) = A_1^a - A_2^a. \tag{2.22}$$

That is, F is the excess of the unionism-induced wage gain A_1^a for black workers over the corresponding gain A_2^a for white workers.

The gain F in the color differential may be decomposed into two parts, one part of which may be estimated from cross-section wage equations and a second part which cannot be so estimated. By definition:

$$\begin{aligned} W_j^a &= \overline{U}_j W_{uj}^u + (1-\overline{U}_j) W_{nj}^n; \\ \overline{W}_{nj} &\equiv \overline{U}_j W_{nj}^u + (1-\overline{U}_j) W_{nj}^n; \\ W_j^a - \overline{W}_{nj} &= \overline{U}_j \, (W_{uj}^u - W_{nj}^u) = \overline{U}_j M_j^u; \end{aligned} \tag{2.23}$$

where W_{uj}^u is the mean of W_{uj} among unionized j workers, W_{nj}^n the mean of W_{nj} among nonunion j workers, W_{nj}^u the mean of W_{nj} among unionized j workers, $\overline{U}_j$ the fraction of j workers who are unionized, and M_j^u the mean of the wage gap M among unionized j workers. Clearly $\overline{U}_j M_j^u$ is the difference, measured in the presence of the existing unionism, between the actual mean wage W_j^a of j workers and the mean wage $\overline{W}_{nj}$ of these workers for nonunion status.

It also follows by definition that:

$$\begin{aligned} V_j^a &= \overline{U}_j V_j^u + (1-\overline{U}_j) V_j^n; \\ \overline{W}_{nj} - V_j^a &= \overline{U}_j (W_{nj}^u - V_j^u) + (1-\overline{U}_j)(W_{nj}^n - V_j^n) \\ &= \overline{U}_j A_{nj}^u + (1-\overline{U}_j) A_{nj}^n \equiv \bar{A}_{nj}; \end{aligned} \tag{2.24}$$

where V_j^i is the mean of V_j among $i = u,n$ workers, A_{nj}^u is the mean of the wage gains A_{nj} among unionized workers, and A_{nj}^n the similar mean for nonunion workers. Since wages V in the "absence" of unionism cannot be estimated from cross-section wage equations (2.1) or (2.2), the wage gains $\bar{A}_{nj}$ cannot be estimated from these equations.

Now plug (2.23) and (2.24) into (2.22) to obtain:

$$F = A_1^a - A_2^a = F^* + (\bar{A}_{1n} - \bar{A}_{2n}); F^* \equiv \overline{U}_1 M_1^u - \overline{U}_2 M_2^u. \tag{2.25}$$

The component $F^* \equiv \overline{U}_1 M_1^u - \overline{U}_2 M_2^u$ of F involves only data in the presence of unionism and can be estimated from cross-section wage equations. The second component $\bar{A}_{1n} - \bar{A}_{2n}$, however, cannot be estimated from such equations, even with respect to sign. Thus there is no assurance that the gain concept F has the same sign as the gap concept F^*.

b) Unionism and Wage Dispersion

Students of trade unionism long have speculated about the effects of unionism on the overall *dispersion* of relative wages among individual workers in the U.S. work force. Here, too, it is important to distinguish sharply between *gap* effects of unionism in which the contrast is between wage dispersion for unionized status and the corresponding dispersion for nonunion status in the presence of the existing unionism and *gain* effects in which dispersion in the presence of unionism is compared to dispersion in the "absence" of unionism.

For present purposes I write the pair of wage equations (2.2) by union status as follows

$$W_i = a_i + a_{ix}x + e_i; i = u,n; \tag{2.26}$$

where now I interpret the a's as true coefficients and the e's as true residuals. I assume that the expected value of e_i, not conditional on union status, is zero and that the unconditional covariance of e_i and x also is zero. Furthermore, to simplify notation I treat the right-hand side of (2.26) as though it contained only one x variable. Then (2.26) leads immediately to

$$\sigma^2(W_i) = a_{ix}^2\sigma^2(x) + \sigma^2(e_i); i = u,n; \tag{2.27}$$

where σ^2 is the variance across all workers of what follows in parentheses. Then the true union/nonunion wage *variance* gap G is

$$\begin{aligned} G &\equiv \sigma^2(W_u) - \sigma^2(W_n) \\ &= (a_{ux}^2 - a_{nx}^2)\sigma^2(x) + \sigma^2(e_u) - \sigma^2(e_n), \end{aligned} \tag{2.28}$$

and the true union/nonunion wage *standard deviation* gap g is

$$\begin{aligned} g &\equiv \sigma(W_u) - \sigma(W_n) \\ &= [a_{ux}^2\sigma^2(x) + \sigma^2(e_u)]^{1/2} - [a_{nx}^2\sigma^2(x) + \sigma^2(e_n)]^{1/2}. \end{aligned} \tag{2.29}$$

At any given time, of course, W_u is observed only for union workers and W_n only for nonunion. Suppose then that the wage equations (2.26) are fitted by ordinary least squares to cross-section data conditional on actual union status, the W_u equation to the data for union workers and the W_n equation to the data for nonunion workers. Then the residual variances calculated from these equations at best will estimate $\sigma^2(e_u)^u$ and $\sigma^2(e_n)^n$ rather than $\sigma^2(e_u)$ and $\sigma^2(e_n)$, where $\sigma^2(e_u)^u$ is the variance of e_u among union workers and $\sigma^2(e_n)^n$ is the variance of e_n among nonunion workers. Since union status selection surely is not random, there is no reason to expect that $\sigma(e_i)^i = \sigma(e_i)$. Therefore, the estimates of G or g derived from such equations are likely to suffer from union status selection bias.

G (or g) measures the gap between wage dispersion for unionized status and wage dispersion for nonunion status in the presence of the existing unionism. I turn now to the gain counterpart of G (or g): the difference between wage dispersion in the presence of unionism and the corresponding dispersion in the "absence" of unionism. Denote by $\sigma^2(W)^a$ the overall variance of actual wages in the presence of unionism and by $\sigma^2(V)^a$ the corresponding overall variance in the "absence" of unionism. Then the wage variance gain H is

$$H \equiv \sigma^2(W)^a - \sigma^2(V)^a; \tag{2.30}$$

and the wage standard deviation gain h is

$$h \equiv \sigma(W)^a - \sigma(V)^a. \tag{2.31}$$

Since wages V in the "absence" of unionism cannot be estimated from cross-section wage equations fitted to data in the presence of unionism, the dispersion gains H and h also cannot be estimated from such information.

However, H (or h) contains a component H^* (or h^*) that can be estimated from these wage equations and underlying data. First notice that

$$\sigma^2(W)^a = \overline{U}\sigma^2(W_u)^u + (1-\overline{U})\sigma^2(W_n)^n + \overline{U}(1-\overline{U})(W_u^u - W_n^n)^2,$$
$$\sigma^2(W_n) = \overline{U}\sigma^2(W_n)^u + (1-\overline{U})\sigma^2(W_n)^n + \overline{U}(1-\overline{U})(W_n^u - W_n^n)^2, \quad (2.32)$$

where $\overline{U}$ is the fraction of workers who are unionized, $\sigma^2(W_u)^u$ is the variance of W_u among unionized workers, $\sigma^2(W_n)^u$ and $\sigma^2(W_n)^n$ are the variances of W_n among unionized and nonunion workers, respectively, W_u^u is the mean of W_u among unionized workers, and W_n^u and W_n^n are the means of W_n among unionized and nonunion workers, respectively. Estimates of $\overline{U}$, $\sigma^2(W_u)^u$, $\sigma^2(W_n)^n$, W_u^u, and W_n^n may be calculated, of course, from the cross-section data. Furthermore, $W_n^u = W_u^u - M^u$, where M^u is the mean wage gap calculated for unionized workers. M^u may be estimated from the wage equations and underlying data. There remains $\sigma^2(W_n)^u$. It follows from (2.26) that

$$\sigma^2(W_n)^u = a_{nx}^2\sigma^2(x)^u + \sigma^2(e_n)^u, \quad (2.33)$$

where $\sigma^2(x)^u$ and $\sigma^2(e_n)^u$ are the variances of x and e_n, respectively, among unionized workers. The cross-section wage equations and data provide estimates of both a_{nx} and $\sigma(x)^u$, but not $\sigma\,(e_n)^u$. The estimate of the residual variance in the W_n equation is for $\sigma^2(e_n)^n$ rather than $\sigma^2(e_n)^u$. However, if there were no union status selection bias, $\sigma(e_n)^u$ would be equal to $\sigma(e_n)^n$. Assume this to be true. Then from (2.31), (2.32), and (2.33):

$$H = H^* + \sigma^2(W_n) - \sigma^2(V)^a; H^* \equiv \sigma^2(W)^a - \sigma^2(W_n);$$
$$h = h^* + \sigma(W_n) - \sigma(V)^a; h^* \equiv \sigma(W)^a - \sigma(W_n); \quad (2.34)$$

where H^* and h^* may be estimated from the cross-section wage equations and related data. However, since the sign of $\sigma(W_n) - \sigma(V)^a$ is unknown, there is no assurance that H (or h) will have the same sign as H^* (or h^*).

3 Estimates from Macro Equations: The Problem of Interpretation

1. Introduction

This is the first of seven chapters surveying union relative wage effect estimates that I have retrieved from post–1963 studies of wage differentials in the U.S. work force. This chapter surveys estimates from *macro* equations fitted to cross-section (CS) data usually by ordinary least squares (OLS). (See Lewis [122] for an earlier version of this chapter.)

Return to equation (2.3) of Chapter 2, which I now write slightly differently as follows:

$$W = a + a_x x + a_y y + \overline{M}U + e, \tag{3.1}$$

where W is the natural logarithm of a worker's wage, the x's are variables characterizing the worker and his employment, y is the fraction of workers who are unionized in the industry (or area, or occupation, etc.) in which the worker is employed, U is the union status of the worker, e is the residual, the a's and $\overline{M}$ are estimated coefficients, and in particular $\overline{M}$ is the estimate of the mean union/nonunion wage gap. The union status variable U is a *micro* concept of collective bargaining coverage. For each worker it distinguishes between two states, unionized and nonunion. Its presence on the right-hand side of wage equations such as (3.1) above permits the estimation of the wage gap $\overline{M}$. I term wage equations that include U as micro equations, whether they also include or, more often, exclude extent of unionism y variables.

Extent of unionism y, whether measured by industry, occupation, locality, etc., is a group or macro concept of union status or collective bargaining coverage. There is a strong presumption, I think, that in the general equilibrium of the economy in the presence of unionism the relative wage of each worker depends not only on his union status, sex, color, schooling, experience, and like variables but also on the extent of unionism in the whole work force and the distribution of workers by union status among work-force sectors. This argues for the presence on the right-hand side of micro wage equations of extent of unionism variables characterizing this distribution, though it does not, of course, settle the question of the proper specification of these variables.

We now have a substantial stock of micro wage equations that include extent of unionism variables, a sample of which is reported in section 4. The estimated coefficients a_y of these variables often are numerically large, of uncertain sign, and have values that are sensitive to the way y is measured, the specification of the wage equation, and the data set used. The large dispersion of the estimated a_y's argues against any simple interpretation of the wage effects picked up in the data by these coefficients. Indeed, I am not by any means convinced that these estimated wage effects are mostly effects of unionism rather than mostly effects of left-out variables correlated with the included y variables.

Until about 1965 there were no large random samples with broad coverage of the U.S. work force containing information on wages and numerous worker and employment characteristics that also classified workers by their union status U. In the absence of the union status data, either one or the other of two alternative procedures were followed in the earlier of the post–1963 studies and in numerous later studies emulating them:

1. The wage equation (3.1) or similar equation was fitted to individual-worker data on W, x, and y omitting union status U. I write the fitted macro wage equation as

$$W = c + c_x x + c_y y + e'. \tag{3.2}$$

Frequently in such equations y was interacted with one or more of the x variables. This is what I call a "Weiss-type" macro equation after Leonard W. Weiss who was the first, I think, to fit such wage equations (see Weiss [198]).

2. The wage equation (3.1) or similar equation, thought of as pertaining to individual workers, was aggregated by industry (or geographic area, etc.) across individual workers and the resulting aggregate or macro equation was fitted to observations on the industry (or area, etc.) aggregates. Assume that the aggregation is by industry and denote the industry mean of a variable by an asterisk superscript. Also assume that y is exactly equal to U^*. Then the aggregation of (3.1) by industry is

$$W^* = a + a_x x^* + (a_y + \overline{M})y + e^*. \tag{3.3}$$

There is no assurance, of course, that the residual e^* in (3.3) is uncorrelated with x^* even though the residual e in the individual-worker equation (3.1) is uncorrelated with x, y, and U. Therefore, the fitted macro equation

$$W^* = d + d_x x^* + d_y y + e'', \tag{3.4}$$

may have coefficients that differ considerably from those of (3.3). Some of the fitted macro equations similar to (3.4) included one or more yx^* interactions. In addition, medians rather than means often were used in the aggregation, and usually W^* was measured as the logarithm of the arithmetic rather than geometric mean wage in the industry. I call (3.4) an *aggregate* macro equation.

The authors of the studies containing macro wage equations differ in the way they interpret the unionism content of these equations. However, the most frequently reported statistic is the partial derivative—call it W_y—of W in (3.2) or W^* in (3.4) with respect to extent of unionism y. In this connection recall that the wage gap $\overline{M}$ is the partial derivative of W in (3.1) with respect to union status U. Thus W_y conceptually has some resemblance to the wage gap $\overline{M}$, and I read some authors as interpreting W_y as though it were $\overline{M}$.

This chapter reports and reacts to estimates of W_y that I have retrieved from the macro equations and underlying data in 42 post-1963 studies containing such equations. The next section identifies the studies and presents the estimated values of W_y for each study (table 3.1).

The critical question, of course, is: What does W_y estimate? This question is the subject of section 3. I show there that if macro and corresponding micro wage equations are fitted by ordinary least squares (OLS), the estimate of W_y in the macro equation contains a combination of the extent of unionism (EU) effect a_y and the wage gap effect $\overline{M}$. Indeed, under certain ideal conditions (exact aggregation), W_y as estimated from an aggregate macro equation is exactly the sum of a_y and $\overline{M}$. Thus with OLS estimation of the wage equations, W_y estimates neither a pure wage gap effect or a pure EU effect.

This raises the question: Is the relation of estimates of W_y to corresponding estimates of $\overline{M}$ sufficiently stable that one can estimate $\overline{M}$ reliably from knowledge of the estimate of W_y? In section 4 I report experiments designed to answer that question. The answer is negative. Thus the bottom line of sections 3 and 4 is that the "union wage effect" measured by W_y is not the union/nonunion wage gap $\overline{M}$ nor can $\overline{M}$ be estimated reliably from W_y.

2. Survey of Estimates of W_y from Macro Equations

Since W in (3.2) and W^* in (3.4) are measured in logarithmic units, the partial derivative W_y also is in these units. (Readers who wish to convert values of W_y to percentage units should calculate $100[e^{W_y} - 1]$.) When the

Table 3.1 Estimates of W_y from Macro Studies

Line No. (1)	Study No. (2)	Estimate and Year: W_y (3)	Estimate and Year: Year (4)	Cross-Section (5)	Coverage (6)
1	18	.38/.43	1960	Industry	Production workers (PW), manufacturing (MFG)
2	19	.36/.40	1967	Industry	White males, private sector, urban
3	19	.65/.74	1967	Industry	Line 2, blue-collar (BC) only
4	19	.42W	1967	Industry	Line 2
5	34	.37/.41	1966–75	City	Private, professional hospital workers
6	34	.30/.42	1966–75	City	Private, nonprofessional hospital workers
7	34	.04/.08	1966–75	City	Government, professional hospital workers
8	34	−.02/.02	1966–75	City	Government, nonprofessional hospital workers
9	41	.1W	1969	Industry	Clerical and BC, MFG and utilities
10	41	.1W	1969	Industry	Clerical and BC, MFG only
11	53,54	.02/.16	1967	City	Municipal workers, noneducational, 10 departments
12	53,54	.06/.16	1967	City	Municipal workers, noneducational, 7 departments
13	63	.10/.22	1966–72	City	Nonprofessional hospital workers
14	63	.18/.29	1966–72	City	Nonprofessional hospital workers, private
15	63	.09/.20	1966–72	City	Nonprofessional hospital workers, public
16	72	.19/.21	1959	Industry	Nonagricultural workers
17	72	.19/.25	1959	Industry	Goods producing industries
18	76	.00	1969–70	State	Public school teachers
19	80	.06/.10	1960–61	City	Selected occupations and cities, MFG only, full-time
20	80	.13/.19	1963–64	City	Line 19
21	80	.03/.06	1966–67	City	Line 19
22	81	.15/.18	1963–71	City	PW, MFG, in selected cities
23	87	.08/.09W	1969	Industry	Male, 7 selected occupations, private sector, full-time, MFG and transportation, communication, utilities (TCU)
24	88	.11/.27	1969	Industry	Males, private sector

25	89	.03	1969	Industry	Males, private sector, MFG
26	89	.17	1969	Industry	Males, private sector, non-MFG
27	92	.18	1970–73	City	Selected occupations in selected cities, private sector
28	92	.22	1978–79	City	Line 27
29	104	.45	1960	Industry	PW, MFG
30	105	.24	1960	Industry	PW, MFG
31	107	–.06/.10	1966–68	State	Public school teachers
32	111	.26/.30	1977	Industry	Nonagricultural full-time workers
33	129	.38/.39	1966–75	City	Private, professional hospital workers
34	129	.33/.38	1966–75	City	Private, nonprofessional hospital workers
35	129	.05/.09	1966–75	City	Government, professional hospital workers
36	129	–.01/.02	1966–75	City	Government, nonprofessional hospital workers
37	139	.28	1976	Industry	Selected mining (MIN), MFG, transportation (TRANS) industries
38	140	.13	1972	Industry	PW, MFG
39	151	–.01/.20	1969	Occupation	Male, full-year, 16 years of age and older
40	154	.32	1959	Industry	MFG
41	163	.15/.42	1969	State	Full-year workers
42	164	.27	1960	Industry	PW, MFG
43	164	.20	1960	Industry	PW in MIN, MFG, TCU, and construction (CONST)
44	171	.19/.66	1959	Industry	Male laborers (n.e.c.), MFG
45	174	.17/.29	1959	Industry	Males in MIN, MFG, CONST, TCU
46	175	.13/.28	1958	Industry	PW, MFG
47	176	.26/.34	1958	Industry	PW, MFG
48	176	.26/.37	1963	Industry	PW, MFG
49	194	.22	1950	Industry	PW in MIN, CONST, MFG, and trade
50	194	.26	1960	Industry	Line 49
51	195	.08/.08	1975	City	Municipal policemen
52	195	.00/.07	1975	City	Municipal firemen
53	195	.07/.14	1975	City	Municipal refuse collection workers
54	198	.25/.28*W*	1959	Industry	Male, BC, in MIN, MFG, CONST, TCU
55	200	.82	1972	State	PW, MFG

Table 3.1 (continued)

Line No. (1)	Study No. (2)	Estimate and Year: W_y (3)	Estimate and Year: Year (4)	Cross-Section (5)	Coverage (6)
56	124	−.01	1969	City	Urban registered nurses
57	162	.60	1958	State	PW, MFG
58	39	.19	1970	Industry	PW, MFG
59	126	.17/.19*W*	1966	Industry	Older males, MFG and TCU
60	126	.17/.19*W*	1971	Industry	Older males, MFG and TCU
61	128	.43/.51	1963	Industry	PW, MFG
62	84	.07/.10	1963	Industry	PW, MFG
63	85	.10/.11	1958	Industry	PW, MFG
64	85	.02/.02	1967	Industry	PW, MFG

Note:

Lines 1, 24–26, 29, 30, 40, 55, 58. See table 3.2 for 2SLS, 3SLS estimates.

Lines 4, 60. See section 4 for corresponding wage gap ($\overline{M}$) estimates from micro wage equations.

Lines 5–8, 11–12, 19–22, 27–28, 33–36, 39, 45, 51–53. See text for discussion of column 3 estimates.

Lines 5–8, 33–36. W_y estimates also available by year for 1966, 1969, 1972, 1975.

Lines 9, 10. Study reported coefficients (W_y) of y variables to only one decimal place, and for several wage equations I could not calculate W_y. W_y estimates by level of industry concentration ratio also available.

Lines 11, 12. W_y estimates also available by municipal department, city size, and union affiliation.

Lines 13–15. W_y estimates also available by year for 1966, 1969, 1972.

Lines 16, 17. Column 3 omits several wage equations for which I could not calculate W_y.

Lines 19–21. W_y estimates by sex and occupation also available.

Line 22. W_y estimates available by year 1963–71.

Line 23. W_y estimates available by occupation.

Lines 24, 32. W_y estimates available by type of extent of unionism y measure (representation vs. membership).

Line 31. Omits equations that include square of y variable and equations that author describes as 2SLS estimates.

Line 54. W_y estimates available by occupation and by regulated vs. unregulated industries.

Line 57. W_y estimates available by region.

Line 58. Separate estimates available for covered members and covered nonmembers.

left-hand wage variable is W or W^* and there are no yx or yx^* interactions on the right-hand side, the value of W_y is the estimated coefficient, c_y in (3.2) and d_y in (3.4), of the extent of unionism variable y. However, when such y-interactions are present, W_y depends on the values of the interacted x or x^* variables. For all such equations I have evaluated W_y at the mean values (over the observations to which each equation was fitted) of the interacted x or x^* variables.

In some of the macro equations discussed in this section the dependent wage variable was in its natural arithmetic units, i.e., the dependent variable was e^W or e^{W^*} rather than W or W^*. The calculation of W_y then involves two steps. First calculate $\partial e^W/\partial y$ or $\partial e^{W^*}/\partial y$ and, if necessary, evaluate the partial derivative at means of interacted x or x^* variables. Then divide this derivative by the mean (over the covered observations) of the dependent variable.

None of the values of the partial derivative W_y presented below should be attributed to the authors of the papers from which I have derived them as their estimates of some type of union-induced relative wage effect. The numbers are my reading and calculations from the reported equations and associated data. They are a convenient way of summarizing the unionism content of these equations. What they mean remains to be seen.

Turn to table 3.1. The "study no." in column 2 corresponds to that given in the reference list at the end of the book. Thus study no. 18 reported on line 1 of table 3.1 is the Ashenfelter-Johnson study. The estimates of W_y appear in column 3. More than half of the studies provided more than one estimate of W_y. In all such cases column 3 shows the range of the estimates. For example, from study no. 18 (on line 1) I drew three estimates ranging from 0.38 to 0.43. The letter W on some lines of column 3 indicates estimates that come from Weiss-type equations. The year to which an estimate pertains is given in column 4. Column 5 shows whether the extent of unionism (y) variable used in the macro wage equation was by industry, city, State, or occupation. Column 6 briefly describes the worker coverage of the observations on the dependent wage variable. The notes to table 3.1 identify the macro studies that (a) provide simultaneous-equations (2SLS, 3SLS) estimates discussed later in this section, or (b) contain interesting details in the estimates of W_y that are not shown in table 3.1, or (c) used wage equation models requiring the special discussion that immediately follows.

In five of the studies [34, 53, 54, 129, 195], all involving "city" cross-sections, some of the W_y estimates were derived from wage equations that included more than one right-hand extent of unionism y variable, one for the group of workers covered by the equation, the "own-y" variable, and the others for other groups of workers in the same city. For all such equations the estimates of the partial derivative W_y in column 3 are with respect to the own-y variable.

For the Cain et al. study [34], each of the W_y estimate ranges on lines 5–8 covers three separate estimates, each from an equation fitted to the pooled 1966, 1969, 1972, 1975 data. The equations differ in their y variables as follows:

Equation 1: own-y only
Equation 2: own-y and y for other occupation (professional versus nonprofessional)
Equation 3: own-y and y for same occupation but other hospital class (private versus government)

The detailed W_y estimates are:

	Eq. 1	*Eq. 2*	*Eq. 3*
Private, professional	.39	.37	.41
Private, nonprofessional	.42	.30	.42
Government, professional	.04	.08	.04
Government, nonprofessional	.02	−.02	.01

The column 3 ranges for the Ehrenberg and the Ehrenberg and Goldstein studies [53, 54] on lines 11 and 12 cover separate estimates by municipal department, 10 departments on line 11 and seven on line 12. The underlying wage equations for these estimates included only one extent of unionism variable, that for own-y. However, the authors also fitted wage equations comparable to those for line 12 that included y variables for several other departments as well as that for own-department. The range of the seven departmental estimates was 0.01/0.07, about half of that on line 12.

Each of the estimate ranges on lines 33–36 for the McLaughlin study [129] covers a pair of estimates from a pair of equations fitted to pooled 1966, 1969, 1972, 1975 data. Both equations included an own-y variable. One of the two equations also included a y variable for the other (professional versus nonprofessional) occupational group of hospital workers.

In the Victor study [195] the ranges for policemen and firemen on lines 51 and 52 cover two equations, one of which included, but the other did not, a y variable for the other occupation (police or fire). The range on line 53 for refuse collectors covers four equations with W_y estimates and y variable specifications as follows:

Equation 1 (W_y = .14): own-y only
Equation 2 (W_y = .07): own-y and police-y
Equation 3 (W_y = .12): own-y and fire-y
Equation 4 (W_y = .08): own-y, police-y, and fire-y.

All of the wage equations in this study were estimated by 2SLS in an equation system in which the second equation was for employment.

In the Hamermesh study [80] (lines 19, 20, 21) the dependent wage variable was the natural logarithm of the ratio of the average wage of white-collar (*WC*) workers to that of blue-collar (*BC*) workers in manufacturing by sex, occupation, and city. There were two right-hand extent of unionism variables for each city: y_{WC} for *WC* workers and y_{BC} for *BC* workers, both for manufacturing. The estimate of W_y for *WC* workers was the coefficient of y_{WC} and that for *BC* was the *negative* of the coefficient of y_{BC}. The numbers on lines 19, 20, and 21 are employment-weighted means of the *WC* and *BC* estimates. The separate estimates for *WC* and BC are:

	White-Collar (*WC*)	*Blue-Collar* (*BC*)
1960–61	−.02/.04	.12/.14
1963–64	.12/.17	.14/.22
1966–67	−.11/−.06	.12/.15

The procedure in the second Hamermesh study [81] was fairly similar. The dependent wage variable was the natural logarithm of the ratio of the wage of unionized bus drivers to the average wage of production workers in manufacturing by city and year. There was of course only one right-hand y variable, that for manufacturing production workers, and I took the negative of its coefficient as the estimate of W_y for these workers. The numbers on line 22 are means of the nine yearly figures as follows:

1963	.25/.26	1968	.12/.14
1964	.25/.27	1969	.12/.15
1965	.23/.26	1970	.04/.08
1966	.18/.21	1971	.06/.10
1967	.15/.18	Pooled data	0.16

The Hirsch-Rufolo study [92] lines 27 and 28 is similar to the first Hamermesh study [80]. The numerator wage was for municipal workers, the denominator wage for private sector workers. There were two corresponding right-hand y variables, one for the government workers and the other for private workers in manufacturing. The estimates of W_y in the table are for the private sector workers. The corresponding estimates for the government workers are:

1970–73	.23
1978–79	.25

In the next section I argue that the procedure followed in these three studies [80, 81, 92] is likely to make the estimates of W_y that I have drawn from them somewhat incomparable to other estimates in table 3.1.

The estimate range on line 39 for the Pashigian study [151] covers estimates from five wage equations. Three of these equations, fitted by OLS and differing slightly in right-hand variables, all yielded W_y estimates of

0.20. Two other wage equations, also differing in right-hand variables, were fitted by 2SLS as part of a simultaneous equations system that also included geographical mobility equations. They yielded W_y estimates of −0.01 and 0.11.

The first Rosen study [174] line 45 fitted by two-stage least squares (2SLS) a simultaneous equations model in which there were two equations, an hours-of-work demand equation by employers and an hours-of-work supply equation by workers, in which the y variable (in the demand equation) was treated as exogenous. The estimates of W_y on line 45 came from the reduced-form wage equations.

The Potthoff study [163] line 41 is one of the few macro studies in which the dependent wage was expressed in both real (cost-of-living deflated) and nominal terms. The low figure 0.15 on line 41 corresponds to the equation in which the real wage was dependent, and the high figure 0.42 to the nominal wage equation. Potthoff also noticed that the observations for Alaska and Hawaii were outliers. When these two states were omitted, the estimate range went from 0.15/0.42 to 0.09/0.24.

In most of the equations from which table 3.1 was derived (excluding W-type equations on indicated lines and the Hamermesh and Hirsch-Rufolo estimates on lines 19–22, 27, 28), the macro wage concept that was used was that of an arithmetic mean or, less often, a median, rather than a geometric mean. Ashenfelter and Taussig [19] lines 2 and 3 experimented with both the arithmetic and geometric means. On line 2 the low figure 0.36 is for the geometric mean and the high figure 0.40 for the arithmetic, while on line 3 the reverse is true. Hirsch [88] line 24 tried all three: arithmetic mean, geometric mean, and median. The estimates of W_y for the geometric mean and median versions were nearly equal and roughly 0.1 higher in log units than for the arithmetic mean.

Two studies, Killingsworth [111] line 32 and Hirsch [88] line 24, experimented with alternative measures of the extent of unionism y variable: extent of collective bargaining *coverage* or representation versus union *membership*. The low figure 0.26 on line 32 (Killingsworth) is for the coverage measure, the high figure 0.30 for membership. The Hirsch study also implies differences in estimates of W_y in the same direction and of about the same size.

The wide range 0.11/0.27 of W_y estimates on line 24 (Hirsch [88]) is entirely accounted for by differences in the wage concept and extent of unionism concept used in the six equations from which the estimates were drawn. The low figure 0.11 is for an equation with an arithmetic mean wage and a coverage extent of unionism measure. The high figure 0.27 is for a median wage measure coupled with a membership union status concept.

The even wider range 0.19/0.66 of the estimates drawn from the Rapping study [71] line 44 is the result of differences in right-hand variables in the eight equations covered in the range.

Those who are familiar with the often-cited Weiss study [198] line 54 undoubtedly will not recognize the numbers reported on line 54. The smaller figure 0.25 is the employment weighted mean of three W_y estimates by major occupation among unregulated industries. The larger figure 0.28 is the corresponding mean among both unregulated and regulated industries. The detailed estimates of W_y by major occupation and industry coverage are:

Major Occupation	*Unregulated*	*All Industries*
Craftsmen	.28	.25
Operatives	.20	.28
Laborers	.34	.33

Weiss also fitted an equation for operatives in manufacturing for which the estimate of W_y is 0.31.

In eight of the table 3.1 studies the wage equation, modeled as a part of a simultaneous equations system containing an extent of unionism equation and sometimes other equations in addition to the wage equation, was estimated by simultaneous equations (SE) methods (2SLS or 3SLS or both). The SE estimates of W_y, which are not shown in table 3.1, are reported below in table 3.2. Column 1 identifies the study, column 2 the table 3.1 line number, column 3 repeats the W_y estimates (by OLS) given in table 3.1, and column 4 gives the corresponding SE estimates. In five of the nine lines of table 3.2, the SE estimates are lower than the corresponding OLS estimates, but the SE estimates are more dispersed than the OLS estimates. (For [155] there is no corresponding OLS estimate.)

Fourteen of the studies in table 3.1, most of which were published before 1973, give estimates of W_y for 1958, 1959, or 1960 (see lines 1, 16, 17,

Table 3.2 Simultaneous Equations Estimates of W_y

Study No. (1)	Line No. (Table 3.1) (2)	Estimates of W_y: OLS (Table 3.1) (3)	Estimates of W_y: SE (4)
18	1	.38/.43	−.09/.18
88	24	.11/.27	−.21/.12
89	25	.03	.10/.17
89	26	.17	.02/.07
104	29	.45	.78
105	30	.24	.55
154	40	.32	.24
200	55	.82	.60/.78
39	58	.19	.42/.53
155[a]	—	—	.27

[a]The estimate in column 4 pertains to workers in manufacturing in 1959.

29, 30, 40, 42–47, 50, 54, 57, and 63). The estimates of W_y from these 14 studies for the three years average 0.27 (or 31%) and range from 0.10 to 0.60 even when only the low sides of estimate ranges are included. (The average is 0.34 or 40 percent when high sides of estimate ranges are substituted for low sides.) In my 1963 book [121] I estimated that the mean wage gap $\overline{M}$ in the U.S. labor force in 1957–58 was 10–15 percent (or 0.10–0.14 in log units). If estimates of W_y are interpreted as estimates of the mean wage gap $\overline{M}$ for the workers covered, as at first I did, then these 14 studies suggest that I underestimated the economy-wide average wage gap in 1957–58 by a factor of one-half or more. Moreover, table 3.1 indicates that there was nothing special about the years 1958–60. The estimates of W_y for later years are roughly at their 1958–60 level.

Of course the table 3.1 figures are disproportionately for workers in manufacturing industries. Is the mean wage gap for these workers well above the economy-wide average? Neither my 1963 book or table 3.1 contains much evidence on this question, but what there is does not suggest that the gap in manufacturing is unusually high. Indeed, recent estimates of the mean gap by industry derived from micro wage equations indicate that the manufacturing wage gap is *lower* than the all-industry average wage gap (see section 5, Chapter 7).

After 1965, as several large micro-data sets became available that contained information on the union status U of individual workers, estimates of the union wage effects came in rapidly increasing proportions from *micro,* rather than *macro,* wage equations. As these micro equations appeared, I noticed that the wage gap estimates that I was obtaining from them were considerably smaller than the W_y estimates I had drawn from the earlier macro equations.

The earlier estimation of macro wage equations (other than Weiss-type) usually involved laborious assembly and processing of data from a variety of sources. As a consequence, the macro equations (except Weiss-type) underlying table 3.1 commonly include relatively few right-hand variables. In contrast, the new micro-data sets made it easy to fit micro wage equations with numerous right-hand variables using data from a single source. Can the differences between the macro W_y estimates and the micro $\overline{M}$ estimates be accounted for by differences in right-hand variables?

The answer to this question is negative. In section 4 I compare micro and macro equations fitted to data from the same source with the same right-hand variables, except of course that in the micro equation the union status variable U is for individuals and in the macro equation it is replaced by an extent of unionism variable y, a macro version of U. Large differences emerge between estimates of $\overline{M}$ and corresponding estimates of W_y.

What is it, then, that W_y estimates? That is the subject of the next three sections.

3. What Do These Estimates of W_y Estimate?

a) *Weiss-Type Equations*

I begin with discussion of estimates of W_y from Weiss-type equations. Return to equations (3.1) and (3.2):

$$W = a + a_x x + a_y y + \overline{M}U + e; \quad (3.1)$$

$$W = c + c_x x + c_y y + e'; \; W_y = c_y. \quad (3.2)$$

Both are fitted to data for individual workers. The first, (3.1), is a micro wage equation; it includes the union status dummy variable U (equal to unity for union workers and zero for nonunion workers). The second, (3.2), is a Weiss-type equation because it excludes U. It follows from the omitted-variable theorem that if both equations are fitted by ordinary least squares (OLS), then

$$W_y = a_y + \overline{M}b_{Uy \cdot x} = J\overline{M}; \; J \equiv \frac{a_y}{\overline{M}} + b_{Uy \cdot x}, \quad (3.5)$$

where $b_{Uy \cdot x}$ is the partial regression coefficient of union status U on extent of unionism y in a regression that also includes the x variables on the right-hand side.

Therefore, unless J is close to unity, W_y and $\overline{M}$ will not be nearly equal. However, even if J were not near unity, it would still be possible to infer $\overline{M}$ from W_y if J varied little across data sets and y variables so that its magnitude could be estimated from a few experiments of the kind reported in the next section. Unfortunately, these experiments suggest that J is not unity and is not by any means invariant to the choice of y variable.

b) *Aggregate Macro Equations*

All of the macro equations except the Weiss-type were fitted to aggregates, say by industry, of individual-worker data. Go back to equation (3.1), interpret it as a micro equation, assume that it has been fitted by OLS, but modify its format as follows:

$$W = a + a_x x + a_x^* x^* + a_y U^* + \overline{M}U + e. \quad (3.6)$$

The modifications consist only of adding to the list of right-hand variables the industry means x^* of all of the x variables and replacing the extent of unionism y variable by the industry mean U^* of the union status dummy variable U. Aggregate (3.6) by industry to obtain

$$W^* = a + d_x x^* + W_y U^* + e^*; \; \mathrm{d}_x \equiv a_x + \mathrm{a}_x^*; \text{ and } W_y \equiv a_y + \overline{M}. \quad (3.7)$$

Since (3.6) has been fitted by OLS, the residual e is uncorrelated across the individual-worker observations with the industry means x^* and U^*. Therefore, the industry mean residual e^* in (3.7) also is uncorrelated with the industry means x^* and U^* in (3.7) provided only that each industry observation is weighted by the number of covered workers employed in the industry. Hence, if (3.7) were fitted by employment-weighted least squares, the coefficient W_y of the extent of unionism variable $y = U^*$ would be exactly equal to the sum $a_y + \overline{M}$ of the coefficients a_y for $y = U^*$ and the wage gap $\overline{M}$ for the union status dummy variable U in the micro equation.

The argument of the preceding paragraph assumes, of course, that the extent of unionism variable y used in the micro and macro equations is the exact aggregation U^* of the union status dummy variable U in the micro equation. However, the only macro equations in table 3.1 for which this was true are those on lines 2 and 3 (Ashenfelter-Taussig study) and line 32 (Killingsworth study). In all of the other studies the extent of unionism variable was not exactly the same as U^*. Of course, if U^* in (3.7) is measured inaccurately by the extent of unionism variable y that is used in the macro equation, the coefficient W_y of y in the fitted equation will not be exactly equal to $a_y + \overline{M}$. Indeed, if the measurement errors are uncorrelated with U^*, W_y will be less than $a_y + \overline{M}$.

There are other reasons why in the table 3.1 macro equations the interpretation of W_y as the sum $a_y + \overline{M}$ of coefficients in an underlying, but not observed, micro equation is not exact. Most of the macro equations reported in the table were fitted without employment weighting of the observations. Frequently some of the right-hand x^* variables were inexact aggregates of their x counterparts in the underlying micro equation. The same was often true of the left-hand wage variable.

The key question, of course, is whether the coefficient a_y of the extent of unionism variable U^* in the micro equation (3.6) typically is positive and so large as to make W_y in the macro equation (3.7) overstate substantially the wage gap $\overline{M}$ for the workers covered in the macro equation, even in the presence of errors in measuring U^* and other variables. The next section reports several experiments addressed to this question.

I turn now to the slightly special problem encountered in the interpretation of the macro equations of the Hirsch-Rufolo study [92] and the two Hamermesh studies [80, 81]. In these studies the left-hand variable (in logarithmic units) was the wage difference between two different groups of workers and there were two right-hand extent of unionism variables in the macro equations, one for each of the two groups of workers. Denote the two groups by subscripts 1 and 2 and write the micro wage equation for each of the two groups as follows:

$$W_k = a_{k1} U_1^* + a_{k2} U_2^* + \overline{M}_k U_k;\; k = 1,2. \tag{3.8}$$

Each equation also includes an intercept and an error term along with x and x^* variables, but I have left them out because their presence is not essential to what follows. Aggregate each of the equations (3.8) and then subtract one equation from the other:

$$W_1^* - W_2^* = W_{y1}U_1^* - W_{y2}U_2^*;\; W_{yk} = a_{kk} - a_{jk} + \overline{M}_k;\; j \neq k = 1,2. \tag{3.9}$$

Thus if the a's are all positive, W_{yk} will overstate $\overline{M}_k$ not by a_{kk} but by the smaller amount $a_{kk} - a_{jk}$. This may account in part for the lowness of the estimates of W_y from these studies relative to the others in table 3.1. I suspect, however, that measurement error in the extent of unionism variables used in these studies and in the Hendricks study, line 23, was the chief reason for their low W_y figures.

Return to equations (3.6) and (3.7). Notice that in the micro equation (3.6) there are two quite distinct "unionism" variables, extent of unionism ($U^* = y$) and the dummy variable U classifying the observations by their union status: unionized or nonunion. It is the presence of U rather than y that is critical for the estimation of the wage gap $\overline{M}$. (It is not at all essential for the estimation of $\overline{M}$ that the observations to which the micro equations are fitted be for individual workers so long as they can be clearly classified as either for a group of union workers or for a group of nonunion workers.)

In going from the micro equation (3.6) to the macro equation (3.7) the distinction between extent of unionism and union status is lost. There is only one unionism variable in (3.7), extent of unionism $y = U^*$ and its coefficient W_y in (3.7) picks up the separate effects in the micro equation (3.6) of both extent of unionism in its coefficient a_y and union status in its coefficient $\overline{M}$.

Rosen [175] was aware of the importance of distinguishing between union status and extent of unionism in the macro as well as in the micro wage equation. The essence of his proposed solution to the problem is this. First rewrite the micro equation (3.6) as follows:

$$W = a_{y1}D_1 + a_{y2}D_2 + \ldots + a_{yk}D_k + \overline{M}U + e, \tag{3.10}$$

where the D's are dummy variables dividing industries into k + 1 classes according to their values of U^* and assume that e is uncorrelated with right-hand variables. (For simplicity I do not show right-hand x and x^* variables.) Now aggregate (3.10):

$$W^* = a_{y1}D_1 + a_{y2}D_2 + \ldots + a_{yk}D_k + \overline{M}U^* + e^*. \tag{3.11}$$

Since e is uncorrelated with the D's (and U) in (3.10), e^* is uncorrelated with the D's in (3.11). Unfortunately, however, zero correlation between e and U in (3.10) does not imply zero correlation between e^* and U^* in the macro equation (3.11). For this reason, when (3.11) is fitted by employment-weighted least squares, there is no assurance that the resulting coefficient W_y for U^* will be equal to $\overline{M}$. Indeed, in the next section I report an experiment in which I fitted both the macro equation (3.11) and its micro counterpart (3.10). The coefficient of U^* in the aggregated equation differed considerably from the estimate of $\overline{M}$ in the micro equation. Nevertheless, the estimates 0.13/0.28 (line 46) of W_y from Rosen's study no. 175 are considerably lower than his corresponding estimates 0.26/0.34 (line 47) for the same workers for the same year using the same data sources from his study no. 176.

4. Macro versus Micro Estimates: Some Experiments

a) Weiss-Type Equations

Return to equations (3.1), (3.2), and (3.5):

$$W = a + a_x x + a_y y + \overline{M}U + e; \quad (3.1)$$

$$W = c + c_x x + c_y y + e'; W_y = c_y; \quad (3.2)$$

$$W_y = a_y + \overline{M}b_{Uy \cdot x} = J\overline{M}; J \equiv \frac{a_y}{\overline{M}} + b_{Uy \cdot x}; \quad (3.5)$$

where $b_{Uy \cdot x}$ is the partial regression coefficient of union status U on extent of unionism y in a regression that also includes the x variables on the right-hand side. (3.1) is a micro wage equation, (3.2) the corresponding Weiss-type macro equation. (3.5) relates the coefficient $c_y = W_y$ of y in the Weiss-type equation (3.2) to the coefficients a_y of y and $\overline{M}$ (the wage gap) of U in the micro equation (3.1) when both (3.1) and (3.2) are fitted by ordinary least squares. Questions: How large is J and how stable is it across data sets and y variables used?

I am surprised that the literature on union wage effects contains so little information on these questions. The needed data have been available for over a decade, and no sophisticated econometrics or computer processing is required. The unpublished Ashenfelter-Taussig paper [19], which exists only in the form of a short set of notes and tables, contains some relevant information. Their notes show that they fitted a Weiss-type equation (3.2) for which the coefficient W_y of extent of unionism y was 0.42 (see line 4 of table 3.1). The corresponding wage gap coefficient $\overline{M}$ of union status U in their fitted version of the micro equation (3.1) was 0.13. However, in fitting (3.1) they omitted the extent of unionism variable y. Had they not omitted y, I suspect that their estimate of $\overline{M}$ would have been about 0.12 instead of 0.13. Thus from their results, I estimate that J was about 3.5, a very large ratio. Long and Link in study no. 126, line 60 of table 3.1, also fitted the micro equation (3.1) without the y variable as well as the Weiss-type equation (3.2). The estimate range for W_y was 0.17/0.19 and for the wage gap $\overline{M}$ was $-0.08/-0.07$.

Table 3.3 presents the key results from several experiments that I have made in an effort to discover the unionism content of W_y when estimated from Weiss-type equations. The table covers 20 micro wage equations and 10 matching Weiss-type equations fitted by OLS to the May 1973 *Current Population Survey* (CPS) data file. The workers covered are white male

Table 3.3 Comparison of Micro Estimates of $\overline{M}$ with Weiss-Type Estimates of W_y (White Males in Private Sector, May 1973 CPS)

Panel A

Line No. (1)	y variable (2)	Weiss-type Equation W_y (3)	Micro Equations: With Uy $\overline{M}$ (4)	With Uy a_y (5)	Without Uy $\overline{M}$ (6)	Without Uy a_y (7)
1	U^* by industry	.365	.180	.234	.172	.224
2	BLS-PW by industry	.342	.183	.254	.166	.249
3	BLS-AW by industry	.323	.181	.206	.175	.201
4	CPS-PW by industry	.437	.184	.332	.164	.313
5	CPS-AW by industry	.395	.183	.268	.173	.246
6	U^* by occupation	.124	.172	−.054	.194	−.031
7	CPS by occupation	.159	.172	−.011	.192	.011
8	U^* by SMSA	.100	.172	−.012	.172	−.012
9	CPS-PW by SMSA	.103	.173	.010	.172	.010
10	CPS-AW by SMSA	.089	.174	−.037	.173	−.040

Panel B

Line No. (1)	$W_y - \overline{M}$: (3) − (4) (8)	$W_y - \overline{M}$: (3) − (6) (9)	$W_y/\overline{M}$: (3)/(4) (10)	$W_y/\overline{M}$: (3)/(6) (11)	$W_y/(a_y + \overline{M})$: (3)/[(4) + (5)] (12)	$W_y/(a_y + \overline{M})$: (3)/[(6) + (7)] (13)
1	.185	.193	2.03	2.12	.883	.922
2	.159	.176	1.87	2.05	.782	.823
3	.142	.148	1.78	1.85	.835	.860
4	.253	.273	2.38	2.67	.847	.916
5	.212	.222	2.15	2.28	.875	.942
6	−.048	−.070	.72	.64	1.049	.758
7	−.012	−.033	.93	.83	.990	.782
8	−.072	−.072	.58	.58	.621	.623
9	−.071	−.069	.59	.60	.560	.568
10	−.085	−.084	.51	.52	.649	.671

wage and salary workers, at least 15 years of age, employed in the private sector, with needed data, but excluding farm and private household workers. Lines 1–5 also exclude workers in CPS detailed industries with fewer than 20 covered workers, lines 6 and 7 exclude workers in CPS detailed occupations with fewer than 20 covered workers, and lines 8–10 exclude workers not residing in an SMSA (Standard Metropolitan Statistical Area). The number of observations (workers) for each of lines 1–5 is 17,546; for each of lines 6 and 7 is 17,758; and for lines 8–10 is 12,647.

In all of the equations covered in table 3.3 the dependent variable is the natural logarithm of a worker's usual hourly earnings—his "usual weekly earnings" divided by his "usual weekly hours." All of the regressions have in common the following right-hand variables: years of school completed, age, one marital status dummy variable, two city-size dummies, a dummy variable for part-time work (usual weekly hours less than 35), five major occupation dummies, three region dummies, four major industry dummies, and an extent of unionism y variable that is different on each line of the table. These are the only variables included in the Weiss-type equations. The micro equations, two for each line of the table, also include the union status dummy variable U and one of the two micro equations also includes the interaction variable Uy as indicated in the column headings.

In lines 1–5 the y variable is by industry (154 CPS detailed industries), in lines 6 and 7 by occupation (91 CPS detailed occupations), and in lines 8–10 by SMSA (98 listed SMSAs and one catch-all category for all other SMSAs). U^* is the fraction of *covered* workers in each industry (line 1), or occupation (line 6), or SMSA (line 8) who are union members as reported in the May 1973 CPS where *covered* means "covered in the fitted wage equations." The remaining seven y variables were estimated by Freeman and Medoff [69] from U.S. Bureau of Labor Statistics (BLS) establishment data for 1968–72 on collective bargaining coverage, separately for production workers (PW) and all workers (AW) by industry (lines 2 and 3), and from May 1973, 1974, and 1975 CPS data on union membership by occupation (line 7) and separately for PW and AW by industry (lines 4 and 5) and by SMSA (lines 9 and 10).

The coefficient W_y of the extent of unionism y variable in each of the 10 Weiss-type wage equations is given in column 3 of table 3.3. The range of these 10 coefficients is quite wide, from 0.09 to 0.44, indicating great sensitivity of W_y to the choice of the extent of unionism y variable used in the regressions. The estimates of a_y (the partial derivative of W with respect to y evaluated in column 5 at the mean of U among covered workers) from the 20 micro equations, given in columns 5 and 7, vary with the chosen y variable in a manner similar to that of W_y in column 3.

In contrast, the estimates of the wage gap $\overline{M}$ (the partial derivative of W with respect to union status U, evaluated in column 4 at the mean of y among covered workers) from the 20 micro equations, shown in columns 4 and 6, are rather insensitive to which of the 10 y variables enters the equation. The range of $\overline{M}$ in column 4 is 0.172 to 0.184 and in column 6 is 0.164 to 0.194.

Panel B of table 3.3 compares the Weiss-type "union wage effect" estimates W_y with the wage gap estimates $\overline{M}$ from the matching micro wage equations in three different ways: the differences $W_y - \overline{M}$ in columns 8 and 9, the ratios $W_y/\overline{M}$ in columns 10 and 11, and the ratios $W_y/(a_y + \overline{M})$ in columns 12 and 13. Both the differences $W_y - \overline{M}$ and the ratios $W_y/\overline{M}$ are too unstable across the 10 lines of the table to permit estimation with much precision of the wage gap $\overline{M}$ from knowledge of W_y estimates from Weiss-type equations. There are some regularities, of course, in columns

8–11: all of the Weiss-type W_y's are larger than corresponding wage gap $\overline{M}$'s when the y variable is by industry and the reverse holds when the y's are by occupation or SMSA.

How closely does W_y approximate the corresponding value of $a_y + \overline{M}$ from the micro equation? The geometric mean of the ratios in column 12 is 0.79, and the range is 0.56 to 1.05. The geometric mean of column 13 is 0.78 and the range is 0.57 to 0.94. The differences $W_y - (a_y + \overline{M})$, calculated from columns 3–5 and not shown in the table, average -0.053 and range from -0.095 to 0.006. Thus these figures suggest that although Weiss-type W_y estimates are somewhat lower than values of $a_y + \overline{M}$ from corresponding micro wage equations, the interpretation of W_y as roughly the sum of the union/nonunion wage gap $\overline{M}$ and the extent of unionism wage differential captured in the coefficient a_y is a valid one.

Table 3.3 reports results of experiments designed to discover what it is that is estimated by Weiss-type W_y figures. In various other contexts, however, I have fitted by OLS a variety of other Weiss-type equations and matching micro equations. These are summarized in table 3.4.

All of the equations covered in table 3.4 were fitted by OLS to May CPS data for individual workers. Lines 1, 2, and 3 cover all nonfarm, not private household wage and salary workers, 16 years of age and older, without missing data, except that line 3 is restricted to operatives (except transport equipment operatives). The worker coverage on lines 4–7 is the same as in table 3.3 except that in table 3.4 the observations come from a 20 percent random subsample of the May 1973 CPS.

The dependent variable in all of the equations is the natural logarithm of usual hourly earnings. All of the equations have an extent of unionism y variable by industry on the right-hand side. Column 3 identifies the y variable used on each line where the shorthand identifications have the

Table 3.4 Other Comparisons of W_y and $\overline{M}$ (May CPS Data)

Line No. (1)	Coverage and Date[a] (2)	y (3)	W_y (4)	Micro Equations: $\overline{M}$ (5)	Micro Equations: a_y (6)	$W_y \div a_y + \overline{M}$ (7)
1	All, 1973–75	BLS-AW	.275	.168	.157	.845
2	All, 1973–75	CPS-AW	.349	[b]	[b]	[b]
3	Operatives, 1973–75	BLS-AW	.368	.182	.219	.917
4	White males, 1973	CPS-PW	.390	.176	.299	.821
5	White males, 1973	BLS-PW	.253	.173	.174	.728
6	White males, 1973	CPS-AW	.348	.172	.235	.855
7	White males, 1973	BLS-AW	.269	.167	.164	.812

[a]See text for details.

[b]Micro equation not fitted.

same meaning in table 3.4 as in table 3.3. The estimated coefficients W_y of y in the Weiss-type equations appear in column 4. All of the micro equations reported in the table include two additional unionism variables: the union membership dummy variable U and its interaction Uy with y. The estimates of $\overline{M}$ and a_y from the micro equations are given in columns 5 and 6 and the ratio of W_y to $a_y + \overline{M}$ in column 7.

The x variables included in the wage equations are as follows:

Lines 1–3: years of school completed and its square, age and its square, the cross-product of age and schooling, two year dummies, two marital status dummies, eight major occupations dummies (omitted, of course, on line 3), 14 major industry dummies, three sex by race dummies, seven region by rural versus urban dummies, and 98 SMSA dummies.

Lines 4–7: schooling and its square, experience (age minus schooling) and its square, three marital status dummies, eight region dummies, five city-size dummies, eight occupation dummies, 11 industry dummies, and one part-time worker dummy.

The numbers in table 3.4 closely resemble those by industry on the first five lines of table 3.3 and lead to the same conclusions.

b) Aggregate Macro Equations

Return to equations (3.6) and (3.7):

$$W = a + a_x x + a_x^* x^* + a_y U^* + \overline{M} U + e; \tag{3.6}$$

$$W^* = a + d_x x^* + W_y U^* + e^*; \mathrm{d}_x \equiv a_x + \mathrm{a}_x^*; W_y \equiv a_y + \overline{M}; \tag{3.7}$$

where (3.6) is a micro wage equation fitted by OLS, (3.7) is the corresponding aggregate (by industry, city, etc.) macro equation fitted by employment-weighted least squares, and the asterisk superscripts denote means (by industry, city, etc.) of the variables to which they are attached. Thus when the aggregation is exact, as in (3.7), the coefficient W_y of the extent of unionism variable U^* is exactly equal to the sum $a_y + \overline{M}$ of the coefficient a_y of U^* and the wage gap coefficient $\overline{M}$ of union status U in the matching micro equation (3.6). However, if the aggregation is not exact—e.g., when the extent of unionism variable y in (3.6) and (3.7) is not U^* or when (3.7) is not fitted with employment weights—then W_y is only approximately equal to $a_y + \overline{M}$, as table 3.5 below shows.

This table covers 10 micro equations all fitted by OLS and 20 macro equations of which 10 were fitted with employment-weighted observations and 10 without weighting the observations. The data sources, worker coverage, extent of unionism y variables, and the dependent variable W and right-hand x variables in the 10 micro equations are exactly the same as in table 3.3. The aggregates W^* of W and the x^*'s of the x variables in the macro equations are all exact. All of the means x^*'s of the x's, as well as the x's, are included as right-hand variables in the micro equations

Table 3.5 Comparison of Micro Estimates of a_y and $\bar{M}$ with Aggregate Macro Estimates of W_y (White Males in Private Sector, May 1973 CPS)

Line No. (1)	y variable (2)	Regression Coefficients: Micro a_y (3)	Micro $\bar{M}$ (4)	Macro: W_y Wtd. (5)	Macro: W_y Unwtd. (6)	$W_y/(a_y + \bar{M})$ Wtd. (7)	$W_y/(a_y + \bar{M})$ Unwtd. (8)
1	U^* by ind.	.216	.174	.390	.452	1.00	1.16
2	BLS-PW by ind.	.157	.177	.257	.269	.77	.81
3	BLS-AW by ind.	.154	.179	.287	.312	.86	.94
4	CPS-PW by ind.	.236	.173	.384	.448	.94	1.10
5	CPS-AW by ind.	.238	.175	.423	.490	1.02	1.19
6	U^* by occ.	−.216	.203	−.013	.061	1.00	[a]
7	CPS by occ.	−.216	.202	−.016	.058	[a]	[a]
8	U^* by SMSA	.242	.168	.410	.366	1.00	.89
9	CPS-PW by SMSA	.204	.169	.327	.237	.88	.64
10	CPS-AW by SMSA	.261	.169	.438	.329	1.02	.76

[a]Not shown because denominator is negative and close to zero.

along with the extent of unionism y variable and the union membership dummy variable U.

Within each column of table 3.5 the figures differ by line only because the extent of unionism y variable is different on each line. The estimates of the wage gap $\bar{M}$ in column 4 vary little across the 10 lines of the table. Furthermore, the $\bar{M}$ estimates in table 3.5 are close to their counterparts in table 3.3 despite the inclusion in table 3.5, but not in table 3.3, of the means x^* of the x's as right-hand variables in the micro equations. In contrast, the estimated coefficients a_y of y in column 3 of table 3.5 show considerable sensitivity to the choice of y variable and several of the a_y estimates in table 3.5 differ by a substantial amount from their table 3.3 counterparts, indicating sensitivity of estimates of a_y to the inclusion or exclusion from the micro equation of the means x^*.

The estimates of W_y from the macro equations in columns 5 and 6 also have much across-lines variability, and some of them are sensitive to weighting. The 20 estimates of W_y range from −0.02 to 0.49, which is fairly similar to the range 0.09 to 0.44 of the Weiss-type W_y estimates in table 3.3.

Columns 7 and 8 show the ratios $W_y/(a_y + \bar{M})$. On lines 1, 6, and 8 of column 7 the macro equation is an exact aggregation in all respects of the matching micro equation and, of course, the ratio $W_y/(a_y + \bar{M})$ then must be unity. None of the other 14 ratios in columns 7 and 8, however, is unity to at least two decimal places and, though the geometric mean of these 14 ratios is 0.91, which is fairly close to unity, the range of the ratios is wide, from 0.64 to 1.19. The differences $W_y - (a_y + \bar{M})$, not shown in the table, average -0.013 (zero differences are excluded in calculating the average) and range from -0.135 to 0.077. Thus though on the average the values of $a_y + \overline{M}$ approximate well the values of W_y from matching aggregate macro equations, the error in a particular approximation may be substantial in magnitude and of ambiguous sign. Furthermore, both the differences $W_y - \overline{M}$ and the ratios $W_y/\overline{M}$ are widely dispersed. The differences range from -0.22 to 0.32 and the ratios from -0.08 to 2.8.

There are, of course, some regularities that may be observed in table 3.5. On lines 1–5, with y by industry, the 10 values of $W_y - \overline{M}$ are all positive with a mean of 0.196 but a wide range from 0.080 to 0.315. Similarly on lines 8–10, with y by SMSA, $W_y - \overline{M}$ also is always positive with a mean of 0.182 and range from 0.068 to 0.269. In contrast, when y is by occupation, lines 6 and 7, $W_y - \overline{M}$ is negative with a mean of -0.180 and range from -0.218 to -0.142.

Return to equation (3.11) which incorporated Rosen's suggestion for maintaining in the macro equation the distinction between extent of unionism effects and wage gap (or union status) effects. I fitted an employment-weighted macro equation exactly like that on line 1 of table 3.5 except for including three dummy variables classifying industries by their values of U^* as in equation (3.11). The estimate of W_y (equal to the estimated coefficient of U^*) was 0.365, more than twice as large as the wage gap $\overline{M}$ estimate from the matching micro equation. Thus in this experiment his suggestion failed to work.

In this section I have presented evidence that:

a) Macro estimates of the union wage effect measured by W_y from wage equations fitted by least squares to aggregated cross-section data tend on the average to estimate the sum of two quite distinct coefficients in corresponding micro equations: the union/nonunion wage gap $\overline{M}$ and the partial derivative a_y of W with respect to the extent of unionism variable y used in the macro equations. A similar proposition holds for Weiss-type W_y estimates, with the qualification that Weiss-type W_y figures tend to be somewhat smaller than values of $a_y + \overline{M}$ from matching micro equations.

b) Ratios of macro W_y's to corresponding values of $a_y + \overline{M}$ from micro equations as well as differences $W_y - (a_y + \overline{M})$ have substantial dispersion.

c) Estimates of a_y are quite sensitive to the choice of y variable and to some other aspects of wage equation specification.

d) Therefore, estimating the wage gap $\overline{M}$ from knowledge of W_y involves much imprecision.

5. The Verdict on the Macro Estimates

Now return to table 3.1. On lines 5–8, 11–15, 18, 31, 33–36, 44, 51–53, and 56 the worker coverage is quite narrow. Omit these 20 lines. Also omit line 39, the only line on which the cross-section was by occupation, and lines 19–22, 27–28 pertaining to the Hamermesh [80, 81] and Hirsch-Rufolo [92] studies. On these 28 lines the mean value of W_y, using lower ends of estimate ranges, was 0.10 and 0.18 using upper ends.

On the remaining 36 lines of the table the corresponding means were 0.26 and 0.29. On seven of these lines the W_y estimates were of the Weiss-type, all with industry cross-sections. On the other 29 lines the estimates were of the aggregate type with industry cross-sections on 26 lines and State cross-sections on 3 lines. On the 33 lines with industry cross-sections the corresponding means were 0.23 and 0.26. Tables 3.3 and 3.5 strongly suggest that these W_y figures substantially overestimate their wage gap $\overline{M}$ counterpart.

By how much? I cannot answer this question with much precision. The W_y figures in table 3.1 pertain disproportionately to production workers in manufacturing in the period from the late 1950s to the middle 1970s, while tables 3.3 and 3.5 refer to white males employed in the private sector in 1973. Furthermore, the estimates of $W_y - \overline{M}$ for industry cross-sections in tables 3.3 and 3.5 range from 0.080 to 0.315. Thus at best there is only a crude suggestion that for the period from the late 1950s to the middle 1970s and for the workers covered in the 33 lines of industry cross-sections in table 3.1 the average wage gap did not exceed 0.18.

4 Simultaneous Equations Estimates: The Problem of Robustness

1. Introduction

Most of the union/nonunion wage gap ($\overline{M}$) estimates surveyed in this book come from wage equations, such as (2.1) and (2.2), fitted by ordinary least squares (OLS) to cross-section (CS), individual-worker data on union status (U), wages, and other variables included to provide at least partial control for differences among workers in their productiveness and in the quality of their working conditions. Chapters 6–9 survey these Micro, OLS, CS wage gap estimates. Universally in the fitted wage equations underlying these estimates the unexplained or residual wage variances were not negligible, indicating that important wage-explanatory variables were omitted from the right-hand side. These omissions would not be worrisome if, conditional on the included right-hand variables (other than U), the union status selection process were random.

However, most students of unionism, I think, would argue that union status selection is not random and that therefore Micro, OLS, CS wage gap estimates may suffer from "selectivity" bias. I have strong priors on the direction of the bias. Let a union through collective bargaining impose on an employer higher wages for his workers than he otherwise would pay them with worker quality not tightly specified in the collective bargaining agreement. The higher wages will lengthen the queue of the applicants for the unionized jobs, including some applicants of greater productiveness than otherwise would have applied. At the same time the employer has an incentive to evade the increase in his labor costs by employing workers of greater quality. The evasions will take time and will be impeded by the costs of screening for worker quality, imperfect substitution in production among worker qualities, and employment constraints in the collective bargaining agreement. Nevertheless, higher wages, I argue, eventually will lead to a higher quality work force. All of this would not matter, of course, if the available data permitted approximately perfect control for worker quality in wage equations. But the data do not permit such control. Hence my priors are that the Micro, OLS, CS wage gap estimates are biased upward—the omitted quality variables are positively correlated with union status *U*.

The likelihood that Micro, OLS, CS wage gap estimates are selectivity biased has not escaped the notice of econometricians, and recently a substantial number of papers have appeared that use techniques designed to reduce this bias. Broadly speaking, these papers fall into two groups according to the technique used:

1. Simultaneous equations (SE) studies that postulate a system of equations consisting of at least the wage equation (or pair of equations by union status) and an equation or equations determining union status. (In some SE studies the equation system contains not only wage and union status equations but also other equations such as one for worker mobility.) The equation system then is fitted to the cross-section data. The SE studies are summarized in this chapter.
2. Panel studies that use longitudinal data, thus permitting wage comparisons "before and after" unionization. Chapter 5 reviews the panel studies.

The next section of this chapter briefly discusses the SE techniques that have been used and presents the Micro, SE, CS wage gap estimates that I have drawn from the simultaneous equations studies. For most of these SE estimates there are corresponding Micro, OLS, CS estimates with which the SE estimates may be compared. The simultaneous equations estimates are much more dispersed than the OLS estimates. They are not consistently smaller than the OLS estimates or consistently larger. Furthermore, a substantial fraction of the SE estimates are, I think, preposterously large or outlandishly negative. There is also considerable evidence in the set of SE estimates that they are sensitive to the set of right-hand variables in the wage and union status equations, the assumptions made regarding the error or residual terms in these equations, the method used to fit the equations to the data, and the data set used.

In a majority of the SE studies the estimation method is one in which the union status equation first is fitted to data on union status and the exogenous variables in the equation system. The predicted value $\hat{U}$ [or a curvilinear function $h(\hat{U})$ of $\hat{U}$] of the union status variable U is then calculated for each worker from the fitted union status equation and is entered on the right-hand side of the wage equation in place of (or in addition to) the observed union status variable in fitting the wage equation.

The third section appraises the simultaneous equations wage gap estimates covered in this chapter.

2. Survey of the Simultaneous Equations Estimates

In this section I survey the simultaneous equations wage gap estimates that I have retrieved from 28 studies. All of the studies are of recent vintage. I have excluded studies in which the fitted wage equations were of the macro type, i.e., in which the unionism variable in the fitted wage equations was extent of unionism y rather than union status U. Chapter 3 briefly discusses the SE estimates from macro equations.

I have divided the estimates into four groups according to the technique used to adjust the fitted wage equations for selectivity bias:

1. The inverse Mills' ratio or IMR method in which the wage equations are augmented by adding each worker's estimated inverse Mills' ratio as a right-hand variable. The estimated IMRs come from a union status equation fitted by probit.
2. The U-hat method in which the estimated probability of being unionized $\hat{U}$ is substituted for the union status dummy variable U in fitting the wage equation. $\hat{U}$ is calculated for each worker from a union status equation usually fitted by OLS, logit, or probit.
3. MLE or maximum likelihood estimation in which the parameters of the simultaneous equations system (consisting of wage, union status, and sometimes other equations) are estimated by maximum likelihood procedures.
4. Other estimates.

a. IMR Estimates.

I first discuss the studies that used the IMR technique to correct for selectivity bias. These studies postulate a wage equation resembling (2.1) or pair of wage equations by union status resembling (2.2) and a reduced-form union status equation. The right-hand variables in the latter frequently, but not necessarily, are the same as those (excluding U) in the wage equation(s). This union status equation is fitted by probit to the cross-section, individual-worker data on union status and the specified right-hand variables. The computer output from this fitting of the union status equation consists of the estimated status equation and for each worker the estimated probability $\hat{U}$ of being unionized and his estimated IMR, h_u if $U = 1$ and h_n if $U = 0$. The specified wage equations are then augmented by adding the inverse Mills' ratio h as a right-hand variable, where $h = h_u$ for a unionized worker and $h = h_n$ for a nonunion worker. The augmented wage equations are then fitted to the cross-section, individual-worker data on wages, union status U, the inverse Mills' ratio h, and other right-hand variables by ordinary least squares (OLS) or generalized least squares (GLS).

Inserting the appropriate inverse Mills' ratio as an additional variable on the right-hand side of the wage equations, according to the proponents of the method (e.g., see study no. 114), will correct for the selectivity bias that otherwise might occur in estimating the parameters of the unaugmented wage equations. Thus in calculating wage gap estimates from the fitted wage equations, the IMR variable should be disregarded, its function being only to adjust for selectivity bias.

Turn now to table 4.1 which summarizes the IMR wage gap ($\overline{M}$) estimates together with corresponding OLS estimates. Column 2 identifies by its number in the references list at the end of the book the study from which the estimates on each line were drawn. Columns 3 and 4 present the wage gap ($\overline{M}$) estimates. None of these estimates should be attributed to the study authors as their estimates. Indeed, many of the numbers appearing in columns 3 and 4 cannot be found in the studies from which I have calculated them. These estimates are in natural logarithmic, not percentage, units. The date to which the estimates pertain is shown in column 5. Column 6 provides a brief and incomplete description of the worker coverage. The notes to the table contain additional explanatory detail.

Except for the figures on lines 3, 4, 8, and 33 for hospital workers and on lines 51, 53, and 55 for library workers, none of the OLS wage gap estimates in column 3 is negative (the lowest is -0.15), and similarly except for the figures on lines 13, 26, and 27 none exceeds 0.22 (the largest is 0.31). The IMR wage gap estimates in column 4 are much more widely dispersed. Their range is incredible: from -3.61 to 1.58 ($e^{-3.61}-1=-0.97$ and $e^{1.58}-1=3.85$!). Twenty of the 55 IMR estimates are above 0.22 and 14 are negative, leaving only 21 in the range 0.00 to 0.22.

On 50 of the 55 lines of the table it is possible to compare the OLS and IMR estimates. In only 22 of the 50 comparisons is the deviation of IMR estimate from OLS estimate as small numerically as 0.10. In 21 of the comparisons the IMR estimates exceed their OLS counterparts by more than 0.10, and in seven comparisons the IMR figures fall short of the OLS figures by more than 0.10. The range of the excess of IMR over OLS estimates is from -3.71 to 1.56.

Four of the studies [34, 61, 62, 129] covered in table 4.1 are for hospital workers, and one [56] is for library workers. Disregard these studies. This leaves 24 lines in the table. The range of the OLS wage gap estimates on these lines is 0.05 to 0.31 with only those on lines 13, 26 and 27 above 0.22. The corresponding range for the IMR estimates is -3.61 to 0.53 with 12 estimates above 0.22, three below 0.05, and nine in the range 0.05 to 0.22. On the 20 lines in which IMR and OLS may be compared, the IMR exceeded the OLS estimates by more than 0.10 in eight comparisons and fell below the OLS figures by more than 0.10 in two comparisons (both in the Podgursky study no. 160). Thus, disregarding the hospital worker studies does not significantly change the message of table 4.1.

Table 4.1 IMR and OLS Wage Gap ($\overline{M}$) Estimates

Line No. (1)	Study No. (2)	$\overline{M}$ Estimate: OLS (3)	$\overline{M}$ Estimate: IMR (4)	Date (5)	Worker Coverage (6)
1	27	.15	.22	1970	NLS Young Men, 1969–71; Young Women, 1970–72
2	34	.03	.29	1973–76	Hospitals, private, nonprofessionals
3	34	−.13	−.03	1973–76	Hospitals, private, registered nurses
4	34	−.15	.01	1973–76	Hospitals, private, technicians
5	34	.13	.26	1973–76	Hospitals, private, practical nurses
6	34	.00	.20	1973–76	Hospitals, government, nonprofessionals
7	34	.03	−.01	1973–76	Hospitals, government, registered nurses
8	34	−.02	−.68	1973–76	Hospitals, government, technicians
9	34	.14	.14	1973–76	Hospitals, government, practical nurses
10	34	.02	1.58	1973–76	Hospitals, private, nonprofessionals
11	49	.13	.30	1969	NLS Older Men, white
12	49	.16	.35	1971	NLS Older Men, white
13	59	.26	.32	1977	See line note
14	62	.06	.49	1977	Hospital registered nurses
15	62	.06	.46	1977	Hospital licensed practical nurses
16	61	.02	−.08	1977–78	Hospital nurses
17	61	.16	.79	1977–78	Hospital nurses' aides
18	61}	.00	{.26	1977–78	Hospital health aides
19	61}		{.25	1977–78	Hospital health technicians
20	86	.11	.53	1974	Male household heads
21	86	.05	.09	1968–74	Male household heads
22	90	.11	.53	1970	Blue-collar workers, manufacturing
23	114	.14	.12	1967	Private full-time operatives
24	119	.10	.33	1969	NLS Older Men, white
25	119	.13	.40	1971	NLS Older Men, white
26	119	.28	.38	1969	NLS Older Men, black
27	119	.31	.47	1971	NLS Older Men, black
28	119	.22	.33	1971	NLS Young Men, white
29	119	.19	.25	1971	NLS Young Men, black
30	129	.06	.22	1973–76	Hospitals, private, nonprofessionals
31	129	.05	.20	1973–76	Hospitals, private, nonprofessionals
32	129	.03	.17	1973–76	Hospitals, private, registered nurses
33	129	−.11	.06	1973–76	Hospitals, private, registered nurses

36	129	.03	−.27	1973–76	Hospitals, government, registered nurses
37	129	.00	−.32	1973–76	Hospitals, government, registered nurses
38	160	.07	.05	1969	Private, blue-collar workers
39	160	.07	.07	1969	Private, blue-collar workers
40	160	.10	−1.01	1969	Private, blue-collar workers
41	160	.10	−3.61	1969	Private, blue-collar workers
42	199	.12	.09	1973	Wage and salary workers 16 and over
43	199	.14	.16	1973	Wage and salary workers 16 and over
44	199	—	.08	1973	Wage and salary workers 16 and over
45	199	—	.20	1973	Wage and salary workers 16 and over
46	199	—	.26	1973	Wage and salary workers 16 and over
47	50	—	−.02	1971	NLS Older Men, white
48	56	.03	.08	1977	City library professionals
49	56	.06	.02	1977	City library technicians
50	56	.07	.11	1977	City library clerical
51	56	−.08	−.10	1977	City library maintenance
52	56	.00	.03	1977	Line 48
53	56	−.05	−.08	1977	Line 49
54	56	.04	.08	1977	Line 50
55	56	−.12	−.14	1977	Line 51

Note:

Line 1. Coverage includes only job changers except the self-employed, construction workers, and persons enrolled in school.

Lines 1, 11, 12, 24–29, 47. NLS means *National Longitudinal Survey*.

Lines 2–10. Line 2 differs from line 10 in that on line 10 two separate wage equations by union status were fitted while on line 2 a single equation was fitted to the data for both union and nonunion workers. *U*-hat estimates also available from this study (see table 4.2).

Line 13. Worker coverage excludes self-employed, managers, sales workers, and construction workers. The corresponding MLE estimate of $\overline{M}$ was −1.01 (see table 4.3).

Lines 14–15. In this study the observations were for hospitals by occupation rather than for individual workers.

Lines 16–19. The OLS and IMR estimates of $\overline{M}$ are not strictly comparable.

Line 21. The dependent variable is the natural log of the present value (as of 1968) of discounted wages for 1968–74; all right-hand variables are for 1968.

Line 23. Coverage is restricted to mining, construction, manufacturing, transportation, and utilities.

Lines 30–37. Coverage is restricted to full-time workers. For each of lines 31, 33, 35, and 37 the underlying wage equations include interactions of union status with color and year, while the equations on lines 30, 32, 34, and 36 do not include these interactions. Corresponding *U*-hat wage gap estimates are available in table 4.2.

Lines 38–41. Coverage is restricted to full-time, year-round nonagricultural workers, 14 years of age and older. On lines 38 and 39, the dependent variable in the wage equation is annual earnings while on lines 40 and 41 the dependent variable is *ln* (annual earnings). In other respects lines 38 and 39 do not differ from lines 40 and 41, respectively. Lines 38 and 39 (and corresponding lines 40 and 41) differ from each other only in the specification of the union status equation. *U*-hat estimates of $\overline{M}$ are available in table 4.2.

Lines 42–46. Coverage is restricted to persons working at least 20 hours per week. The wage equation specifications differ from line to line.

Line 47. Worker coverage and right-hand variables in wage and union status equations were not quite the same on this line as on line 12. See table 4.2 for *U*-hat estimates.

Lines 48–55. In this study the observations were for libraries by occupation. On lines 48–51 the dependent variable was *ln* (annual starting salary), but on lines 52–55 was *ln* (annual maximum salary).

That the excess of the IMR over the OLS wage gap estimate varies with worker coverage is to be expected. What is surprising, however, is the extent of the variation in this excess as shown in the following line comparisons:

Lines Compared	*Range of Excess*
2–9	–.66 to .26
14, 15	.40 to .43
16, 17	–.10 to .63
24, 26	.10 to .23
25, 27–29	.06 to .27
30, 32, 34, 36	–.30 to .16
or 31, 33, 35, 37	–.32 to .17
48–51	–.04 to .05
or 52–55	–.03 to .04

There is also evidence in table 4.1 that the excess of the IMR over the OLS wage gap estimate is sensitive to the specification of the wage and union status equations:

Lines Compared	*Range of Excess*
2, 10	.26 to 1.56
20, 21	.04 to .42
30, 31	.15 to .16
32, 33	.14 to .17
34, 35	–.26 to –.28
36, 37	–.32 to –.30
38–41	–3.71 to .00
42, 43	–.03 to .02

In this connection also compare lines 12 and 47 both based on studies by the same authors (Duncan and Leigh). The worker coverage and right-hand variables in the wage and union status equations differ slightly between the two lines. Yet the IMR wage gap $\overline{M}$ estimates in column 4 are quite different: 0.35 on line 12 and –0.02 on line 47!

One of the assumptions underlying the IMR method is that the errors in the reduced-form union status equation are normally distributed. This is not, I judge, an innocuous assumption. In a recent study [115] Lee used a two-stage procedure somewhat similar to the IMR method in fitting the wage and union status equations, but instead of the normal distribution he assumed other distribution forms: student's *t*, Chi-square, and one of the bivariate Edgeworth expansions. He used the same data set and equation specifications as in his earlier study [114] on line 23 of table 4.1. Below are the resulting estimates of the wage gap $\overline{M}$ (df = degrees of freedom):

Distribution Form	*Estimate of $\overline{M}$*
Normal—i.e., IMR	.22
Student's *t* (5 df)	.15
Chi-square (100 df)	.25
Chi-square (3 df)	.57
Bivariate Edgeworth	.02

According to Lee, the best-fitting wage equations were those based on the bivariate Edgeworth expansion and the worst-fitting were their normal (IMR) counterparts. The differences in goodness of fit (adjusted residual variance), however, were small compared to the above differences in $\overline{M}$ estimates. (Notice that the above IMR estimate 0.22 is not the same as that 0.12 given on line 23 of table 4.1. I judge that Lee in [115] intended to replicate the IMR wage equation estimates in his earlier study [114]. Lee noted his failure to replicate and stated that it was "because the computer systems and least square subroutines used" were not the same.)

Adamache and Sloan [3] in their study of unions and hospital wages used an IMR-like procedure proposed by Olsen [149]. Assume that the errors in the union status equation have a rectangular distribution with a minimum of zero and a maximum of unity. Then Olsen showed that the coefficients of the union status equation may be estimated consistently by least squares (linear probability model) and that to correct for selectivity bias in the wage equation, the wage equation should be augmented by the predicted value $\hat{U}$ of U for a nonunion worker and $\hat{U}-1$ for a union worker, where $\hat{U}$ is calculated from the union status equation. Unfortunately, the wage gap estimates reported by Adamache and Sloan are not conceptually comparable to those shown in table 4.1, and I could not calculate comparable estimates from data reported in their paper.

b) U-Hat Estimates

The *U*-hat method of adjusting the wage equation for selectivity bias differs from the IMR method in the following respects:

1. The reduced-form union status equation may be fitted by OLS (linear probability model) or logit as well as by probit.
2. For each worker his predicted probability $\hat{U}$ of being unionized, instead of his IMR, is calculated from the fitted reduced-form union status equation.
3. In fitting the wage equation the value of the union status variable assigned to each worker is $\hat{U}$ rather than his observed union status *U*.

For the econometric argument underlying the *U*-hat method see [34] and [50] and the references cited there.

Table 4.2 summarizes the *U*-hat wage gap estimates and compares them to corresponding OLS and IMR estimates whenever the latter are available. The format of the table is similar to that of table 4.1. Only nine studies provide *U*-hat wage gap estimates, four of which also have IMR estimates covered in table 4.1.

The story told by table 4.2 about the *U*-hat wage gap estimates is similar to that told by table 4.1 for the IMR estimates: incredible dispersion of the estimates and great sensitivity to worker coverage and specification of the underlying wage and union status equations. For example, compare the *U*-hat estimates on lines 19 and 44 where the specifications of the equation system differed substantially. Similarly, Duncan and Stafford in study no. 48 line 17 report only one *U*-hat estimate, but they mention that in experimenting with various specifications they found that the *U*-hat estimates varied considerably across the specifications.

On 20 lines of table 4.2, *U*-hat, IMR, and OLS estimates may be compared. On 14 of the 20 lines the deviations, taken numerically, of *U*-hat from OLS wage gap estimates were larger than the corresponding deviations of IMR from OLS estimates. For both the *U*-hat and IMR estimates, positive deviations and negative deviations from OLS occurred with roughly equal frequency. Furthermore, the deviations of *U*-hat from IMR estimates, taken numerically, exceeded 0.20 in 10 of 21 comparisons, indicating marked sensitivity of simultaneous equations gap estimates to the particular method used to correct for selectivity bias.

c) MLE Estimates

The six studies whose maximum likelihood wage gap estimates are presented in table 4.3 are a somewhat heterogenous group. Therefore I discuss these studies individually, beginning with study nos. 180 and 181 on lines 5 and 6 of the table. These two studies have in common an author (Schmidt), a data set, and fairly similar views of the underlying simultaneous equations model. Study no. 181, which came first, postulates a wage equation with an endogenous union status variable *U* on the right-hand side and a union status equation in logit form with an endogenous wage variable on the right-hand side. The coefficients of the pair of equations were estimated by maximum likelihood procedures. (However, Olsen [148] has pointed to a flaw in the authors' likelihood function.)

In study no. 180, line 5, the specification of the wage equation was changed to include several interactions of union status *U* with other right-hand variables, permitting the wage gap to vary with these variables, and in the logit union status equation the *wage* variable was replaced by the *wage gap* variable. In addition, Schmidt assumed that the error term in the wage equation was distributed independently of the right-hand variables, thus assuming away selectivity bias in the wage equation. Thus I do not find it surprising that on line 5 the OLS and MLE estimates are the same.

Turn now to study nos. 1, 57, and 59 on lines 1–4 of table 4.3. These three studies have an author (Farber) in common and therefore somewhat

Table 4.2 *U*-Hat, OLS, and IMR Wage Gap ($\overline{M}$) Estimates

Line No. (1)	Study No. (2)	$\overline{M}$ Estimate OLS (3)	*U*-Hat (4)	IMR (5)	Date (6)	Worker Coverage (7)
1	34	.06	.46	—	1973–76	Hospitals, private, nonprofessionals
2	34	.03	.58	.29	1973–76	Hospitals, private, nonprofessionals
3	34	.03	−.02	—	1973–76	Hospitals, private, registered nurses
4	34	−.13	.02	−.03	1973–76	Hospitals, private, registered nurses
5	34	−.17	−.08	—	1973–76	Hospitals, private, technicians
6	34	−.15	.27	.01	1973–76	Hospitals, private, technicians
7	34	.02	.13	—	1973–76	Hospitals, private, practical nurses
8	34	.13	.05	.26	1973–76	Hospitals, private, practical nurses
9	34	.04	.53	—	1973–76	Hospitals, government, nonprofessionals
10	34	.00	.79	.20	1973–76	Hospitals, government, nonprofessionals
11	34	.01	−.33	—	1973–76	Hospitals, government, registered nurses
12	34	.03	−.03	−.01	1973–76	Hospitals, government, registered nurses
13	34	−.02	−.59	—	1973–76	Hospitals, government, technicians
14	34	−.02	−.65	−.68	1973–76	Hospitals, government, technicians
15	34	.13	.02	—	1973–76	Hospitals, government, practical nurses
16	34	.14	.23	.14	1973–76	Hospitals, government, practical nurses
17	48	.17	.21	—	1976	Blue-collar with regular work schedules
18	118	.13	−.12	—	1969	NLS Older Men, white
19	118	.16	−.05	—	1971	NLS Older Men, white
20	118	.28	.54	—	1969	NLS Older Men, black
21	118	.29	.47	—	1971	NLS Older Men, black
22	118	.18	−.01	—	1969	NLS Older Men, both
23	118	.20	.01	—	1971	NLS Older Men, both
24	118	.22	.13	—	1969	NLS Young Men, white
25	118	.23	.23	—	1971	NLS Young Men, white
26	118	.18	.39	—	1969	NLS Young Men, black
27	118	.20	.31	—	1971	NLS Young Men, black
28	118	.21	.22	—	1969	NLS Young Men, both

Table 4.2 (continued)

Line No. (1)	Study No. (2)	$\overline{M}$ Estimate: OLS (3)	*U*-Hat (4)	IMR (5)	Date (6)	Worker Coverage (7)
29	118	.23	.29	—	1971	NLS Young Men, both
30	129	.06	.45	.22	1973–76	Hospital workers, private, nonprofessionals
31	129	.05	.36	.20	1973–76	Hospital workers, private, nonprofessionals
32	129	.03	.25	.17	1973–76	Hospital workers, private, registered nurses
33	129	−.11	.16	.06	1973–76	Hospital workers, private, registered nurses
34	129	.04	.05	−.22	1973–76	Hospital workers, government, nonprofessionals
35	129	.01	−.12	−.27	1973–76	Hospital workers, government, nonprofessionals
36	129	.03	−.23	−.27	1973–76	Hospital workers, government, registered nurses
37	129	.00	−.57	−.32	1973–76	Hospital workers, government, registered nurses
38	160	.07	.03	.05	1969	Private, blue-collar, wage and salary workers
39	160	.07	.23	.07	1969	Private, blue-collar, wage and salary workers
40	160	.06	−.88	—	1969	Private, blue-collar, wage and salary workers
41	160	.10	−1.32	−1.01	1969	Private, blue-collar, wage and salary workers
42	160	.10	−2.25	−3.61	1969	Private, blue-collar, wage and salary workers
43	160	.09	−1.59	—	1969	Private, blue-collar, wage and salary workers
44	50	—	.25	−.02	1971	NLS Older Men, white
45	24	.06	.14	—	1973	Police
46	25	.07	.09	—	1974	Schoolteachers
47	25	.21	.26	—	1977	Schoolteachers
48	183	.02	−.16	—	1973	Registered nurses

Note:
Lines 1–16. The wage equations for the odd-number lines exclude (those on the even-number lines include) 3 interactions of union status with other right-hand variables.
Lines 18–29, 44. NLS means *National Longitudinal Survey*.
Lines 30–37. See the notes for lines 30–37 in table 4.1.
Lines 38–43. Coverage is restricted to full-time, year-round, nonagricultural workers, 14 years of age and older. On lines 38, 39, and 40 the dependent variable is annual earnings, while on lines 41–43 the dependent variable is *ln* (annual earnings). Lines 38 and 39 (and correspondingly 40 and 41) differ from each other only in the specification of the union status equation. Line 40 differs from lines 38 and 39 (and similarly line 43 from lines 41 and 42) in both union status and wage equation specifications.
Line 45. Estimates in columns 3 and 4 are means of 4 separate estimates. In this study the observations were for police departments.
Line 48. In this study the observations were for individual hospitals.

Table 4.3 MLE and OLS Wage Gap ($\bar{M}$) Estimates

Line No. (1)	Study No. (2)	$\bar{M}$ Estimates OLS (3)	MLE (4)	Date (5)	Worker Coverage (6)
1	1	.07	.12	1975	Male household heads, excluding self-employed and construction
2	57	.28	.41	1970	NLS Young Men, out of school, <12 years of schooling
3	57	.28	.42	1970	NLS Young Men, out of school, <12 years of schooling
4	59	.26	−1.01	1977	Excludes managers, sales, construction, self-employed
5	180	.06	.06	1967	Private, full-time, 14–65 years of age
6	181	.10	.07	1967	Private, full-time, 14–65 years of age
7	157	.41	.46	1973–75	Male construction craftsmen

similar views regarding the underlying economics and econometrics. The data sets used, however, are quite different.

Study no. 1 on line 1 sets up a four-equation system consisting of a pair of wage equations by union status similar in form to equations (2.2) and a unique pair of union status equations in bivariate probit form. The first of the probit status equations, for the probability that a worker would be in the queue for a union job, reflects individual-worker choice regarding unionization. The second probit status equation, for the probability that a worker in the queue would get a union job, reflects choices of unions and unionized employers. The system was fitted both by maximum likelihood estimation and by an extension of the IMR method to the bivariate probit case. In this extension, the pair of union status equations is first fitted by bivariate probit, two (instead of one) IMRs are calculated for each worker, the wage equations are then augmented by these two IMRs and fitted by OLS. The IMR wage gap estimate, not shown on line 1, was 0.24, which is considerably larger than the OLS and MLE estimates given on line 1.

The equation system in study no. 57, lines 2 and 3, consists of a wage equation, a union status equation in probit form, and a turnover equation also in probit form. Union status was a right-hand variable in both the wage and turnover equations. There are two MLE wage gap estimates corresponding to the two different ways worker turnover was measured: by *quitting* a job or by being *separated* from it.

In Farber's study no. 59 the equation system is the somewhat standard one used in the IMR studies: a probit union equation and a pair of wage equations by union status. Indeed, Farber used the IMR method to estimate the pair of wage equations. The IMR wage gap estimate, 0.32, is on line 13 of table 4.1. He also estimated the equation system by maximum likelihood. The MLE wage gap estimate, on line 4 of table 4.3, is a highly implausible -1.01.

In the Perloff-Sickles study no. 157 on line 7 of table 4.3 the equations system contained three equations, one for union status, a second for hours worked per week, and the third for the hourly wage. In the wage and hour equations union status was interacted with all of the other right-hand variables including the constant. The authors reported their maximum likelihood wage gap estimate as 58.2 percent. The figure in column 4 of table 4.3 is ln (1.582). This estimate is conditional on a positive (>0) value of hours worked as predicted by the hours equation. The corresponding estimate not subject to this condition is $0.731 = ln\ (2.077)$.

d) Other Simultaneous Equations Studies

The remaining study, no. 111 by Killingsworth, is distinctly different. The data set used is one in which the observations are by industry and union status. Thus there are two wage observations for each industry, one is the mean for union workers and the other the mean for nonunion workers. The equation system consists of a pair of wage equations by union status and a corresponding pair of employment equations as follows:

$$\begin{aligned} \ln W_u^* &= a_o + a_x x^* + a_1 y + a_2 y^2 + e_u, \\ \ln W_n^* &= a_o + a_x x^* + a_3(a_1 y + a_2 y^2) + e_n, \\ \ln N_u &= b_u + b(\ln W_u^* - a_o - a_x x^*) + e_u', \\ \ln N_n &= b_n + b(\ln W_n^* - a_o - a_x x^*) + e_n', \end{aligned} \qquad (4.1)$$

where W_u^* and W_n^* are the mean wages of union and nonunion workers, respectively, N_u and N_n are the corresponding employments, the e's are error terms, the a's and b's are coefficients to be estimated, the x^*'s included median schooling by sex and means of sex and color dummies, and $y = N_u/(N_u + N_n)$. The system was estimated by weighted nonlinear three stage least squares and yielded a wage gap estimate of 0.02. There was no corresponding OLS wage gap estimate from this study.

3. Summary

In this chapter I have presented 108 simultaneous equations (SE) wage gap estimates for which there were matching ordinary least-squares (OLS) estimates. What do these estimate pairs tell us about the direction and numerical size of the suspected selectivity bias in the OLS estimates?

More than half (58 out of 108) of the pairs of estimates are for somewhat narrow groups of workers in hospitals, libraries, schools, and police departments. The mean excess of the OLS over the SE wage gap estimate in this set of 58 estimate pairs is −0.07. If this number is taken seriously, it suggests that OLS wage gap estimates, at least for these workers, are substantially *downward* biased, a result that for me is quite counterintuitive. However, I do not take this number seriously: the dispersion (standard deviation) among the 58 OLS minus SE estimate differences is 0.35!

In the remaining 50 pairs of estimates, with broader worker coverage, the mean excess of OLS over SE estimates is +0.19 suggesting that OLS wage gap estimates are markedly *upward* biased. But here, too, the standard deviation of the estimate differences is so large—0.73—as to make estimation even of the sign of the bias quite uncertain. However, 10 of these 50 pairs of estimates came from one study, that by Podgursky [160]. When the estimates from this study are ignored, the mean excess of OLS over SE wage gap estimates in the remaining estimate pairs is −0.03, and the standard deviation is 0.26. Again the sign of the bias is not transparent.

The selectivity bias problem in OLS wage gap estimates is one of omitted variables, a lack of information. I admire the ingenuity that has gone into the development of simultaneous equations econometrics to deal with this problem. Yet in the present context the techniques are not working. I know little more about the magnitude of the selectivity bias in OLS wage gap estimates after completing the survey of this chapter than if I had ignored the SE estimates reported here.

5 Estimates from Panel Data: The Problem of Measurement Error

1. Introduction

This chapter surveys wage gap estimates that I have drawn from wage equations fitted to *panel* or longitudinal data on individual workers. The key feature of panel data is that the same set of individuals, the "panel," is observed at more than one date. Thus panel data consist of a cross-section of individual-worker time series. All of the studies covered in this chapter explicitly exploit this time series aspect of panel data.

The two chief sources of panel data used in these studies are the University of Michigan Survey Research Center's *Panel Study of Income Dynamics* (PSID) and the Ohio State University's *National Longitudinal Survey* (NLS) with four panels, Young Men (14–24 years of age in 1966), Older Men (45–59 in 1966), Young Women (14–24 in 1968), and Older Women (30–44 in 1967). The data supplied by these sources may be regarded, of course, as simply a set of cross-sections differing by date. Indeed most of the studies reporting wage equations fitted to the NLS and PSID data have ignored their time series feature. Some of these were covered in Chapter 4 and the rest in later chapters, especially Chapter 9.

The problem that the panel studies attempt to solve is the same as that faced in the simultaneous equations studies covered in Chapter 4: omitted wage-explanatory variables that are correlated with the included union status variable in the wage equation. The simultaneous equations studies deal with this problem by first postulating a system of equations consisting of at least a wage equation and a union status equation. The equation system is then fitted to the data. The fitting procedure commonly is one in which the union status equation is fitted to data on the exogenous variables in the system and the predicted value (or a curvilinear function of the predicted value) of union status is entered on the right-hand side of the wage equation in place of (or in addition to) the observed union status variable in fitting the wage equation.

The panel studies treat the omitted variables problem rather differently. Central to their treatment is the notion that a worker's position in the wage distribution, as measured by his relative wage *w*, though subject to life cycle and transitory variations, tends to persist over time. A considerable part of the permanent or fixed component of his relative wage, as well as the life cycle and transitory components, undoubtedly can be captured by right-hand variables such as schooling, age, experience, and other commonly used right-hand variables. But even after controlling for these variables, a substantial part of the permanent relative wage component may remain in an unobserved (to the econometrician) fixed effect portion of the error term in the wage equation. This portion of the error term, fixed for each worker, but varying across workers, undoubtedly includes effects of omitted worker-quality and working-conditions variables likely to be correlated with the union status of workers. It may be eliminated, of course, by comparing the relative wage of each worker at one date with *his* relative wage at another date. Thus write the relative wage equation at the individual worker level at date *t* as follows:

$$W_t = a_t + a_{xt}x_t + \overline{M}_t U_t + e^f + e_t, \tag{5.1}$$

where e^f is the fixed (time-invariant) part of the error term and e_t is the remaining part. (The other symbols have their usual meanings.) Then if t' is a date different from t,

$$\begin{aligned} W_{t'} - W_t = a_{t'} - a_t + a_{xt'}x_{t'} - a_{xt}x_t \\ + \overline{M}_{t'}U_{t'} - \overline{M}_t U_t + e_{t'} - e_t. \end{aligned} \tag{5.2}$$

Not surprisingly, the fixed effect e^f does not appear in (5.2). Thus if the remaining error $e_{t'} - e_t$ in (5.2) were uncorrelated with union status ($U_{t'}$, U_t) and if $U_{t'}$ were not equal to U_t for all workers, unbiased estimates of the wage gaps $\overline{M}_{t'}$ at date t' and $\overline{M}_t$ at date t could be obtained by regressing $W_{t'} - W_t$ on $x_{t'}$, x_t, $U_{t'}$, and U_t.

What I have just described is not exactly the procedure followed in any of the studies surveyed in this chapter, though for several of the studies the description does not err seriously, I trust. In the next section I summarize each of the studies, amplify the description of estimation procedures used, and report the resulting wage gap estimates. There is much agreement among the studies that panel estimation procedures lead to reduced, but on average positive, wage gap estimates. That is, the studies suggest that wage gap estimates from wage *level* equations fitted by least squares to *cross-section* micro-data are substantially upward biased. This suggestion is in accord with my priors.

Nevertheless, I do not regard this evidence from the panel studies as settling definitively this question of bias. If union status were a permanent characteristic of workers ($U_{t'} = U_t$ for all t', t, and all workers), then, as suggested by (5.2), the panel estimation procedures used in the studies would have failed to yield wage gap estimates. All of the studies thus rely heavily on accurate distinction in the panel data between union status changers and nonchangers and on observing a substantial number of changers.

Section 2 presents data from the panel studies showing that the fraction of workers who changed union status typically was small and strongly suggesting that appreciable fractions of those who *reported* a change in union status did not really experience a union status change. Such inaccuracy in the status change data is very likely to lead to downward bias in wage gap estimates from panel data. Indeed, in section 3 I present evidence indicating that a large part, perhaps most, of the excess of cross-section over panel wage gap estimates may be the result of misclassification of workers by union status change.

Section 4 gives a summary appraisal of the panel estimates.

2. Survey of Panel Estimates

This section reports the wage gap estimates that I have drawn from 17 panel studies. All of the studies are recent; only four appeared before 1980. Furthermore, only nine of the 17 studies focus primarily on unions and wages. The unionism content of the other eight papers is incidental.

Later in this section I present a table (table 5.10) summarizing the panel wage gap estimates retrieved from these 17 studies and comparing them with corresponding cross-section estimates that ignore the panel or time-series feature of the underlying data. Because the studies differ in their estimation techniques or in other important but not easily tabulated respects, I first present study-by-study reviews, grouping together studies using similar techniques.

a) Studies Using the "Deviation-from-Own-Mean" Method

Return to equation (5.1) and assume that its coefficients a_t, a_{xt}'s, and $\overline{M}_t$ do not vary over the time period, $t = 1,2, \ldots, T$, covered by the panel data. Then (5.1) becomes

$$W_t = a + a_x x_t + \overline{M} U_t + e^f + e_t. \tag{5.3}$$

Now express each of the variables for each worker in the panel as a deviation from the worker's own T-period mean of the variable. I denote this deviation by a prefixed D; thus DW_t for a worker is the deviation of W_t from his T-period mean of W_t. Then (5.3) with this transformation of variables becomes

$$DW_t = a_x Dx_t + \overline{M} DU_t + De_t. \tag{5.4}$$

The potentially biasing unobserved individual-worker fixed effect e^f has been eliminated. If the remaining error term De_t in (5.4) is uncorrelated with the transformed union status variable DU_t, an unbiased estimate of the wage gap $\overline{M}$ may be obtained by regressing DW_t on DU_t in the presence of the Dx_t's using the panel data pooled over the period $t = 1,2, \ldots, T$. I term this procedure as the "deviation-from-own-mean" or DOM method. For any x variable that is time invariant, such as sex, color, and ethnicity, Dx_t, of course, will be zero and will not appear in (5.4). Similarly DU_t will be zero for all workers who did not change union status during the period.

The DOM method was used in the Baugh-Stone [25], Brown [32], Chowdhury-Nickell [38], Kenny [109], Moore-Raisian [144], and Raisian [167, 168] studies. Baugh-Stone used the May *Current Population Survey* data for elementary and secondary school teachers. They made cross-section estimates separately for 1974 and 1977 and panel estimates separately for the two year pairs 1974, 1975 and 1977, 1978. Their panel estimates covered only teachers who were nonunion in the first year of the year pairs. Brown used the NLS data for Young Men for the years 1966–71 and 1973, covering workers 14–24 years of age in 1966, not college graduates, not enrolled in school in any of these years, with complete data for the whole period. The Chowdhury-Nickell panel estimates were based on the PSID (random portion) data for 1968–76 for male household heads with needed data for every year 1968–76. Workers whose reported union status in 1974 was not the same as in 1972 were deleted. (For the remaining workers union status in 1973 was assumed to be the same as in 1972 and 1974.) Kenny used the PSID data for 1970 and 1974 for males whose estimated annual average hourly earnings were less than $9.98. Moore-Raisian and Raisian used the PSID data for 1967–77 for male household heads not over 65 years of age, not in the military, and not self-employed. Raisian [167] also excluded workers with less than 1.5 years of current employment tenure. As I noted in Chapter 4, the sampling design used with the NLS panels was one in which blacks were heavily oversampled. The same is true of the so-called nonrandom portion of the PSID data which Moore-Raisian, Raisian [167], and, I judge, Kenny did not exclude. None of these studies (Brown, Moore-Raisian, Raisian) in fitting their wage equations weighted the individual-worker observations by the inverse of each worker's sampling probability ratio (see section 7 of Chapter 6 for discussion of the resulting bias potential).

The Baugh-Stone panel wage gap estimates for school teachers were: 1974–75 = 0.04, 1977–78 = 0.12. The corresponding cross-section estimates were: 1974 = 0.07, 1977 = 0.21. Thus the Baugh-Stone panel estimates were roughly 60 percent of the cross-section estimates. The 1970s were years of rapid growth of unionism among school teachers: 14 percent of the teachers who reported themselves as nonunion in May 1974 reported that in May 1975 they were unionized; the corresponding figure for the year May 1977–May 1978 was 29 percent.

In the NLS data for Young Men for 1966–71, 1973, union status (collective bargaining coverage) was reported only for the three years 1969, 1970, and 1971 so that Brown was forced to impute values of U_t for 1966–68 and 1973. His imputations were:

1. If the worker had the same employer in 1973 as in 1971, then $U_{1973} = U_{1971}$.
2. If the worker had the same employer in 1966 or 1967 or 1968 as in 1969, then $U_t = U_{1969}$.
3. Otherwise, $U_t = y_t$ where y_t is the extent of unionism as estimated by Freeman and Medoff [69] from U.S. Bureau of Labor Statistics data by industry separately for office and nonoffice employees.

About one-fourth of the worker-year observations were of the third type, $U_t = y_t$. The resulting measurement errors may account in part for the somewhat lower estimates of the wage gap than others have obtained from the NLS data for Young Men for 1969–71 (see table 5.10). The panel (DOM) estimates of the wage gap that I have drawn from the Brown paper [32] are:

$\overline{M}$ = .08 from four equations that include Dy_t;
$\overline{M}$ = .12 from four equations that exclude Dy_t.

Fortunately Brown also fitted corresponding cross-section (CS) equations (5.3) that ignore the time-invariant feature of the fixed effect e^f. These estimates of the wage gap are:

$\overline{M}$ = .13 from four equations that include y_t;
$\overline{M}$ = .17–.18 from four equations that exclude y_t.

Thus the panel (DOM) wage gap estimates from Brown's paper are about 60–70 percent as large as the corresponding cross-section (CS) estimates. (I suspect that the unusually large effect on the wage gap estimates of including the extent of unionism y variable is a consequence of using y also as the value of union status U in about one-fourth of the worker-year observations.)

Chowdhury-Nickell presented seven DOM wage gap estimates for male household heads for 1972–76 and one for 1971–76:

1972–76: range = .07/.10, mean = .08;
1971–76: .10.

(Three of the estimates for 1972–76 used the Hausman-Taylor [83] modification of the DOM technique.) They reported no matching cross-section (CS) estimates by ordinary least squares. However, I judge from other studies using the PSID data (see, e.g., table 5.10) that the matching CS estimates would have been close to 0.20. If so, the Chowdhury-Nickell DOM gap estimates are roughly 40 percent of the corresponding CS estimates. (In section 3 I discuss experiments by Chowdhury-Nickell designed to estimate downward bias in DOM panel estimates produced by union status measurement error.)

Kenny [109] fitted only one DOM equation to the PSID data for males for 1970 and 1974. The resulting estimate of $\overline{M}$ was 0.08. I judge that had he fitted a matching cross-section (CS) wage equation to the pooled data for 1970 and 1974, the estimate of the wage gap would have been roughly 0.2, or about 2.5 times his panel estimate.

Two aspects of the use by Moore-Raisian [144] and Raisian [167, 168] of the DOM method on the PSID data for 1967–77 should be mentioned:

1. Union status U was not reported in the 1973 survey but was imputed from data on U in 1972 and 1974 and evidence on job change.

2. In each year, union status was reported as of about April while the dependent wage was an average for the whole of the preceding year. This lack of simultaneity in the timing of U_t and W_t may lead to bias in the DOM estimates of the wage gap.

Moore and Raisian [144] fitted both the cross-section (CS) equation (5.3) and the panel (DOM) equation (5.4) separately by union status, class of worker (government, educational services, and private nonagricultural), and occupation (blue-collar versus white-collar), 12 equations by each method, and separately by union status and class of worker without the occupation breakdown, six equations by each method. The wage gap $\overline{M}$ estimates that I have calculated from these equations, and related data are given in table 5.1.

The panel (DOM) estimates, without exception, are lower than the corresponding cross-section (CS) estimates. For all covered workers the DOM figure 0.07 is only about one-third of the CS figure 0.20/0.21. However, the ranking of the DOM figures is almost the same as that of the CS figures. In particular, the panel and cross-section figures both show higher wage gaps for blue-collar than for white-collar workers.

Raisian [167] fitted the DOM equation (5.4) with four slightly different sets of right-hand variables. The $\overline{M}$ estimates from these equations ranged from 0.056 to 0.058. He also fitted these four DOM equations separately by union status yielding wage gap estimates ranging from 0.055 to 0.057. He did not fit matching cross-section CS equations, but I judge (from the Moore-Raisian study and from two other papers by Raisian using the 1967–77 PSID data) that, had he done so, the CS estimates of $\overline{M}$ would have been close to 0.20, or about 3.5 times the DOM estimates.

Table 5.1 Wage Gap Estimates from the Moore-Raisian Study [144]

Line	Worker Group	Cross-Section (CS)	Panel (DOM)
1	Government, all	.15	.03/.04
2	Government, blue-collar	.20	.05
3	Government, white-collar	.11	.03
4	Educ. services, all	.06/.08	.02/.03
5	Educ. services, blue-collar	.14	.06
6	Educ. services, white-collar	.05	.01
7	Private, nonagric., all	.22	.07/.08
8	Private, nonagric., blue-collar	.30	.10
9	Private, nonagric., white-collar	.03	.01
10	Blue-collar, all	.29	.09
11	White-collar, all	.04	.02
12	All workers	.20/.21	.07

Raisian [168] contains two DOM gap estimates for 1967–77 for male household heads. The first, based on the random portion of the PSID for this period, is 0.08; the second, 0.10, is based on the PSID full sample, both the random and the nonrandom portions. No matching CS estimates are reported in this paper, but their order of magnitude surely is close to 0.20.

b) Studies Using "Fixed-Effect-Function" or FEF Methods

Seven studies, Chamberlain [36], Duncan-Stafford [48], Freeman [68], Ichniowski [99], Leigh [120], Mellow [131], and Mincer [136], used what I term "fixed-effect-function" or FEF methods. The econometrics are set out rather fully in Chamberlain [36] which I will discuss shortly. But first I adapt his argument to the procedures used in the other FEF studies to help me interpret their empirical equations.

Return to the cross-section (CS) wage equation (5.1).

$$W_t = a_t + a_{xt}x_t + \overline{M}_t U_t + e^f + e_t;\ t = 1,2. \tag{5.1}$$

For the purpose of discussing these papers, I assume that the panel data span two dates: $t = 1,2$. Presumably the fixed effect e^f is correlated (in the presence of the x variables) with union status U_t across workers. Hence express the fixed effect of e^f as a function of the worker's two-period union status history as follows:

$$e^f = m_1U_1 + m_2U_2 + m_{12}U_1U_2 + f, \tag{5.5}$$

where f is the residual in (5.5). Now plug (5.5) into (5.1) and collect terms:

$$W_t = a_t + a_{xt}x_t + (\overline{M}_t + m_t)U_t + m_{t'}U_{t'} + m_{12}U_1U_2 + f + e_t, \tag{5.6}$$

where $t' \neq t = 1,2$.

Now define:
$U11 = 1$ if $U_1 = U_2 = 1$ and zero otherwise, the "always union" group;
$U10 = 1$ if $U_1 = 1 - U_2 = 1$ and zero otherwise, the "leavers" group;
$U01 = 1$ if $1 - U_1 = U_2 = 1$ and zero otherwise, the "joiners" group.

(The remaining group, "never union," is $U00 = 1$ if $U_l = U_2 = 0$ and is zero otherwise.) Equations (5.6) and these definitions imply that

$$\begin{aligned} W_1 &= a_1 + a_{x1}X_1 + (\overline{M}_1 + m_1 + m_2 + m_{12})U11 \\ &\quad + (\overline{M}_1 + m_1)\,U10 + m_2 U01 + f + e_1, \end{aligned} \tag{5.7}$$

$$\begin{aligned} W_2 &= a_2 + a_{x2}X_2 + (\overline{M}_2 + m_1 + m_2 + m_{12})U11 \\ &\quad + m_1 U10 + (\overline{M}_2 + m_2)U01 + f + e_2. \end{aligned}$$

Subtract the first equation of (5.7) from the second to obtain the first-difference wage equation:

$$\begin{aligned} W_2 - W_1 &= a_2 - a_1 + a_{x2}X_2 - a_{x1}X_1 + (\overline{M}_2 - \overline{M}_1)U11 \\ &\quad + \overline{M}_2\,U01 - \overline{M}_1 U10 + e_2 - e_1. \end{aligned} \tag{5.8}$$

Notice that (5.8) does not contain the residual fixed effect f.

In (5.8), as I have written it, there are three U variables on the right-hand side, but only two wage gap coefficients $\overline{M}_l$ and $\overline{M}_2$ for these variables. Thus to avoid ambiguity in the interpretation of a fitted equation (5.8), the three unionism variables should be combined into two variables, $U11 + U10$ and $U11 + U01$. Suppose, however, that (5.8) is fitted with three union status variables ($U11$, $U10$, and $U01$) and that in the fitting no restrictions are placed on the coefficients of these variables. Denote the estimated union status coefficients by B_{11}, B_{10}, and B_{01}, respectively, where, with (5.8) in mind, B_{11} is read as an estimate of $\overline{M}_2 - \overline{M}_1$, B_{10} as an estimate of $-\overline{M}_1$, and B_{01} as an estimate of $\overline{M}_2$. There is no assurance, however, that B_{11} will be equal to $B_{10} + B_{01}$ even in sign. Hence the fitted equation will yield two, rather than one, estimates of $\overline{M}_1$ and two of $\overline{M}_2$ as follows

	Estimate 1	*Estimate 2*
$\overline{M}_1$	$-B_{10}$	$B_{01} - B_{11}$
$\overline{M}_2$	B_{01}	$B_{11} - B_{10}$

What I have just said applies also to the fitting of the pair of equations (5.7).

In both the Mellow and Mincer papers the years 1 and 2 were close together. It is likely, therefore, that in truth $\overline{M}_1$ will be close to $\overline{M}_2$ and that any difference between the two will be estimated imprecisely. Therefore, in presenting my FEF wage gap estimates from these studies I will show the range of the four estimates drawn from each equation (5.8) as though the range was for the average of $\overline{M}_1$ and $\overline{M}_2$. However, for the convenience of the reader I will also show the estimated coefficients B_{11}, B_{10}, and B_{01}.

Fitting (5.7) without coefficient restrictions provides not only the four FEF wage gap estimates discussed above but also cross-section (CS) wage gap estimates that ignore the fixed effects e^f. To see this, write equations (5.7) as

$$\begin{aligned} W_1 &= a_1 + a_{x1}x_1 + B_{1,11}U11 + B_{1,01}U01 + B_{1,10}U10, \\ W_2 &= a_2 + a_{x2}x_2 + B_{2,11}U11 + B_{2,01}U01 + B_{2,10}U10, \end{aligned} \tag{5.9}$$

where the B's are the coefficients estimated from OLS fitting of (5.7). Denote the mean of Uij over the workers covered in the fitting of (5.7) by $\overline{Uij}$. Then the cross-section (CS) wage gap estimates are:

$$\begin{aligned} \overline{M}_1(\text{CS}) &= \frac{\overline{U11}B_{1,11} + \overline{U10}B_{1,10}}{\overline{U}_1} - \frac{\overline{U01}B_{1,01}}{1 - \overline{U}_1}, \\ \overline{M}_2(\text{CS}) &= \frac{\overline{U11}B_{2,11} + \overline{U10}B_{2,01}}{\overline{U}_2} - \frac{\overline{U10}B_{2,10}}{1 - \overline{U}_2}. \end{aligned} \tag{5.10}$$

I turn now to the Mellow study [131]. His data sources were the May CPS for two pairs of adjacent years, 1974–75 and 1977–78. In each pair of years he covered nonagricultural wage and salary workers with needed data in both of the two years. Table 5.2 shows the distributions of these covered workers by union status. The second column shows the fraction who were joiners, the third column the corresponding fraction who were leavers, and the fourth and fifth columns the fractions who were never union and always union, respectively. Notice that except for blacks fewer

Table 5.2 Distribution of Workers by Union Status: Mellow Study [131]

Year Pair and Worker Group	Union Status Category			
	*U*01	*U*10	*U*00	*U*11
1974–75, all	.041	.041	.695	.222
1977–78, all	.047	.039	.686	.228
1977–78, blacks	.074	.056	.626	.244
1977–78, whites	.044	.037	.693	.226
1977–78, males	.047	.042	.617	.294
1977–78, females	.047	.034	.780	.138
1977–78, age ≤ 25	.058	.039	.779	.124
1977–78, age > 25	.045	.039	.664	.252

than 10 percent of the workers apparently were union status *changers* (joiners or leavers).

Mellow did not follow exactly the format of (5.7) and (5.8). In particular, he used U_1 instead of $U11$. This presents no problem in interpreting his equations. The implied coefficient for $U11$ in the (5.7) or (5.8) format is his reported coefficient for U_1 and, correspondingly, the implied coefficient for $U10$ in the (5.7) or (5.8) format is the sum of his reported coefficients for U_1 and $U10$.

Table 5.3 tabulates the wage gap estimates I have calculated from the Mellow study. Column 3 shows the pair of years (74–75 of course means 1974–1975 and 77–78 means 1977–1978) to which the panel (FEF) estimates pertain. Column 4 indicates whether the estimates were derived by fitting the first-difference equation (5.8) or from fitting the pair of wage level equations (5.7). The estimated coefficients of $U11$, $U10$, $U01$ in (5.8) are given in columns 5, 6, and 7. The range of the four FEF wage gap $\overline{M}$ estimates appears in column 8 and the mean of the four estimates in column 9. The year to which the cross-section wage gap estimates pertain is shown in column 10; column 11 indicates whether the estimate was derived from a CS equation of the form of (5.1) or of the form of (5.7). The CS wage gap estimates appear in column 12.

Unfortunately Mellow's study does not provide cross-section estimates of $\overline{M}$ for lines 1 and 10–12. Evidence on other lines of the table strongly suggests that the missing figure for $\overline{M}$ on line 12 is about 0.18/0.19. Similarly, evidence in section 2 of Chapter 9 indicates that the missing estimate of $\overline{M}$ on line 1 is roughly 0.15/0.20.

Ignore lines 10 and 11 for which there are no cross-section wage gap estimates. The message from the remaining lines is loud and clear: the panel (FEF) wage gap estimates are much below their cross-section counterparts. On the lines in which there are entries in column 12 the ratios of column 9 to column 12 range from 0.23 for blacks to 0.49 for males. Notice also that the panel (FEF) wage gap estimates on line 2 derived from fitting the first difference equation (5.8) to 1977–78 data differ little from corresponding estimates on line 3 derived from fitting the pair of wage level equations (5.7) to the same data.

Lines 13, 14, and 15 differ from line 2 in the following respects:

Line 13 includes among the right-hand variables a dummy variable for change in census 3-digit occupation and its interactions with $U10$ and $U01$.

On line 14 the occupation-change variable pertains to the census 1-digit rather than 3-digit occupation.

Line 15 adds to line 14 on the right-hand side a dummy variable for change in census 1-digit industry and its interactions with $U10$ and $U01$. Thus from these equations (5.8) it is possible to derive FEF estimates separately for occupation and/or industry changers. I have done so below for the equation on line 15.

Table 5.3 Wage Gap Estimates from the Mellow Study [131]

		Panel (FEF) Estimates							Cross-Section (CS)		
Line (1)	Worker Group (2)	Years (3)	Eq. (4)	B_{11} (5)	$-B_{10}$ (6)	B_{01} (7)	Range (8)	Mean (9)	Year (10)	Equations (11)	$\overline{M}$ (12)
1	All	74–75	5.8	.00	.08	.07	.07/.08	.08	—	—	—
2	All	77–78	5.8	−.02	.07	.08	.05/.09	.07	77,78	5.1, 5.7	.18/.19
3	All	77–78	5.7	−.02	.07	.08	.05/.10	.07	77,78	5.1, 5.7	.18/.19
4	Blacks (B)	77–78	5.8	.00	.07	.02	.02/.08	.04	77	5.7	.20
5	Whites (W)	77–78	5.8	−.02	.07	.09	.05/.11	.08	77	5.7	.19
6	B and W	77–78	—	—	—	—	—	.08	77	5.7	.19
7	Males (M)	77–78	5.8	−.02	.08	.09	.07/.10	.09	77	5.7	.17
8	Females (F)	77–78	5.8	−.02	.05	.06	.03/.08	.06	77	5.7	.21
9	F and M	77–78	—	—	—	—	—	.07	77	5.7	.19
10	Age ⩽ 25	77–78	5.8	−.03	.07	.20	.04/.23	.13	—	—	—
11	Age > 25	77–78	5.8	−.02	.07	.04	.04/.07	.06	—	—	—
12	⩽ 25, > 25	77–78	—	—	—	—	—	.07	—	—	—
13	All	77–78	5.8	−.02	.07	.06	.05/.08	.07	77,78	5.1, 5.7	.18/.19
14	All	77–78	5.8	−.02	.07	.07	.05/.08	.07	77,78	5.1, 5.7	.18/.19
15	All	77–78	5.8	−.02	.05	.05	.04/.07	.05	77,78	5.1, 5.7	.18/.19

Note:

Lines 2–3, 13–15. The estimate of $\overline{M}$ for 1978, based on (5.7) for that year, is 0.18. There are 2 estimates of $\overline{M}$ for 1977, both 0.19, based on equations (5.1) and (5.7).

Line 6, column 9. Figure shown is the employment-weighted mean of figures for blacks and whites.

Line 9, column 9. Employment-weighted mean of separate figures for males and females.

Line 12, column 9. Employment-weighted mean of figures for Age ⩽ 25 and Age > 25.

Worker Group (2)	Range (8)	Mean (9)
Changed 1-digit occupation and 1-digit industry	.21/.24	.23
Changed neither	.01/.03	.02

These are startling differences. They are consistent, however, with my view that panel wage gap estimates may suffer from downward bias resulting from errors in reporting union status (see the next section).

This brings me to Mincer's study [136]. Mincer's data were from the NLS panels for Young Men (14–24 in 1966) and Older Men (45–59 in 1966) for 1969 and 1971 and the random (or self-weighting) portion of the PSID for 1968–78. He covered only white males, not students, not over 65 years of age with needed data. (He treated the PSID for 1968–78 as a time series of adjacent year pairs, pooling the year pairs.) As I noted earlier, lack of simultaneity in the timing of reported union status and hourly earnings in the PSID may create downward bias in panel wage gap estimates. (For the period 1976–78 Mincer estimated that the downward bias was about one-fifth.)

In the two NLS panels the basic union status question was with respect to collective bargaining coverage. If a worker stated that he was covered, he was also asked whether he was a member of the covering union. Mincer used both a coverage and a membership concept of union status. In the PSID he imputed the unreported union status (membership) for 1973 as follows:

1. If $U_{72} = U_{74}$, then $U_{73} = U_{72} = U_{74}$.
2. If $U_{72} \neq U_{74}$, then first, if the worker had the same employer in 1973 as in 1974, then $U_{73} = U_{74}$; and second, if the worker had the same employer in 1973 as in 1972, then $U_{73} = U_{72}$.
3. Otherwise, the worker was excluded for 1973.

Mincer classified workers by their two-period union status in the same way as in (5.7) and (5.8), namely, always union $U11$, leavers $U10$, joiners $U01$, and never union $U00$. In addition, he divided workers within each of these four categories into two groups, the *movers,* those with a different employer in year 2 than in year 1, and the *stayers,* those with the same employer in both years. (He also included tenure in current job and its square as right-hand x variables in his wage equations [5.7].) Thus in his wage equations he had seven union status categories as follows:

$MU11$, $MU10$, $MU01$, and $MU00$
$SU11$, $SU10$, $SU01$

with *M* and *S* signifying movers and stayers, respectively, and with *SU*00, the stayer-never union group, as the omitted comparison group. This format presents no problem in using (5.8) to interpret his equations, provided that the coefficient for *MU*00 (mover-never union) is subtracted from the coefficients for each of *MU*11, *MU*10, and *MU*01.

Table 5.4 shows the distribution of workers by union status-employer change in the NLS data for Young Men and Older Men, 1969 and 1971, and in the PSID data by age for the period 1968–78. In the NLS data years 1 and 2 were 1969 and 1971, respectively, while in the PSID data years 1 and 2 were adjacent years in the period 1968–78. Except for the NLS Young Men, fewer than 10 percent changed union status from year 1 to year 2. Furthermore, with the same exception, stayers considerably outnumbered movers among union status changers—by more than four to one for the older men in both data sets. This finding suggests to me, as it did to Mincer, that "the figures for job stayers who change union status appear to be inflated by misreporting or misclassification."

Table 5.4 Distribution of Workers by Union Status and Employer Change: Mincer Study [136]

Category	NLS Young Men		NLS Older Men	
	Covered	Member	Covered	Member
Movers, all	.377	.377	.104	.104
Always union *MU*11	.057	.044	.027	.026
Leavers *MU*10	.052	.044	.008	.005
Joiners *MU*01	.049	.046	.010	.008
Never union *MU*00	.219	.243	.059	.065
Stayers, all	.623	.623	.896	.896
Always union *SU*11	.203	.180	.327	.312
Leavers *SU*10	.020	.015	.028	.020
Joiners *SU*01	.040	.042	.047	.042
Never union *SU*00	.360	.386	.494	.522
	PSID			
	All	Age < 30	Age $\geqslant 30$	
Movers, all	.105	.192	.066	
Always union *MU*11	.013	.020	.010	
Leavers *MU*10	.009	.018	.005	
Joiners *MU*01	.010	.020	.005	
Never union *MU*00	.073	.134	.046	
Stayers, all	.895	.808	.934	
Always union *SU*11	.278	.221	.303	
Leavers *SU*10	.023	.024	.023	
Joiners *SU*01	.026	.027	.025	
Never union *SU*00	.568	.536	.583	

Table 5.5 contains wage gap estimates I have calculated from Mincer's study. The format of the table is essentially the same as that of table 5.3. For each data set Mincer fitted both the pair of wage-level equations (5.7) and the first-difference equation (5.8). However, the panel (FEF) wage gap estimates from (5.7) were so similar to those from (5.8) that I show only the latter in the table, the estimate ranges in column 6 and the estimate means in column 7. The cross-section (CS) wage gap estimates, in columns 8 and 9, are based on Mincer's fittings of equations (5.7). For the NLS Young Men the wage gap estimates, not shown in the table, from wage equations using a membership concept of union status are quite

Table 5.5 Wage Gap Estimates from the Mincer Study [136]

		Panel (FEF) Estimates					Cross-Section (CS) $\bar{M}$	
Line (1)	Worker Group (2)	B_{11} (3)	$-B_{10}$ (4)	B_{01} (5)	Range (6)	Mean (7)	Year 1 (8)	Year 2 (9)
	NLS Young Men (Coverage Concept of Union Status)							
1	Movers	.02	.35	.07	.06/.37	.21	.33	.29
2	Stayers	.04	.06	.06	.02/.11	.06	.14	.18
3	Both	—	—	—	—	.12	.21	.22
	NLS Older Men (Coverage Concept of Union Status)							
4	Movers	.10	.16	.16	.05/.27	.16	.43	.54
5	Stayers	.05	−.02	.06	−.02/.06	.02	.01	.03
6	Both	—	—	—	—	.04	.05	.08
	NLS Older Men (Membership Concept of Union Status)							
7	Movers	.11	.04	.11	.00/.15	.08	.47	.53
8	Stayers	.05	−.03	.05	−.03/.05	.01	.00	.04
9	Both	—	—	—	—	.02	.05	.09
	PSID Men, Age < 30							
10	Movers	−.02	.08	.06	.06/.08	.07	.25	.27
11	Stayers	−.01	.04	.04	.03/.05	.04	.20	.21
12	Both	—	—	—	—	.05	.21	.22
	PSID Men, Age ≥ 30							
13	Movers	.08	.02	.03	−.04/.10	.03	.19	.26
14	Stayers	−.01	.02	.00	.00/.02	.01	.14	.14
15	Both	—	—	—	—	.01	.15	.15
	PSID Men, All							
16	Movers	.02	.06	.05	.03/.08	.05	.23	.27
17	Stayers	−.01	.03	.02	.02/.03	.02	.16	.16
18	Both	—	—	—	—	.03	.17	.17

similar to those shown for the collective bargaining concept. The figures on lines 3, 6, 9, 12, 15, and 18 are employment-weighted means of the figures on the preceding two lines.

The most conspicuous features of the table are these:

1. Both the panel (FEF) and cross-section (CS) wage gap estimates are substantially higher for movers than for stayers. Indeed, for the stayers among NLS Older Men both are close to zero, as is the FEF estimate for older male stayers in the PSID data.

2. The mean FEF estimates in column 7, except for stayers among NLS Older Men, are much lower than the corresponding CS estimates in columns 8 and 9. Indeed, except for NLS Young Men movers and NLS Older Men stayers, even the tops of the FEF estimate ranges in column 6 fall well below the lower of the CS estimates in columns 8 and 9.

3. There is no consistent tendency for the joiner coefficient B_{01} to exceed that $-B_{10}$ for leavers among either movers or stayers.

4. Both the panel (FEF) and cross-section (CS) wage gap estimates, by and large, are larger for young men than for older men.

Mincer also fitted first-difference wage equations (5.8) in which movers were classified by quit versus layoff and alternatively by whether they moved within (W) or between (B) industries at the 2-digit level. The FEF estimate ranges and means that I have calculated from these equations are given in table 5.6. (For the NLS data sets the figures are from equations using the coverage concept of union status.) The four data sets all show

Table 5.6 FEF Wage Gap Estimates for Movers by Industry Change and Quit versus Layoff (Mincer [136])

	By Industry Change					
	Estimate Range			Mean		
Data Set	Between	Within	Both[a]	B	W	Both[a]
NLS Young	.13/.39	−.01/.19	.06/.37	.26	.09	.21
NLS Older	.05/.39	−.06/.24	.05/.27	.22	.09	.16
PSID < 30	−.04/.25	−.03/.09	.06/.08	.11	.03	.07
PSID ⩾ 30	−.08/.18	−.12/.01	−.04/.10	.05	−.06	.03
	By Quit (Q) versus Layoff (L)					
	Estimate Range			Mean		
	Q	L	Both[a]	Q	L	Both[a]
NLS Young	.07/.35	.12/.35	.06/.37	.21	.23	.21
NLS Older	.07/.28	.01/.31	.05/.27	.17	.16	.16
PSID < 30	.07/.22	−.04/.10	.06/.08	.15	.03	.07
PSID ⩾ 30	−.08/.07	−.14/.06	−.04/.10	.00	−.04	.03

[a]From table 5.5.

rather higher wage gap estimates for movers who changed their 2-digit industry than for movers who did not. For the PSID young male movers the estimates for those who quit also were much higher than for those who were laid off. For the other three data sets, however, the quit versus layoff estimate differences were small.

I come now to the Chamberlain study [36] in which what I have called the FEF method is most fully developed. He applied the method to the NLS data for Young Men for the three years 1969, 1970, and 1971, excluding those enrolled in school in any of these years and those with missing data on left-hand or right-hand variables in one or more of the years.

Return to equation (5.1) and write it for three years:

$$W_t = a_t + a_{xt}x_t + \overline{M}_tU_t + e^f + e_t;\, t = 1,2,3. \tag{5.1}$$

For benchmarking his panel (FEF) wage gap estimates against corresponding cross-section (CS) estimates he fitted (5.1) by OLS to the cross-section data for each of the three years. The resulting CS estimates of $\overline{M}$ are

Year 1 (1969):	.195
Year 2 (1970):	.189
Year 3 (1971):	.191
Mean 1969–71:	.192

He then wrote the "fixed effect function," similar to (5.5), essentially as follows

$$e^f = m_1U_1 + m_2U_2 + m_3U_3 + f, \tag{5.11}$$

or more generally

$$e^f = m_1U_1 + m_2U_2 + m_3U_3 + m_{12}U_1U_2 + m_{13}U_1U_3 + m_{23}U_2U_3 + m_{123}U_1U_2U_3 + f. \tag{5.12}$$

(I have not shown it, but he also included in [5.11] and [5.12] the three-period history x_1, x_2, and x_3 of two x variables in his wage equations [5.1].) Plug (5.11) into (5.1) to obtain:

$$W_t = (\overline{M}_t + m_t)U_t + m_{t'}U_{t'} + m_{t''}U_{t''};\, t'' \neq t' \neq t = 1,2,3, \tag{5.13}$$

where I have omitted all except the terms in the union status variables in order to simplify the writing. He fitted (5.13) by OLS to the data for each of the three years without any restrictions on the coefficients of the union status variables. The resulting CS wage gap estimates are

Year 1 (1969):	.193
Year 2 (1970):	.188
Year 3 (1971):	.190
Mean 1969–71:	.191

which are very close to the corresponding figures from fitting (5.1).

The three wage equations (5.13), fitted without coefficient restrictions, also yield six FEF wage gap estimates, two for each year, as follows:

Year 1 (1969):	.123, .125
Year 2 (1970):	.108, .109
Year 3 (1971):	.122, .141
Range 1969–71:	.108 / .141
Mean 1969–71:	.121

Now go back to (5.12) and plug it into (5.1) to obtain

$$W_t = (\overline{M}_t + m_t)U_t + m_{t'}U_{t'} + m_{t''}U_{t''} + m_{12}U_1U_2 + m_{13}U_1U_3 + m_{23}U_2U_3 + m_{123}U_1U_2U_3, \tag{5.14}$$

where again I have omitted all terms except those in the union status variables. He fitted (5.14) by OLS without coefficient restrictions, which gave me the following CS and FEF wage gap estimates:

	CS	*FEF*
Year 1 (1969)	.192	.146, .177
Year 2 (1970)	.186	.061, .086
Year 3 (1971)	.187	.050, .063
Range 1969–71	.186 / .192	.050 / .177
Mean 1969–71	.188	.097

The CS figures are close to those from fitting (5.1) and (5.13), but the FEF estimates have a wider range and a lower mean than were obtained from the unrestricted fitting of (5.13).

Chamberlain then fitted the equation triplet (5.14) by minimum distance estimation (MDE) subject to the following alternative restrictions on the coefficients:

A. The coefficients (m's) in the fixed effect function (5.12) and the wage gap coefficient $\overline{M}$ are time invariant.

B. As in A, except that $\overline{M}$ may vary by year.

C. As in A, except that $\overline{M}$ may not be the same for union joiners as for union leavers.

The resulting FEF wage gap estimates are:

A. .107

B. Year 1 (1969): .105
Year 2 (1970): .103
Year 3 (1971): .114
Mean 1969–71: .107

C. Joiners .097, leavers .119, both .107.

Chamberlain also fitted (5.14) by conventional generalized least squares (GLS) subject to the restrictions A; the estimate of $\overline{M}$ was 0.121. He tested statistically the restrictions A, B, and C and could not reject them. As an added test, he fitted (5.14) by MDE subject to the restrictions A plus the restriction that all the coefficients (m's) in the fixed effect function (5.1) be zero and strongly rejected the additional restriction.

Table 5.7 summarizes the wage gap estimates from this Chamberlain study. The CS estimates for 1969–71 average about 0.19; the corresponding average among the FEF estimates is about 0.11, or about 60 percent of the CS average.

In the data used in this study, 15.8 percent of the workers (joiners 9.2 percent, leavers 6.6 percent) reported a different union status in 1970 than in 1969. The corresponding figure for 1970 and 1971 was 12.0 percent (joiners 6.1, leavers 5.9) and for 1969 and 1971 was 17.6 percent (joiners 10.2, leavers 7.4); 77.3 percent reported the same union status at all three dates.

Table 5.7 Wage Gap Estimates from the Chamberlain Study [36]

			FEF Estimates		CS Estimates	
Line	Equation	Fitted by	Range	Mean	Range	Mean
1	5.1	Unrestricted OLS	—	—	.189/.195	.192
2	5.13	Unrestricted OLS	.108/.141	.121	.188/.193	.191
3	5.14	Unrestricted OLS	.050/.177	.097	.186/.192	.188
4	5.14	Restricted (A) MDE	—	.107	—	—
5	5.14	Restricted (A) GLS	—	.121	—	—
6	5.14	Restricted (B) MDE	.103/.114	.107	—	—
7	5.14	Restricted (C) MDE	.097/.119	.107	—	—

Ichniowski's study [99] deals with fire fighters in the two years 1966 and 1976. The observations were by city and, in the results I report here, the observations covered 307 cities in which union status was reported, presumably without error, in both 1966 and 1976. (Forty-seven percent of the cities changed fire fighter union status between 1966 and 1976, most of them becoming unionized in that interval.)

For each year 1966 and 1976 Ichniowski reported four CS wage gap estimates:

1966: range = −.014/.002, mean = −.005,
1976: range = .025/.043, mean = .033,
Both: range = −.014/.043, mean = .014.

These estimates were derived from OLS, CS wage equations in the form of (5.1) with four alternative dependent wage variables.

He also fitted the corresponding four wage difference equations (5.8), which I have interpreted in the same way as in the Mellow and Mincer studies to obtain the following panel (FEF) wage gap estimates:

$$1966\text{–}76\text{: range} = -.036/.061, \text{ mean} = .014.$$

Thus both the cross-section and panel estimates agree that the wage gap for city fire fighters was very close to zero.

Freeman [68] made cross-section and panel (FEF) wage gap estimates from four different data sets:

Set A: May CPS for the year pair 1974 and 1975,
Set B: PSID for the year pair 1970 and 1979,
Set C: NLS, Young Men, for the year pair 1970 and 1978,
Set D: *Quality of Employment Survey* for the year pair 1973 and 1977.

He describes the worker coverage only in the sentence: "I sought the largest possible sample for which the outcome variables and the union variable were reported." The fraction of workers whose reported union status was not the same in the two years varied widely across the data sets:

Data Set	*Joiners (%)*	*Leavers (%)*	*Both (%)*
A	2.8	3.4	6.2
B	9.8	9.4	19.2
C	16.0	8.7	24.7
D	5.7	10.1	15.8

For each data set Freeman reported a single CS wage gap estimate. I presume that each such estimate came from an OLS, CS wage equation (5.1) fitted to the pooled data for the year pair with what he describes as a "standard set of controls for demographic and human capital variables." He also fitted for each data set the wage difference equation (5.8) *but without any right-hand variables other than the union status dummy variables.* I interpret these equations in the same way as equations (5.8) in the Mellow and Mincer studies.

Table 5.8, which has basically the same format as tables 5.3 and 5.5, summarizes the CS and FEF wage gap estimates from Freeman's study. I suspect that the FEF estimates in column 6 would have been lower had Freeman subjected them to the same "standard set of controls for demographic and human capital variables" he used in his cross-section wage equations. Nevertheless, only for data set D (*Quality of Employment Survey*) do the FEF estimates in column 6 exceed two-thirds of the corresponding CS estimates in column 7.

Freeman's paper was chiefly concerned with biases in panel estimates produced by union status misclassification and by sample selectivity

Table 5.8 CS and FEF Wage Gap Estimates from Freeman Study [68]

Data Set (1)	Panel (FEF) Estimates B_{11} (2)	$-B_{10}$ (3)	B_{01} (4)	Range (5)	Mean (6)	CS Est. (7)
A	−.01	.09	.09	.08/.10	.09	.19
B	.06	.20	.08	.02/.26	.14	.23
C	−.16	.25	.12	.09/.28	.18	.28
D	−.03	.14	.19	.11/.22	.16	.14

among union status changers. I make extensive use of his analysis in section 3.

I deal only briefly with the Duncan-Stafford [48] and Leigh [120] papers. The panel (FEF) estimates that I have drawn from these papers are crude (i.e., the estimates are subject to no controls for variables other than union status in explaining wage change differences among workers), and they provide no matching CS estimates.

The Duncan-Stafford estimates, based on PSID data, pertain to the pair of years 1968 and 1971 and cover male household heads who held blue-collar jobs in 1968. In this data set 8.0 percent of the workers were union joiners and 5.6 percent union leavers. The FEF estimates were:

$$-B_{10} = .26;\ B_{01} = .10;\ B_{11} = -.05;$$
$$\text{range} = .10/.26;\ \text{mean} = .18.$$

These estimates are fairly close to similar estimates in Freeman's paper (see table 5.8, data set *B*).

The Leigh estimates are based on the NLS data for Young Men in 1971 and 1976 who were blue-collar workers in 1971. Union joiners comprised 11.4 percent of the workers and union leavers 9.7 percent. The FEF wage gap estimates were:

$$-B_{10} = .22;\ B_{01} = .18;\ B_{11} = -.06;$$
$$\text{range} = .16/.24;\ \text{mean} = .20.$$

These estimates, too, are fairly close to similar estimates from the Freeman study (see table 5.8, data set *C*).

c) Other Studies

Chamberlain's study no. 35 preceded his study no. 36, discussed above, by about two-and-a-half years, so that no. 36 reasonably may be regarded as having superseded no. 35. (Indeed, no. 36 contains no references to no. 35). Nevertheless, the wage gap estimates in no. 35 based on the same NLS data for Young Men, 1969–71, as were used in no. 36, are close to those in no. 36, and they are helpful in interpreting the two Duncan studies yet to be discussed.

Return to equation (5.1) and modify it as follows:

$$W_t = a_t + a_{xt}x_t + \overline{M}_t U_t + g_t W_{t-1} + f_t e^f + e_t;\ t = 1,2,3. \qquad (5.15)$$

Equation (5.15) adds to (5.1) the lagged value W_{t-1} of the dependent variable and permits the fixed effect e^f to have a time-varying coefficient f_t. Write (5.15) for $t = 2$ (1970) and $t = 3$ (1971), solve the $t = 2$ equation for the fixed effect e^f, plug the solution for e^f into the $t = 3$ equation and collect terms. The result is

$$\begin{aligned} W_3 = {} & (a_3 + f_{32}a_2) + a_{x3}x_3 - f_{32}a_{x2}x_2 + \overline{M}_3 U_3 - f_{32}\overline{M}_2 U_2 \\ & + (g_3 + f_{32})W_2 - f_{32}g_2 W_1 + (e_3 - f_{32}e_2); f_{32} \equiv f_3/f_2. \end{aligned} \qquad (5.16)$$

Unfortunately, as (5.15) makes clear, W_2 in (5.16) is correlated with e_2 and, if the e's are serially correlated, W_2 is also correlated with e_3, while W_1 is correlated with both e_2 and e_3. Hence if (5.16) is fitted by OLS, the coefficient estimates are likely to be biased. To overcome this source of bias, Chamberlain fitted (5.16) by the instrumental variable technique in which the instruments for W_2 and W_1 included the time-invariant x's and the three-year histories x_1, x_2, x_3, and U_1, U_2, and U_3 of the other right-hand variables. The estimated coefficients of U_2, U_3, W_1, and W_2 were

$$-f_{32}\overline{M}_2 \text{ of } U_2\text{: } -.110;\ -f_{32}g_2 \text{ of } W_1\text{: } -.021;$$
$$\overline{M}_3 \text{ of } U_3\text{: } .122;\ g_3 + f_{32} \text{ of } W_2\text{: } 1.01.$$

Thus the panel estimate of the wage gap for 1971 is 0.122.

Furthermore, it seems reasonable to suppose that $\overline{M}_2 \cong \overline{M}_3$ and $g_2 \cong g_3$. Assume first that $g_2 = g_3 = g$. Then $g_2 = g_3 = g = -0.02$, close to zero, $f_{32} = f_3/f_2 = 1.03$, close to unity, and $\overline{M}_2 = 0.11$. Alternatively suppose that $\overline{M}_2 = \overline{M}_3 = 0.12$. Then $f_{32} = 0.90$, $g_3 = 0.11$, and $g_2 = 0.02$. Under either of these assumptions both $\overline{M}_2$ and $\overline{M}_3$ are close to 0.12, f_{32} is close to unity, and both g_2 and g_3 are close to zero. But then (5.16) is approximately the DOM equation (5.4). Indeed, Chamberlain fitted (5.4) by OLS to the 1970–71 data and obtained the wage gap estimate $\overline{M}$ of 0.117.

He also fitted (5.16) under the assumption that the error e's in (5.15) are not serially correlated. Then W_1 is not correlated with $e_3 - f_{32}e_2$ in (5.16) and may be included as an instrument for W_2. The resulting estimates were close to those discussed in the two preceding paragraphs. In particular, the estimate of the wage gap for 1970–71 was 0.115.

In summary, the panel wage gap estimates for 1970–71 from this Chamberlain study [35] averaged slightly below 0.12. The corresponding CS figure for 1970–71 (from Chamberlain [36]) was 0.19. Thus the panel estimates averaged about 40 percent below the CS estimates.

Turn next to the Duncan study [47]. He used the PSID data, 1972–77, for male household heads, 23–38 years old in 1972, whose annual average hourly earnings were between \$0.50 and \$25.00, and annual hours worked were at least 250 in each year 1971–76. In the appendix to his paper he reports FEF first-difference wage equations (5.8) fitted by OLS separately by color (black and white), in which W_1 was for 1971 and W_2 for 1976. (The union status variables $U11$, $U10$, and $U01$ were based on reports for Spring 1972 and Spring 1977). In the text of the paper, however, the first difference wage equations that he discussed at length (all fitted by OLS) included among the right-hand variables the year 1 value W_1 of the wage variable. Thus the text equations strongly resemble (5.16) above of the Chamberlain study [35].

Chamberlain argued against fitting (5.16) by OLS. Nevertheless, for reference purposes he did so, omitting W_1 in one of the fittings and including it in the other. The resulting equations cannot be nicely interpreted with (5.16) as the interpreter. However, if the estimated coefficient for U_3 is interpreted as an estimate of $\overline{M}_3$, and that for U_2 as an estimate of $\overline{M}_2$, the four estimates average 0.09, about 0.03 below the panel wage gap estimates of close to 0.12 reported above for the Chamberlain study [35].

Therefore, in interpreting Duncan's wage equations I have proceeded as follows:

1. Equations that excluded W_1 (for 1971) on the right-hand side were treated as FEF equations (5.8) in the same manner as for comparable equations in the Mellow and Mincer studies.

2. Equations that included W_1 on the right-hand side were interpreted as though they were FEF equations (5.8), and the coefficient for W_1 was ignored. I expected that the resulting wage gap estimates would be, perhaps, about 0.03 lower than those from the equations that excluded W_1 as a right-hand variable. My expectation was fulfilled (see table 5.9 below).

Unfortunately, in this study Duncan does not report corresponding cross-section (CS) wage gap estimates. However, I judge from other CS

Table 5.9 Panel Wage Gap Estimates from the Duncan Study [47]

Line (1)	Worker Group (2)	B_{11} (3)	$-B_{10}$ (4)	B_{01} (5)	Mean (6)	Range (7)	With W_1(?) (8)
1	White	.07	.11	.18	.15	.11/.18	No
2	White	.13	.09	.15	.12	.07/.17	Yes
3	Black	−.04	.29	.15	.22	.15/.29	No
4	Black	.21	.10	.28	.19	.06/.31	Yes
5	Both	—	—	—	.15[a]	—	No
6	Both	—	—	—	.12[a]	—	Yes

[a]Employment-weighted mean of separate figures for black and white workers.

studies using the PSID data that are reported in this chapter, in Chapter 4, and especially in Chapter 9, that the missing CS figures are somewhat higher than the panel estimates given in table 5.9.

The format of table 5.9 is similar to that of tables 5.3 and 5.5. Columns 3, 4, and 5 report the estimated coefficients of the union status variables *U*11, *U*10, and *U*01. These coeficients yield four wage gap estimates whose mean appears in column 6 and range in column 7. Column 8 indicates whether the first difference wage equation includes (Yes) or excludes (No) the 1971 wage variable W_1 as a right-hand variable. Notice that inclusion of W_1 reduced the wage gap estimate means for both white and black workers by about 0.03.

I have left to the last Duncan's study no. 46 because it presents problems of interpretation that at best I have solved only crudely. Study no. 46 used the PSID data for 1970–75 for male household heads, 25–55 years of age in 1975, who worked at least 500 hours in each year 1970–74. He first fitted cross-section (CS) wage-level equations (5.1) separately for black workers and white workers. In these equations the wage concept was an average of hourly earnings over the two-year period 1970–71. The union status variable on the right-hand side of the equation, however, classified a worker as unionized only if he was a union member in both 1970 and 1971. Thus the coefficient of the union status variable in these equations is an estimate of a wage differential between workers unionized (members) in both years and other workers including some who were union members in one but not both of the two years. These estimated differentials for 1970–71 were 0.215 for white workers and 0.158 for black workers, with a weighted (10 percent for blacks) mean of 0.209. The level, about 0.2, of these figures is not unusual for cross-section (CS) wage gap estimates for males from PSID data (see section 4, Chapter 9). They are quite atypical, however, in putting the level for blacks below rather than above that for whites (see section 3, Chapter 7).

Strictly speaking, however, these wage differentials are not what I have termed *union/nonunion wage gaps.* Nevertheless, data from the Mincer and Mellow studies suggest that, unless Duncan's sample is unusual in having quite high fractions of union status changers, the above differentials should be fairly close to corresponding CS wage gap estimates, and I treat them here as such.

Duncan also fitted a wage-change equation similar to equation (5.8) but different from it in three respects:

1. The base "year" 1 was the period 1970–71 and the end "year" 2 the period 1973–74.
2. As in the Duncan study no. 47, the base year wage variable W_1 was included as a right-hand variable.
3. The wage change equations included only two right-hand union status variables. The first, which I denote by u_1, was equal to unity for a

worker who was a union member in both 1970 and 1971. The second, denoted by u_{01}, was equal to unity if u_1 was equal to zero *and* the worker was a union member in 1974. Thus the omitted base or comparison group included workers who were nonunion in 1970–71 and 1973–74, plus some workers who were union members in 1970 or 1971 or 1973 but not in 1974.

In interpreting the resulting wage equations to obtain panel wage gap estimates as for the Mellow and Mincer studies, I have (1) treated the dummy variables u_1 and u_{01} as though they were U_1 and $U01$, respectively; (2) assumed that the coefficient for the missing union status variable $U10$ (leavers), submerged in the base group with $U00$, was the negative of that reported for u_{01}; (3) assumed that the fraction $\overline{U}10$ of union leavers was the same as that $\overline{U}01$ for union joiners; (4) and then proceeded as in the Mellow study. The resulting, surely crude, panel wage gap estimates are 0.15 for blacks, 0.12 for whites, and 0.12 as their weighted mean.

Table 5.10 compares panel and cross-section (CS) wage gap estimates from the 17 panel studies discussed above. (In order to make table 5.10 readable I have left out many of the detailed comparisons shown in earlier tables.) There is much agreement among the studies covered in the table that the use of panel methods typically tends to produce wage gap estimates lower than corresponding CS estimates. On only two (lines 28 and 29) of the 20 lines for which there are entries in both columns 5 and 6 are the panel estimates as large as the CS estimates. On these 20 lines the mean ratio of column 5 to column 6 is about one-half, but the ratios range from close to zero (line 23) to close to unity (lines 28 and 29), and their standard deviation is about one-fourth. Thus if the excess of CS over panel estimate is interpreted as evidence that the CS estimates are upward biased by correlation of unobserved fixed effects with union status, the magnitude of the bias can be estimated only imprecisely from these studies.

Furthermore, I am not yet convinced that all or even most of the differences between CS and panel estimates reflect upward bias in the CS estimates rather than downward bias in the panel estimates produced by union status measurement error (and, perhaps, sample selectivity). There were hints of such measurement error in the Mincer study. And table 5.10 contains additional evidence.

Column 7 shows the mean fraction (%) of workers who reported a change of union status between the pairs of years given in column 4. (In the Chamberlain study on line 11, the pairs of years are 1969 and 1970, 1970 and 1971, and 1969 and 1971. In the Mincer study on lines 22 and 23, the pairs of years are all of the adjacent years in the period 1968–78.) On the 16 lines for which there are entries in all of columns 5, 6, and 7, the simple correlation between column 7 and the ratio of column 5 to column 6 is about 0.6, and the simple regression coefficient of the ratio on the fraction reporting union status change is 1.4. That is, in the table there is a marked tendency for the ratio of panel to CS estimate to rise as the frac-

Table 5.10 Comparison of Panel and Cross-Section (CS) Wage Gap Estimates

Line No. (1)	Study No. (2)	Panel Method (3)	Years (4)	Gap Estimates: Panel (5)	Gap Estimates: CS (6)	Changers % (7)	Worker Coverage (8)
May CPS							
1	25	DOM	1974, 1975	.04	.07	14	Teachers
2	25	DOM	1977, 1978	.12	.21	29	Teachers
3	68	FEF	1974, 1975	.09	.19	6	
4	131	FEF	1974, 1975	.08	—	8	Wage and salary
5	131	FEF	1977, 1978	.07	.18/.19	9	Wage and salary
NLS Older Men (45–59 in 1966)							
6	136	FEF	1969, 1971	.04	.05/.08	9	White
7	136	FEF	1969, 1971	.02	.05/.09	8	White
NLS Young Men (14–24 in 1966)							
8	32	DOM	1966–71, 1973	.12	.17	—	
9	35	DOM	1970, 1971	.12	.19	12	
10	35	Other	1970, 1971	.12	.19	12	
11	36	FEF	1969–71	.11	.19	15	
12	68	FEF	1970, 1978	.18	.28	25	
13	136	FEF	1969, 1971	.12	.21/.22	17	White
14	120	FEF	1971, 1976	.20	—	21	Blue-collar
PSID							
15	38	DOM	1972–76	.08	—	—	Male
16	38	DOM	1971–76	.10	—	—	Male
17	46	Other	1970–71, 1973–74	.12	.21	—	Male, 25–55 in 1975

19	48	FEF	1968, 1971	.18	—	14	Male, blue-collar
20	68	FEF	1970, 1979	.14	.23	19	
21	109	DOM	1970, 1974	.08	—	—	Male
22	136	FEF	1968–78	.05	.21/.22	9	White male < 30
23	136	FEF	1968–78	.01	.15	6	White male ⩾ 30
24	144	DOM	1967–77	.09	.29	—	Male, blue-collar
25	144	DOM	1967–77	.02	.04	—	Male, white-collar
26	167	DOM	1967–77	.06	—	—	Male
27	168	DOM	1967–77	.08	—	—	Male
			Other				
28	68	FEF	1973, 1977	.16	.14	16	
29	99	FEF	1966, 1976	.01	.01	47	Fire fighters

Note:

Lines 1 and 2. See text discussion of Baugh-Stone study. CS estimate on line 1 is for 1974, on line 2 is for 1977.

Line 3. See line A in table 5.8 and text discussion of Freeman study. Worker coverage presumably is broad.

Lines 4 and 5. See table 5.2, table 5.3 lines 1 and 2, and text discussion of Mellow study.

Lines 6 and 7. See table 5.4, table 5.5 lines 6 and 9, and text discussion of Mincer study.

Line 8. See text discussion of Brown study.

Lines 9 and 10. See text discussion of this Chamberlain study. Figures in column 7 are from Chamberlain [36], see text.

Line 11. See lines 1, 4, 6, and 7 of table 5.7 and text discussion of this study.

Line 12. See line C of table 5.8 and text discussion of Freeman study.

Line 13. See table 5.4, table 5.5 line 3, and text discussion of Mincer study.

Line 14. See text discussion of Leigh study.

Lines 15 and 16. See text discussion of Chowdhury-Nickell study.

Line 17. See text discussion of this Duncan study.

Line 18. See table 5.9 line 5 and text discussion of this Duncan study.

Line 19. See text discussion of Duncan-Stafford study.

Line 20. See table 5.8 line B and text discussion of Freeman study. Worker coverage presumably is broad.

Lines 22 and 23. See table 5.4, table 5.5 lines 12 and 15, and text discussion of Mincer study. The corresponding estimates for both age groups are: panel = 0.03, CS = 0.17.

Lines 24 and 25. See table 5.1 lines 10 and 11 and text discussion of Moore-Raisian study. The corresponding estimates for both blue- and white-collar workers are: panel = 0.07, CS = 0.20/0.21.

Lines 26 and 27. See text discussion of these two Raisian studies.

Line 28. See table 5.8 line D (*Quality of Employment Survey*) and text discussion of Freeman study. Worker coverage presumably is broad.

Line 29. See text discussion of Ichniowski study.

tion reporting union status change rises. This correlation, in my judgment, is rather more easily explained by measurement error than by fixed effects. This is the subject of the next section.

3. Fixed Effect or Measurement Error?

The union status questions in household surveys such as the CPS, NLS, and PSID are couched in simple language and are not conceptually difficult. For this reason, I would expect that in these and similar surveys only a small fraction of workers would be misclassified by union status. (Some workers or their proxy respondents may misunderstand the union status questions, not know the answer, or have reason to answer falsely. And, of course, allowance must be made for clerical error.) A small amount of such misclassification, my instincts tell me, should lead to small errors in cross-section wage gap estimates. (See section 5 of Chapter 6 for further discussion of this issue.) On the other hand, since the panel estimates rest basically on observation of union status change and since the fraction of workers reporting such change typically is small, even a small amount of misclassification may lead to large downward bias in the panel estimates. Thus the key question examined in this section is: Could union status misclassification account for all or almost all of the differences between cross-section CS and panel wage gap estimates shown in the studies surveyed in the proceeding section, given the available data on union status measurement error?

The differences between the CS and panel estimates are large. If union status measurement errors are mainly responsible for these differences, then confirmation of this fact should not require the use of highly sophisticated econometrics. Accordingly, the statistical model that I use is the rather simple one used by Freeman [68] in calculating his tables 4 and 5.

Write the CS wage equations at two dates in the form

$$W_t = a_t + a_x x_t + MU_t + e_t; t = 1,2; \qquad (5.17)$$

where U_t is the true value of the union status variable, the wage gap M is assumed to be time invariant, and the errors e_t are well-behaved—in particular, there are no fixed effects or other unobservables correlated with right-hand variables. The corresponding two-date wage-difference panel DOM equation is

$$\Delta W = a_2 - a_1 + a_x \Delta x + M \Delta U + \Delta e; \qquad (5.18)$$

where $\Delta W \equiv W_2 - W_1$, and so on. Then the wage gap may be estimated without bias (in what follows the unbiased estimate is denoted by M) by fitting by OLS either (5.17) or (5.18).

Now let union status measurement error intrude. Denote the measured union status by U_m and the measurement error by $m \equiv U_m - U$. Substitute $U_m - m$ for U in (5.17) and $\Delta U_m - \Delta m$ for ΔU in (5.18) to obtain:

$$W_t = a_t + a_x x_t + MU_{mt} - Mm_t + e_t; t = 1,2; \quad (5.19)$$

$$\Delta W = a_2 - a_1 + a_x \Delta x + M \Delta U_m - M \Delta m + \Delta e. \quad (5.20)$$

Both m_t and Δm are unobservable and therefore must be omitted in fitting (5.19) and (5.20). Let M_c be the CS estimate of M when (5.19) is fitted by OLS omitting m_t. Similarly let M_p be the panel estimate of M when (5.20) is fitted by OLS with Δm omitted. Then it follows from the left-out variable theorem and the definition of m that

$$M_c = Mb_{UU_m \cdot x}; M_p = Mb_{\Delta U \Delta U_m \cdot x}; \quad (5.21)$$

$$r \equiv M_p / M_c = b_{\Delta U \Delta U_m \cdot x} / b_{UU_m \cdot x};$$

where $b_{UU_m \cdot x}$ is the regression coefficient for U_m in the regression of U on U_m and the x's and $b_{\Delta U \Delta U_m \cdot x}$ is the regression coefficient for ΔU_m in the regression of ΔU on ΔU_m and the Δx's. The chief task of the statistical model is to imply or predict the value of the ratio r.

Assume that union status misclassification is random with time-invariant probabilities of misclassification p_u for unionized status and p_n for non-union status. Assume also that the true mean fraction unionized $\overline{U}$ is time invariant and that $\overline{U} p_u = (1 - \overline{U}) p_n$. Several propositions follow from these assumptions:

Proposition 1: The expected value $E(U_m)$ of U_m is equal to $\overline{U}$ so that the measured fraction unionized $\overline{U}_m$ is an unbiased estimate of the true fraction $\overline{U}$.

Proposition 2: Denote the expected value of the *simple* regression coefficient of U on U_m by b_{UU_m}. Then $b_{UU_m} = 1 - R$ where $R \equiv p_u + p_n$. (R is the key measure of the amount of union status misclassification.) For the proof of this proposition see Freeman [68], the page 8 discussion underlying his equation (9).

Proposition 3: Denote the expected value of the *simple* regression coefficient of ΔU on ΔU_m by $b_{\Delta U \Delta U_m}$. Then

$$b_{\Delta U \Delta U_m} = (1 - R)c / E(|\Delta U_m|), \quad (5.22)$$

$$E(|\Delta U_m|) = c(1 - R)^2 + 2R(2 - R)\overline{U}(1 - \overline{U}),$$

where c is the true fraction of workers changing union status and $E(|\Delta U_m|)$ is the expectation of $|\Delta U_m|$. The measured fraction of workers reporting change of union status, which I denote by c_m, is an unbiased estimate of $E(|\Delta U_m|)$. For proof of (5.22) see Freeman [68], pages 9–11.

I assume, as Freeman did in his numerical calculations, that $b_{\Delta U \Delta U_m}/b_{UU_m}$ is a good approximation of $r \equiv b_{\Delta U \Delta U_m \cdot x}/b_{UU_m \cdot x}$. Then propositions 2 and 3 imply that

$$c \simeq rE(|\Delta U_m|). \tag{5.23}$$

In (5.22) and (5.23) replace $E(|\Delta U_m|)$ by c_m, $\overline{U}$ by $\overline{U}_m$; then from (5.22) and (5.23):

$$c_m[1 - r(1 - R)^2] \simeq 2R(2 - R)\overline{U}_m(1 - \overline{U}_m). \tag{5.24}$$

Without information on the amount of measurement error $R \equiv p_u + p_n$, (5.24) leads only to not very convincing speculation that panel estimates may suffer seriously from measurement error bias. Fortunately there is some such information, though not nearly as much as I would like. The January 1977 CPS asked the union status question (collective bargaining coverage) first of the surveyed workers and then for a random sample of these workers of their employers. In the May 1979 CPS a random sample of the surveyed workers was asked the union coverage question twice, first on the main survey and then again on a supplemental survey.

Freeman [68] has tabulated the responses from these two surveys in his table 3, a condensed version of which follows:

January 1977 CPS:	
Both said $U = 1$	21.44%
Both said $U = 0$	75.10
Worker said $U = 1$, employer $U = 0$	1.73
Worker said $U = 0$, employer $U = 1$	1.73
May 1979 CPS:	
Both answers $U = 1$	21.78
Both answers $U = 0$	74.97
First answer $U = 1$, second $U = 0$	1.49
First answer $U = 0$, second $U = 1$	1.76

The results of the two surveys are in close agreement. The four estimates of p_u ranged from 0.064 to 0.075 and averaged 0.072; the four estimates of p_n ranged from 0.019 to 0.023 and averaged 0.022. Thus the average for R was 0.094. At my request Freeman also tabulated the May 1979 CPS responses by color and by sex. The resulting estimates of R are:

black workers	.106
white workers	.089
male workers	.085
female workers	.115
all workers	.092

Because of some differences in the timing of the pair of union status questions these "measures" of R may overestimate the true R. In order to be conservative in testing for measurement error bias, I shall take as my estimates of R figures that are 0.01 lower than the preceding five figures.

Return now to equation (5.24) and write it as an equality. Then insert the estimate R_m of R in the equation in place of R and solve for r, the ratio of panel to CS wage gap estimate predicted by the measurement error model. The solution—call it $r(R_m)$—then may be compared to the observed ratio r_m. I have calculated $r(R_m)$ for each of the surveyed studies (except the Ichniowski study no. 99 which did not use household survey data) that provided the needed information on the fraction c_m of workers reporting union status change and the measured fraction unionized $\overline{U}_m$.

Table 5.11 shows for each study the observed r_m, the calculated value of the prediced $r(R_m)$, and the estimates R_m used in the calculation of $r(R_m)$. From the CPS data I discussed above I have five estimates of R_m: all workers 0.082, black 0.096, white 0.079, male 0.075, and female 0.105, and these are the estimates used on lines 4 and 7–12. On lines 1 and 2 I adjusted the all-worker estimate of R_m upward to take into account the much

Table 5.11 Testing for Measurement Error Bias in Surveyed Studies

Line No. (1)	Study No. (2)	R_m (3)	r_m (4)	$r(R_m)$ (5)	Year Pair (6)	Data Source (7)	Worker Coverage (8)
1	25	.097	.57	.55	74,75	CPS	Teachers
2	25	.095	.56	.84	77,78	CPS	Teachers
3	35,36	.079	.57	.49	70,71	NLS	Young men
4	68	.082	.47	.04	74,75	CPS	All
5	68	.085	.61	.69	70,79	PSID	All
6	68	.079	.66	.89	70,78	NLS	Young men
7	68	.082	1.18	.67	73,78	QES	All
8	131	.082	.41[a]	.23	74,75	CPS	All
9	131	.096	.23	.49	77,78	CPS	Black
10	131	.079	.43	.32	77,78	CPS	White
11	131	.075	.49	.32	77,78	CPS	Male
12	131	.105	.27	.35	77,78	CPS	Female
13	136	.070	.55	.72	69,71	NLS	White young men
14	136[b]	.070	.39	.39	69,71	NLS	White older men
15	136	.070	.22	.44	[c]	PSID	White men < 30
16	136	.070	.06	$-.02$[d]	[c]	PSID	White men $\geqslant 30$

[a]Cross-section wage gap estimate not reported; figure used was that reported in Freeman [68].

[b]Calculations are from means of separate figures reported for coverage and membership concepts of union status.

[c]Pooled adjacent years in the period 1968–78.

[d]Value of $r(R_m)$ as calculated from equation (5.24). However, by definition $r(R_m)$ cannot be negative.

higher proportion of teachers than of all workers who are female. On lines 3 and 6 I adjusted the male R_m upward because of heavy overweighting of blacks in the NLS data. On line 5 I made a similar adjustment of the all-worker R_m for the overweighting of blacks in the PSID data used by Freeman. And on lines 13–16 I used the estimates by sex and by color to make an estimate of R_m for white males. I suspect that measurement error R decreases with age (labor market experience), but I have no information confirming the suspicion, and the estimates R_m of R in table 5.11 do not differ by age. Similarly I have no information on R_m for teachers during a period of rapid growth of unionization among teachers, though I suspect that the values of R_m on lines 1 and 2 are too low.

The mean of r_m across the 16 lines of the table is 0.48, the mean of $r(R_m)$ is 0.46. The dispersion of both r_m and $r(R_m)$ is large. The values of r_m range from 0.06 to 1.18 and their standard deviation is 0.25, while $r(R_m)$ ranges from zero to 0.89 and has a standard deviation of 0.26. The simple correlation between r_m and $r(R_m)$ is 0.54.

I am reluctant, however, to give much weight to the figures on lines 4 and 7, both from Freeman's study. The high figure (1.18) for r_m on line 7 is the largest that I have seen in any panel study and may be the result of the crudeness of Freeman's panel wage gap estimate. The low value (0.04) of $r(R_m)$ on line 4 is mainly a consequence of a quite low figure (0.062) for c_m. Mellow (line 8) used the same data source but covered a substantially greater (one-third) number of workers. The value of c_m reported by Mellow for 1974–75 was 0.083, which was close to that (0.086) reported by him for 1977–78 for all workers.

Hence ignore lines 4 and 7. The 14 remaining values of r_m range from 0.06 to 0.66, average 0.43, and have a standard deviation of 0.18. The corresponding figures for $r(R_m)$ are: range 0.00/0.89, mean 0.48, standard deviation 0.24. And the simple correlation between r_m and $r(R_m)$ rises to 0.72. Thus table 5.11 supports a finding that the typically low (well below unity) ratios r_m may be largely a consequence of union status measurement error rather than union status selectivity.

This judgment is supported by a simple experiment that I made with data from the random portion of the PSID surveys for the years 1968–80. The experiment covered all male household heads 16–65 years of age in 1968 who headed the same household throughout the period, with positive annual earnings and annual hours worked in each of the surveys, and with reported data in each survey on union status (the union status question was not asked in the 1973 survey so that the 1973 survey was not used except to provide wage data for 1972) and other right-hand wage explanatory variables. The data were carefully screened to insure that the 11 observations in each worker's time series pertained to the same worker. The sample comprised 832 workers.

For each year t = 1968–72, 1974–79 I computed OLS cross-section (CS) wage gap estimates by regressing W_t, the natural logarithm of annual average hourly earnings for the year, on the following right-hand variables for the survey week of the year: union status (membership concept), schooling (eight dummy variables), age, age squared, region (South vs. non-South), city size (SMSA vs. non-SMSA), color (white vs. nonwhite), and occupation (blue-collar vs. white-collar). The resulting CS wage gap estimates are:

1968 = .24, 1971 = .16, 1975 = .18, 1978 = .17,
1969 = .18, 1972 = .17, 1976 = .21, 1979 = .20,
1970 = .19, 1974 = .20, 1977 = .20, 11-year mean = 0.19.

The corresponding estimates of the fraction unionized $\overline{U}_m$ are:

1968 = .29, 1971 = .30, 1975 = .29, 1978 = .29,
1969 = .30, 1972 = .30, 1976 = .29, 1979 = .28,
1970 = .30, 1974 = .28, 1977 = .28, 11-year mean = .29.

Let t', t = 1968–72, 1974–79, where $t' > t$. In these years there are 55 year pairs t, t' in which the between-years interval ranges from one to 11 years. For each of these 55 pairs of years I computed c_m, the reported fraction of union status changers, and the panel wage gap estimate by regressing $ln\, W_{t'} - ln W_t$ on $U_{mt'} - U_{mt'}$, $(\text{Age})^2{}_{t'} - (\text{Age})^2{}_t$, schooling t' − schooling t (eight dummy variables), South t' − South t, SMSAt' − SMSAt, and blue-collar t' − blue-collar t. The 55 panel wage gap estimates ranged from 0.03 to 0.21, averaged 0.105, and had a standard deviation of 0.050. (Twenty-six of these 55 estimates had t-ratios less than 1.96.) There were very marked differences in the panel wage gap estimates by date. The 10 estimates in which 1979 was one of the pair of years ranged from 0.12 to 0.21 and averaged 0.17. At the other extreme the 10 gap estimates in which 1969 was one of the year pair ranged from 0.03 to 0.12 (this high figure was for 1969, 1979) and averaged 0.07.

For each of the 55 year pairs t', t I calculated r_m as the ratio of the panel wage gap estimate for that pair of years to the mean of the CS estimates for years t' and t. The 55 values of r_m ranged from 0.16 to 1.01, averaged 0.54, and their standard deviation was 0.24. Furthermore, the strong date differences that appear in the panel wage gap estimates also appear, not surprisingly, in the figures for r_m. The 10 values of r_m involving 1979 ranged from 0.63 to 1.01 and averaged 0.86. The corresponding figures for 1969 ranged from 0.22 to 0.63 and averaged 0.37.

It is difficult to rationalize such great dispersion in the ratio of panel to cross-section wage gap estimates for a fixed group of workers as the result of fixed effects correlated with union status in the cross-section estimates. Does the measurement error model help to understand this dispersion? In calculating $r(R_m)$ for each of the year pairs t', t, I estimated $\overline{U}_m$ as the mean of $\overline{U}_{mt}$ and $\overline{U}_{mt'}$ and R_m at 0.07. This figure for R_m is a bit lower than that (0.075) used for males in table 5.11. I chose the lower figure because I suspect that year after year questioning of union status in the PSID has lowered union status mesurement error. Nevertheless, R_m at 0.07 resulted in negative calculated values of $r(R_m)$ for three of the 55 year pairs. I have replaced these negative values by zero.

Since R_m is fixed at 0.07 and $\overline{U}_m(1 - \overline{U}_m)$ ranges from 0.204 to 0.211 in the 55 year pairs, dispersion in the calculated values of $r(R_m)$ is almost entirely the result of dispersion in a single variable, the fraction c_m of workers reporting union status change. In table 5.12 I have grouped the 55 year pairs into 11 groups, each with five pairs, according to the value of c_m for each pair. The c_m group means of r_m appear in column 2, the group means of $r(R_m)$ in column 4, and the corresponding standard deviations in columns 3 and 5.

The overall standard deviations of both r_m and $r(R_m)$ are large and are approximately equal, 0.24 for r_m and 0.23 for $r(R_m)$. Similarly both overall means are close to one-half, with the r_m mean 0.54 a bit above the mean 0.50 for $r(R_m)$. I noted earlier that values of r_m for year pairs involving 1979 were outliers. When these 10 values of r_m are omitted, the overall mean of r_m falls to 0.47 and the s.d. to 0.20. Thus these data indicate that *on the average* measurement error may account for all or almost all of the excess of CS over panel wage gap estimates.

Furthermore, measurement error accounts for a substantial part of the between-c_m group dispersion in r_m. The simple correlation between columns 2 and 4 is 0.69. (The fit of column 4 to column 2 is good except when c_m falls below R_m, at which point the calculated values of $r(R_m)$ are quite sensitive to changes in c_m. Thus the simple correlation between columns 2 and 4 is 0.82 when the first two lines are omitted.)

However, as table 5.12 suggests, union status measurement error explains little of the substantial within-c_m group dispersion of r_m. It is therefore no surprise that the overall simple correlation between r_m and $r(R_m)$ across the 55 pairs of years is a modest 0.41.

In my discussion of the Chowdhury-Nickell paper [38] I mentioned that they, too, were worried about union status measurement error in panel wage gap estimates. They used two rather different methods to overcome this bias.

Recall that their data covered male household heads in the random portion of the PSID with needed data for every year in the period 1968–76. Their panel (DOM) wage gap estimate for the period 1971–76 was 0.101, which is very close to the mean (0.105) of the 55 panel estimates underly-

Table 5.12 Comparison of r_m and $r(R_m)$, 55 Year Pairs, 1968–79 PSID Data

c_m Range (1)	r_m Mean (2)	r_m s.d. (3)	$r(R_m)$ Mean (4)	$r(R_m)$ s.d. (5)
.048–.060	.37	.31	.02	.04
.063–.068	.53	.20	.18	.04
.074–.085	.38	.23	.34	.04
.086–.098	.35	.13	.44	.03
.0985–.105	.48	.16	.52	.02
.1058–.115	.62	.30	.57	.02
.1154–.121	.59	.18	.61	.01
.122–.132	.54	.22	.65	.02
.133–.142	.67	.14	.68	.01
.143–.153	.67	.17	.72	.01
.157–.177	.73	.14	.77	.02
.048–.177	.54	.24	.50	.23

ing table 5.12. They did not report any CS, OLS wage gap estimates, but I presume that had they done so, the figures would have been close to the mean (0.19) of the 11 CS estimates underlying table 5.12.

One method to reduce measurement error is to average over individual measurements. Thus they divided the period 1971–76 into two periods 1971–73 and 1974–76 of three years and fitted the panel DOM equation to the three-year means for individual workers. The resulting panel estimate was 0.145. Similarly they divided the years 1969–76 into the two four-year periods 1969–72 and 1973–76 and used the four-year means to obtain a panel estimate of 0.184. From these equations they estimated that with full elimination of measurement error the panel estimate would be about 0.19 to 0.22, or close to the CS estimate.

Their second method was much more elaborate (for the details see their paper). Two panel (DOM) equations were fitted to the data. The first was the standard DOM equation, but the second instrumented union status on union status lagged one year. Neither of the two resulting wage gap estimates, they argued, is free of measurement error bias, but a properly weighted mean of the two is unbiased, with weights computed from the data. They produced four such estimates ranging from 0.162 to 0.220. They concluded that "omitted quality variables bias the union effect upwards by about as much as measurement error problems bias it downwards and the 'old style' cross-section estimates are of the right order of magnitude after all."

4. Summary Appraisal of the Panel Estimates

The panel wage gap estimates surveyed in the chapter on the average are roughly half as large as the corresponding cross-section estimates. On one interpretation, this difference is the consequence of upward bias in the cross-section estimates, caused by correlation of unobserved fixed effects with union status. This difference is large but not incredible. And the direction of the bias in the cross-section estimates accords with my priors.

Nevertheless, I am reluctant to accept this interpretation. First, the ratio r_m of panel to cross-section estimate is widely dispersed, from near zero to close to unity, even for a given group of workers with broad worker coverage. The fixed effect interpretation provides no rationale for this dispersion.

Moreover, there were hints, especially in Mincer's study discussed in section 2, that the difference might be the result of union status measurement error. Indeed, the evidence presented in section 3 indicates that union status misclassification, of the quite modest amounts suggested by CPS data, could account fully or almost fully for the average *difference* between panel and cross-section wage gap estimates and, in addition, explain part of the dispersion in the ratio r_m of the two estimates. This evidence convinces me that the panel wage gap estimates presented in section 2 suffer more seriously than their cross-section counterparts from downward bias produced by union status misclassification. Hence I view the typically positive differences between cross-section and panel estimates as unreliable estimates of an upward selectivity bias in the cross-section estimates.

However, the measurement error story told in section 3 does not explain a substantial part of the dispersion in the ratios of panel to cross-section estimates. For this reason I do not interpret section 3 as indicating that there is no selectivity bias in the cross-section estimates. I still suspect that this bias is indeed upward, but I cannot present convincing evidence that my suspicion is correct.

6 Micro, OLS, CS Estimates: Data Problems

1. Introduction

Most of our evidence on union/nonunion wage gaps in the United States in recent years comes from Micro, OLS, CS wage equations, i.e., from wage equations fitted by ordinary least squares (OLS) to cross-section (CS) data for individual workers (or, less frequently, establishments) on wages, the union status variable *U*, and other variables. I survey this evidence in the next three chapters.

Micro, OLS, CS wage gap estimates, I have argued, are subject to upward bias stemming from correlation of omitted right-hand variables with the union status variable *U*. This is the union status selectivity problem discussed in Chapters 4 and 5. But this selectivity is not the only source of possible bias. In this chapter I examine a variety of estimate errors arising from imperfections in the reported data rather than from failure to observe unobservables:

Section 2. The omission of fringe benefits in the dependent wage variable.
Section 3. Hourly versus weekly or annual wage.
Section 4. Real versus money wage.
Section 5. Union status measurement error.
Section 6. Union membership versus collective bargaining coverage.
Section 7. Nonrandomness by design in the NLS, SEO, and PSID data sets.
Section 8. Nonrandomness produced by missing data.

2. Errors Resulting from Omissions of Fringe Benefits

In the most commonly used household surveys—the *Current Population Surveys* (CPS), the *National Longitudinal Surveys* (NLS), the *Survey of Economic Opportunity* (SEO), and the *Panel Study of Income Dynamics* (PSID)—the wage measures that may be routinely calculated from the data are the more or less conventional ones of hourly, weekly, and annual wages or earnings. All of these wage measures surely exclude employer expenditures for fringe benefits that are not paid directly to workers and hence do not show up promptly in worker pay envelopes. Indeed, some of the wage measures derived from household survey data and used in wage gap estimation probably omit some employer fringe expenditures that are paid directly to workers.

In the discussion of wage, compensation, and fringe benefit concepts that follows, I use the U.S. Bureau of Labor Statistics (BLS) *Employee Compensation Surveys* as a reference benchmark. These are probability sample surveys of U.S. private nonfarm establishments in which data are gathered separately for office and nonoffice employees in each establishment. In these surveys total employee *compensation* is the sum of employer expenditures under three broad and mutually exclusive headings: (A) the *gross payroll,* the total of employer payments directly to workers; (B) *legally required* employer contributions to insurance funds; and (C) *private welfare plan* contributions of employers. The detailed compensation items under these headings are shown in table 6.1.

Which of the compensation items in table 6.1 have been omitted from the wage measures routinely derived from the household surveys (CPS, NLS, SEO, PSID) most often used in Micro, OLS, CS wage gap estimation? This question cannot be answered precisely with presently available data. The wage and hours questions in the household surveys were designed to be answered by workers or other household members acting as their proxies rather than by the personnel offices of employing firms. Therefore the questions were short, couched in simple language, and lacking in the qualifying detail required to elicit precise responses. As a consequence one can only speculate regarding the compensation items included in the household survey wage measures.

My speculations follow:

1. First, it is very likely that none of these wage measures includes either the legally required (B) or private welfare plan (C) expenditures.

2. Second, annual earnings measures probably include all or most of the gross payroll (A) items and thus exclude only B and C.

3. Third, measures of annual average hourly earnings obtained by dividing reported annual earnings by reported annual hours worked are likely to exclude not only B and C but also for some, perhaps most, respondents will exclude paid leave (A4) and severance leave pay (A6). This will be true of respondents whose reported annual hours worked includes time paid for but not worked.

4. Fourth, none of the household survey wage measures is as exclusive of compensation items as A1 (straight-time pay) in table 6.1. (In particu-

Table 6.1 Employer Expenditures for Employee Compensation

Expenditure Item
A. *Gross payroll,* the total of employer payments directly to workers, the sum of items A1–A6.
A1. Straight-time pay
A2. Overtime pay
A3. Shift differentials
A4. Paid leave, the sum of A4a, A4b, A4c, A4d
A4a. Vacations
A4b. Holidays
A4c. Sick leave
A4d. Civic and personal leave
A5. Nonproduction bonuses
A6. Severance pay for either permanent or temporary severance
B. *Legally required* contributions to insurance funds, the sum of B1–B4
B1. Social Security and Railroad Retirement
B2. Unemployment insurance
B3. Workmen's compensation
B4. Other
C. *Private welfare plan contributions,* the sum of C1–C6
C1. Life, health, and accident insurance plans
C2. Pension and retirement plans
C3. Vacation and holiday funds
C4. Severance and supplementary unemployment benefit plans
C5. Savings and thrift plans
C6. Other private welfare plans
D. *Compensation,* the sum of A, B, and C

lar, household respondents are likely to include regular overtime and shift premia.) That is, all of these measures include A1 and more. However, household survey questions on a worker's hourly wage or salary or his usual weekly earnings and usual weekly hours worked are likely to yield wage measures that are almost as exclusive as A1.

Thus in my judgment all of the household survey wage measures include straight-time pay (A1) and exclude legally required (B) and private welfare plan (C) expenditures. Annual earnings measures, I speculate, include most of the gross payroll (A) items, but other wage measures probably omit part or most of the expenditures under the headings A2–A6.

In what follows I adopt the BLS definition of *compensation* at item D of table 6.1. Denote by C the natural logarithm of compensation (per hour, week, or year) and by C_i the natural logarithm of any of the 19 mutually exclusive and exhaustive detailed components (per hour, week, or year) of compensation listed in table 6.1. Then, since $e^C = \sum_{i=1}^{19} e^{C_i}$,

$$M_C = \sum_{i=1}^{19} a_i M_i; \; a_i = e^{C_i - C}; \; \sum_{i=1}^{19} a_i = 1; \tag{6.1}$$

where M_C is the union/nonunion wage gap measured with compensation as the wage concept, M_i is the corresponding gap for the i-th compensation component, and a_i is the share of this component in total compensation.

Let $i = 1,2, \ldots, 9$ for the nine gross payroll (A) items ($A1$, $A2$, $A3$, $A4a$, $A4b$, $A4c$, $A4d$, $A5$, and $A6$) where $i = 1$ for the straight-time pay item $A1$, but the ordering of the other A items is arbitrary. Let

$$e^W = \sum_{i=1}^{m} e^{C_i}; \; e^F = \sum_{i=m+1}^{19} e^{C_i};$$

and

$$a = \sum_{i=m+1}^{19} a_i;$$

where $1 \leq m \leq 9$, e^W is the measured wage concept, e^F that for the omitted fringe expenditures, and a is the ratio of the omitted fringes to compensation. Then

$$M_C - M_W = a(M_F - M_W) = \sum_{i=m+1}^{19} a_i(M_i - M_W), \tag{6.2}$$

and if $m > 1$,

$$(M_C - M_1) - (M_C - M_W) = M_W - M_1 = \sum_{i=2}^{m} a_i(M_i - M_1). \tag{6.3}$$

$M_C - M_W$ is the error in the measured wage gap M_W; i.e., it is the amount that should be added to M_W because of the omission from e^W of the fringe expenditures e^F.

When $m = 1$, $e^W = e^{C_1}$ is the straight-time wage which is approximated by several hourly wage measures derived from household surveys. When $m = 9$, $e^W = \sum_{i=1}^{9} e^{C_i}$ is the gross pay wage concept which, I have said, is approximated by annual earnings. The content of other wage measures derived from household surveys is unclear in terms of included A items. Thus for these measures the value of $M_C - M_W$ is ambiguous.

In the studies that I have used to estimate the error $M_C - M_W = a(M_F - M_W)$ from omitting fringe benefit expenditures two different approaches have been used. The most obvious method is to fit wage equations in pairs differing only in the dependent variable, C in one equation and W in the other. This *direct* approach leads to matched estimates of M_C and M_W.

The second approach involves the fitting of a fringe benefits equation—i.e., an equation in which the dependent variable is F (or e^F), or $F - C$ (or e^{F-C}), or $F - W$ (or e^{F-W}), and the right-hand variables include the union status dummy variable U, control variables x, and usually the measured wage W (or e^W) or compensation C (or e^C) variable. To illustrate, let the fringes equation be:

$$F - W = b + b_w W + b_U U + b_x x + e. \tag{6.4}$$

Then $M_C - M_W = a(M_F - M_W) = a(b_w M_W + b_U)$. Thus unless b_w is zero, it is not possible to calculate $a(M_F - M_W)$ from knowledge only of a and the coefficients b_w and b_U of the fringe benefits equation. A matching estimate of either M_W or M_C also is required. Some of the studies using the second approach also provide matching estimates of M_W or M_C. For the rest of the studies using the second approach, I have used an approximately matching estimate of M_W drawn from the stock of such wage gap estimates that I have accumulated. Fortunately, the partial derivative of $F - W$ with respect to W (the coefficient b_w in 6.4) was close enough to zero in the fitted fringe equations that a precise estimate of M_W was not required for good estimation of $a(M_F - M_W)$.

Table 6.2 reports the estimates of $a(M_F - M_W)$ that I have calculated from 23 different studies. Column 2 identifies each study by its number in the reference list. Thus on line 1 the estimates are from the two Alpert studies [8, 9]. The estimates or estimate ranges (lowest estimate/highest estimate) of $a(M_F - M_W)$ that I have drawn from the studies appear in column 3 and the year or period to which they pertain in column 4. Whenever a range of estimates is given in column 3, the line notes to the table state the number of separate estimates covered in the range. Thus on line 1 the range 0.028/0.036 covers six estimates. Column 5 states the method used to estimate $a(M_F - M_W)$ as follows: *Direct* implies that the study provided separate matching estimates of M_F or M_C and M_W; *F( )* indicates that I have calculated $a(M_F - M_W)$ from a fringe benefits equation and an assumed value of M_W shown in the parentheses. Thus on line 1 the second or *F( )* approach was used and the assumed value of M_W was 0.10.

Column 6 reports the compensation items (by their table 6.1 shorthand identifications) included in the measured wage concept e^W underlying the wage gap M_W in $a(M_F - M_W)$. Thus on line 1, e^W includes all of the compensation items except item *C* (private welfare plans). Column 7 identifies the compensation items (by their table 6.1 identifications) treated as fringes in the fringes equation. On line 1 the covered fringes are those in item *C* (private welfare plans). Notice that on some of the lines of the table the compensation items included in columns 6 and 7 taken together do not exhaust the items of table 6.1, so that the estimate of $a(M_F - M_W)$ in column 3 is only a partial estimate of $M_C - M_W$. For example, on lines 11 and 12 the measured wage column 6 includes only item A1 and the covered fringes column 7 only items *C*1 and *C*2, so that the column 3 estimates 0.022 of $a(M_F - M_W)$ are partial estimates of $M_C - M_W$. All such estimates are identified by the letter *P* in column 3.

Column 8 briefly describes the worker coverage of the estimates and the notes to the table call attention to special features of some of the studies.

On five lines (22–24, 34, 35) of the table the covered fringe expenditures were somewhat crudely estimated. The data sources underlying the estimates of $a(M_F - M_W)$ on these lines provided information for each worker

Table 6.2 Estimates of $a(M_F - M_W)$

Line No. (1)	Study No. (2)	Estimate of $a(M_F - M_W)$ (3)	Date (4)	Method (M_W) (5)	Measured Wage (6)	Covered Fringes (7)	Worker Coverage (8)
				A. Estimates from BLS Employee Compensation Survey Data			
1	8,9	.028/.036	1972	F(.10)	D − C	C	Nonoffice, manufacturing
2	8,9	.013/.027	1972	F(.10)	D − C	C	Office, manufacturing
3	8	.044/.049	1972	F(.15)	D − C	C	Nonoffice, non MFG
4	8	.011/.014	1972	F(.15)	D − C	C	Office, non MFG
5	12	.023/.028	1977	Direct	A1	D − A1	Office, see notes
6	12	.035/.042	1977	Direct	A	D − A	Office, see notes
7	21,22	.030	1977	Direct	A1	D − A1	Office, see notes
8	21,22	.036	1977	Direct	A1 + A2 + A3	D − A1 − A2 − A3	Office, see notes
9	22	.088	1977	Direct	A1	D − A1	Office, MFG, see notes
10	22	.065	1977	Direct	A1 + A2 + A3	D − A1 − A2 − A3	Office, MFG, see notes
11	23	.022P	1968	F(.15)	A1	C1 + C2	Office
12	23	.022P	1968	F(.15)	A1	C1 + C2	Nonoffice
13	44	.016/.021P	1967–72	F(.10)	A1 + A2 + A3 + A4	B + C1 + C2 + C5	Nonoffice, manufacturing
14	65	.025	1967–72	Direct	A1	D − A1	Nonoffice
15	65	.023/.033	1967–72	F(.15)	A1 + B or A1	D − A1 − B	Nonoffice
16	65	.023	1967–72	Direct	A1	D − A1	Nonoffice, manufacturing
17	65	.022/.036	1967–72	F(.08)	A1 + B or A1	D − A1 − B	Nonoffice, manufacturing
18	71	.024/.026	1967–72	Direct	A1	D − A1 − B	Nonoffice, manufacturing
19	71	.022/.023	1967–72	Direct	A	C	Nonoffice, manufacturing
20	136	.022P	1967–72	F(.10)	A1 + A2 + A3 + A4	B + C1 + C2 + C5	Nonoffice, manufacturing
21	191	.024P	1972	F(.10)	A1	C1 + C2	Nonoffice, manufacturing
				B. Other Estimates			
22	4	.030/.031P	1972	Direct	Annual earnings	≃C1 + C2	White, male, blue-collar
23	12	.009/.012P	1979	Direct	UHE	≃C1 + C2	White-collar

24	132,133	.017/.018P	1979	Direct	UHE	≃C1 + C2	Wage and salary
25	116	.03P	1978	Direct	AHE	A4a + A4c + C1	Full-time, 6 locations
26	51	.033/.038P	1974	Direct	AHE	A4a + A4c + B1 + C1 + C2	Refuse collectors
27	51	.033/.038P	1974	F	AHE	A4a + A4c + B1 + C1 + C2	Refuse collectors
28	51	.037/.037P	1974	Direct	AHE	A4a + A4c + B1 + C1 + C2	Truck drivers
29	51	.031/.037P	1974	F	AHE	A4a + A4c + B1 + C1 + C2	Truck drivers
30	26	.030	1976	F(0.06)	AHE	D − AHE	Hospital nonprofessionals
31	34	.00P	1975	F(0.07)	A1	A4	Registered nurses, private
32	202	.004/.014P	1977	F(0.15)	Annual salary	C1 + C2	Public school teachers
33	99	.008/.021P	1976	Direct	Hourly salary	C1 + C2	Municipal fire fighters
34	11	.003/.008P	1979	Direct	UHE	≃C1 + C2	White-collar
35	14	.011P	1979	Direct	UHE	≃C1 + C2	White-collar
36	24	.032	1973	Direct	Annual salary	≃D − B − A1	Policemen

Note:

Lines 1–4. Estimate ranges on lines 1 and 2 cover 6 estimates, on lines 3 and 4 ranges cover 2 estimates. Estimates, not shown in table, of $a_i(M_i - M_W)$ separately for items C1 (insurance) and C2 (pensions) are available.

Lines 5–10. Worker coverage includes professional, technical, and clerical workers in 95 establishments appearing both in the 1977 BLS *Employee Compensation Survey* and in a 1976–78 BLS *Area Wage Survey*. The covered establishments comprise a quite nonrandom sample of U.S. establishments.

Lines 5–6. Estimate ranges cover 6 estimates. Comparable estimates by sex and major occupation are also available.

Lines 7–8. Comparable estimates by sex and establishment size also available.

Lines 11–12. Estimates of $a_i(M_i - M_W)$ also available separately for C1 and C2.

Line 13. Estimate range covers 3 estimates.

Lines 15, 17. Estimate ranges cover 6 estimates. See text for discussion of comparable estimates of $a_i(M_i - M_W)$ separately for compensation items A2, A3, A4, A5, C1, and C2.

Lines 18, 19, 22, 24, 28, 29. Estimate ranges cover 2 estimates.

Lines 22–24, 34, 35. The fringe expenditures were somewhat crudely estimated (see text).

Lines 23, 24, 34, 35. UHE in column 6 means "usual hourly earnings."

Line 23. Estimate range covers 10 estimates. Comparable estimates by sex and major occupation are also available.

Line 24. Comparable estimates by establishment size also available.

Lines 25–30. AHE means average hourly earnings.

Line 25. Worker coverage comprises full-time workers enrolled in the *Rand Health Insurance Study* in 6 cities or counties in 4 states.

Lines 26–29. The workers covered include only public employees engaged in refuse collection.

Lines 26–27. Estimate ranges cover 4 estimates.

Line 33. Estimate range covers 6 estimates.

Line 34. Estimate range covers 9 estimates.

on his measured wage e^W and whether the worker was covered by a fringe benefit plan for each covered fringe item. For a worker not covered by a fringe plan e^{C_i} was equated to zero. For a worker who was covered e^{C_i} was estimated to be the national mean for such plan (lines 22 and 24) or the national mean in the worker's industry (lines 23, 34, 35).

First consider the estimates on lines 1–21, all of which are based on BLS *Employment Compensation Survey* data. These surveys provide much detail at the establishment level on the employee compensation items but little on worker characteristics. Thus all of the estimates on these lines pertain to quite broad groups of workers, differentiating workers only by office versus nonoffice and manufacturing versus nonmanufacturing. (The Antos study no. 12, lines 5 and 6, does provide separate estimates by sex and major occupation, and the Atrostic study nos. 21 and 22, lines 7 and 8, contain estimates by sex and firm size. However, these studies are based on a quite nonrandom sample of U.S. establishments.)

Only the Alpert studies [8, 9] and the Bailey-Schwenk study [23] provide matching estimates of $a(M_F - M_W)$ for office and nonoffice workers. In the Bailey-Schwenk study there was no office versus nonoffice difference, but in the Alpert studies the matched estimate pairs in both manufacturing and nonmanufacturing yielded nonoffice estimates above those for office workers. Thus in what follows I focus attention on nonoffice workers, presuming that $a(M_F - M_W)$ for office workers is not greater than $a(M_F - M_W)$ for nonoffice workers. In proceeding in this way I am ignoring the estimates for office workers on lines 5–10 which include the largest estimates in the table. These estimates, I think, are badly tainted by nonrandomness of the establishment sample on which they are based.

The estimates for nonoffice workers on lines 1, 3, and 12–21 are not strictly comparable in part because of differences in measured wage concept and in covered fringes. Do these differences matter? First notice that the estimates on lines 1 and 3 include the legally required items B in the measured wage but not in the covered fringes. Similarly all of the estimates on lines 15, 17, 18, and 19 exclude B from the covered fringes and some of them include B in the measured wage. I strongly suspect that switching B from covered fringe to measured wage has the effect of increasing $a(M_F - M_W)$ by a positive but *negligible* amount. The legally required contribution (tax) rates are the same for all workers regardless of union status except that the marginal tax rates are zero above the maxima on taxable earnings. Thus unionism can have only the effect of producing a positive union/nonunion gap in the fraction of workers with earnings above the cap on taxable earnings. Antos [12] made matching wage gap estimates with compensation (D) as one wage measure, and compensation less legally required items (D-B) as his second wage measure. The two estimates were identical. Thus I think that the differences in the treatment of the legally required expenditure items do not matter.

Second, observe that the measured wage on lines 1, 3, 13, 19, and 20 includes all or most of the gross payroll (A) items, while on lines 12, 14–18, and 21 the measured wage is essentially that corresponding to straight-time pay ($A1$). It follows from equation (6.3) that for a given specification of compensation e^C, the addition to $A1$ in the measured wage of any other compensation item e^{C_i} will lower the estimate of $a(M_F - M_W)$ by $a_i(M_i - M_1)$. Freeman [65] has fitted equations for most of the compensation items with $A1 + B$ as the wage concept. The estimates of $a_i(M_i - M_1)$ that I have calculated from his study are given below in table 6.3. (In calculating the estimates, I have assumed that $M_i - M_1$ is zero for the legally required B items.)

These estimates—see especially line 9 of table 6.3—suggest that the estimates of $a(M_F - M_W)$ on lines 13 and 20 of table 6.2 would have been higher by perhaps as much as 0.009 if compensation items $A2$, $A3$, and $A4$ had been included in the covered fringes rather than in the measured wage. Similarly, lines 10 and 13 of table 6.3 indicate that the estimates on lines 1, 3, and 19 of table 6.2 would be increased by about 0.004 if items $A2$–$A6$ had been switched from measured wage to covered fringes.

Third, notice that on lines 12 and 21 of table 6.2 the covered fringes include only employer contributions to insurance ($C1$) and pension ($C2$) plans though the measured wage is that of straight-time pay ($A1$). Comparison of lines 12 and 14 of table 6.3 indicate that omission of other compensation items $A2$–$A6$ and $C3$–$C6$ may have lowered these estimates of $a(M_F - M_W)$ by about 0.007 or 0.008.

In table 6.4 I have adjusted the table 6.2 estimates of $a(M_F - M_W)$ on lines 1, 3, 12, 13, 18–21 for nonoffice workers to make them comparable in measured wage concept ($A1$) and covered fringes (D-$A1$) to the estimates on lines 14–17 in accordance with the suggestions of the immediately preceding paragraphs.

The estimates on lines 1 and 3 clearly are outliers. The estimates on lines 12–21 bunch fairly closely about 0.028. Hence I judge from table 6.4 that on the average for nonoffice workers the compensation gap M_C exceeds the measured wage gap M_W by about 0.028 when the measured wage is that of straight-time pay. Evidence presented in tables 6.2 and 6.3 indicates that on average $M_C - M_W$ may be closer to 0.020 than to 0.028 when the measured wage is that of gross pay or earnings and that, for both the straight-time and gross pay concepts of the measured wage, $M_C - M_W$ is not larger and may be smaller for office than for nonoffice workers. I do not regard 0.020 as negligibly small.

Return now briefly to lines 22–36 of table 6.2, panel B. I do not regard the estimates of $a(M_F - M_W)$ in panel B as contradicting the empirical judgments stated in the preceding paragraph. The estimates on lines 25–33 and 36 pertain to workers in narrowly defined occupations (lines 26–33 and 36) or in only a few locations (line 25). And though the worker cover-

Table 6.3 Estimates of $a_i(M_i - M_l)$ from Freeman Study [65]

Line No.	Compensation Item	Estimate of $a_i(M_i - M_1)$ MFG	Non-MFG	Both
1	A2. Overtime premia	−.0042	—	−.0014
2	A3. Shift premia	.0012	—	.0009
3	A4a. Paid vacations	.0084	—	.0045
4	A4b. Paid holidays	.0048	—	.0023
5	A4c. Paid sick leave	−.0012	—	−.0001
6	A5. Bonuses	−.0051	—	−.0040
7	C1. Insurance plans	.0134	—	.0136
8	C2. Pension plans	.0087	—	.0111
9	Sum of lines 1–5	.0090	—	.0062
10	Sum of lines 1–6	.0039	.001	.0022
11	Sum of lines 1–8	.0260	—	.0269
12	D − A1 − B	.030	—	.032
13	Line 12 − line 11	.004	.006	.005
14	Sum of lines 7 and 8	.0221	—	.0247

age of the estimates on lines 22–24 and 34–35 is broad, the estimates come from wage equations in which the covered fringe expenditures were rather crudely estimated.

Table 6.4 Adjusted Estimates of $a(M_F - M_W)$ for Nonoffice Workers

Table 6.2 Line No.	Adjusted Estimate	Industry
1	.032/.040	MFG
3	.048/.053	Non-MFG
12	.029	MFG and non-MFG
13	.025/.030	MFG
14	.025	MFG and non-MFG
15	.023/.033	MFG and non-MFG
16	.023	MFG
17	.022/.036	MFG
18,19	.024/.027	MFG
20	.031	MFG
21	.031	MFG

3. Hourly versus Weekly and Annual Wage Concepts

For an individual worker let W be his hourly wage or earnings, $W1$ his weekly wage, $W2$ his annual wage, $H1 = W1 - W$ his weekly hours worked, $H2 = W2 - W$ his annual hours worked, and $H3 = H2 - H1$ his annual weeks worked, where the wage (W) and hours (H) concepts are measured in natural logarithmic units. In a substantial fraction of the studies from which I have drawn wage gap estimates, the dependent wage variable was $W1$ or $W2$ rather than W. Clearly, if unionism produces a union/nonunion differential or gap in hours worked, then wage gaps estimated from $W1$ or $W2$ will differ from the corresponding wage gap estimated from the hourly wage W. In particular, $M_{W1} - M_W = M_{H1}$ and $M_{W2} - M_W = M_{H2} = M_{H1} + M_{H3}$ where each M denotes the union/nonunion gap in the subscripted variable.

Table 6.5 shows the hours gap estimates that I have drawn from 16 different papers. On only five of the 21 lines of table 6.5 are the estimated hours gaps *not negative,* and the largest estimate numerically is that (-0.07) for fire fighters on line 15. Thus these studies suggest that typically the hours gaps M_{H1}, M_{H2}, and M_{H3} are negative and may not be negligible in size. Among the studies with at least moderately broad worker coverage (lines 1–14), the mean estimate of M_{H1}, the hours per week gap, is about -0.018 and that for M_{H2}, the hours per year gap, is about -0.030. These estimates of M_{H1} and M_{H2} in turn are consistent with the estimates of M_{H3} from the Raisian studies shown on lines 9, 11, and 14.

4. Real versus Money Wage

In the great majority of the Micro, OLS, CS wage equations surveyed in Chapters 7–9 the dependent wage variable was a money rather than real (cost-of-living deflated) wage. Unionized workers to a greater extent than nonunion workers reside in areas (large cities and the non-South) in which the cost of living is relatively high. Hence there is a danger that unless cross-section cost-of-living differences are controlled for, use of a money rather than real wage will lead to upward biased wage gap estimates.

The most common method of adjusting for these cost-of-living differences was to include region and city-size variables among the right-hand variables in the wage equation. Several studies *also* deflated the dependent money wage variable by U.S. Bureau of Labor Statistics cost-of-living indexes which have been available for some cities and outside of these cities by region and urban versus rural residence.

Four studies covered in table 6.6 fitted both real and money wage equations. All of the equations included some right-hand controls for cross-section cost-of-living differences. Let M_R be the wage gap estimate from a real wage equation and M_N the corresponding gap estimate from the money wage equation. Column 3 of table 6.6 shows the values of $M_R - M_N$ that I have calculated from the four studies. These estimates of $M_R - M_N$ differ in sign and are all close to zero. Thus the four studies suggest that if cost-of-living differences are at least roughly controlled by variables on the right-hand side of the wage equation, it makes little difference whether the dependent variable is a money or real wage. (Gay also fitted wage equations comparable to those underlying line 1 of table 6.6 except that the control

Table 6.5 Hours Gap Estimates

Line No. (1)	Study No. (2)	Estimated Gap (3)	Date (4)	Gap Concept (5)	Worker Coverage (6)
1	4	.00	1972	H2	White, male, blue-collar
2	64	−.03/−.02	1973–75	H1	Male, blue-collar, manufacturing
3	64	−.04/−.02	1973–75	H1	Male, blue-collar, nonmanufacturing
4	66	−.04	1971	H2	Male, household heads, 26–28 years of age
5	71	.01	1973–75	H1	Blue-collar, construction
6	81	−.05	1967	H2	Full-time, white, male, household heads
7	150	−.05/−.04	1973	H1	Full-time workers
8	157	−.04	1973–75	H1	Male craftsmen, construction
9	166	−.02	1967–74	H3	Male household heads
10	165	−.01	1967–74	H1	Male household heads
11	165	−.02	1967–74	H3	Male household heads
12	167	.00	1967–77	H1	Male household heads
13	168	.00/.00	1967–79	H1	Male household heads
14	168	−.01/.01	1967–79	H3	Male household heads
15	15	−.07	1961–66	H1	Fire fighters
16	24	−.01	1973	H1	Police privates
17	25	−.02	1974	H1	Elementary and secondary school teachers
18	25	−.04	1977	H1	Elementary and secondary school teachers
19	52	−.05	1969	H2	Fire fighters
20	99	−.05/−.02	1966	H1	Fire fighters
21	99	−.01/.00	1976	H1	Fire fighters

Note:
Column 5. H1 = hours per week; H2 = hours per year; H3 = weeks per year.
Lines 2, 3, 13, 14. Estimate ranges cover 2 estimates.
Line 4. Estimate is from an hours equation.
Line 6. Estimates also available separately for government and private workers.
Lines 7, 20. Estimate ranges cover 3 estimates.
Line 8. Estimate is from an hours equation in a simultaneous equations system fitted by maximum likelihood.
Lines 9–14. Estimates are from hours and weeks equations.
Lines 12–14. Panel technique used to estimate H1 and H3 gaps.
Line 15. Estimates also available by year, region, and city size.
Line 19. Estimates also available by city size.
Line 21. Estimate range covers 6 estimates.

variables included only major occupation and for each worker's industry an extent of unionism and a concentration ratio variable. The estimate of $M_R - M_N$ from these equations was -0.028, which is not negligible.)

5. Union Status Measurement Error

Measurement error in the union status variable U (= 1 for a unionized worker and zero otherwise) used in fitted Micro, OLS, CS wage equations

Table 6.6 Wage Gap Estimates: Real versus Money Wage

Line (1)	Study No. (2)	$M_R - M_N$ (3)	Date (4)	Worker Coverage (5)
1	73	.008	1967	Male blue-collar
2	172	.000	1973	Males, 32 large cities
3	178	−.003	1973	29 large cities
4	178	−.002	1978	29 large cities
5	190	−.005	1978	44 large cities

Note:

Line 1. Column 3 is the mean of separate estimates by occupation. Right-hand variables include both regional and city-size variables.

Line 2. Right-hand variables include region and seven city variables.

Lines 3, 4. Column 3 is the mean of separate estimates by sex and region.

Line 5. Right-hand variables include 4 city variables and in the money wage equation the cost-of-living deflator.

may arise for two reasons. First, for some workers union status may be misreported by the worker or by a proxy respondent reporting for him. Second, the date to which the reported union status pertains may not match that of the dependent wage variable in the wage equation. For example, in the Michigan PSID surveys union status pertains to the reference week of the survey, while the annual earnings and annual hours worked questions refer to the preceding calendar year. Thus when the dependent variable in a fitted wage equation is either annual earnings or annual average hourly earnings, the date of the union status variable cannot match that of the wage variable. Unfortunately, I know of no studies that cast much light on the effect of such timing mismatches on Micro, OLS, CS wage gap estimates.

In the commonly used household surveys the union status questions are rather simple. Even so, some workers or their proxy respondents may respond incorrectly to them and, of course, clerical errors between the household interview and the final edited tape cannot be ruled out. Nevertheless I would expect that only a small fraction of workers would be misclassified by union status. The resulting bias in cross-section wage estimates then would be small though perhaps not negligible.

One way of learning about response error in household surveys is to check the household responses for a given worker against corresponding responses by the worker's employer. This was done in the January 1977 *Current Population Survey* (CPS). That survey contained two supplements in addition to the usual battery of questions on labor force status, sex, age, schooling, occupation, industry, and the like. First, a random subsample of those surveyed were asked additional questions on union status (collective bargaining coverage), usual weekly earnings, and usual weekly hours worked. Second, each of the subsample was asked to give the name and address of his employer. The employer in turn was asked to report the worker's occupation, industry, union status (collective bargaining coverage), usual weekly earnings, and usual weekly hours worked. The timing of the employer responses, of course, was not quite the same as that of the workers.

The May 1979 CPS contained two sets of supplemental questions (the first about "dual jobs," the second about "pensions") asked of a random subsample of workers. Both supplements asked workers about their collective bargaining status. Thus each worker was reinterviewed regarding his union status.

Freeman [68] has tabulated the union status responses from both of these surveys. For the January 1977 survey he reported that for 3.5 percent of the 3,297 workers covered in his tabulations, the employer and worker responses differed. For the May 1979 survey 3.2 percent of 18,257 workers gave a different response when reinterviewed.

Mellow and Sider [134] also tabulated the data from the January 1977 survey. Their tabulation covered 4,523 workers (instead of 3,297 in the Freeman tabulations), and they reported that for 7.1 percent (instead of 3.5 percent as reported by Freeman) of the workers employer and worker responses differed. (I regard the Freeman 3.5 percent figure as more credible than the Mellow-Sider figure of 7.1 percent.)

Mellow and Sider fitted five wage equations to the January 1977 CPS subsample data for 2,571 private-sector workers employed full time. The specifications of the first four of the equations were:

Dependent: $W1 = ln$ (wage) as reported by the worker, or $W2 = ln$ (wage) as reported by the employer, where the wage was the ratio of usual weekly earnings to usual weekly hours worked.

Right-hand: common to all of the equations were sex, color, schooling years, experience (age minus schooling minus six years) and its square as reported by the worker. In addition, the equations included either worker-reported ($RH1$) or employer-reported ($RH2$) industry (nine dummy variables), occupation (eight dummy variables), and the union status dummy variable U. The resulting wage gap estimates (coefficients of U) were:

Dependent	*Right-Hand Set*	*Wage Gap*
$W1$	$RH1$	.173
$W2$	$RH1$	.175
$W1$	$RH2$	.146
$W2$	$RH2$	.150

In the fifth equation all of the variables, except for union status, were measured from worker responses. However, both worker and employer responses were used to classify workers into four union status groups: ($U11$) both say $U = 1$; ($U00$) both say $U = 0$, the base group; ($U01$) worker says $U = 0$, employer $U = 1$; ($U10$) worker says $U = 1$, employer $U = 0$. Thus the fifth wage equation contained three union status dummy variables for the three groups ($U11$), ($U01$), and ($U10$). The estimated coefficients for these variables were: ($U11$) = 0.180, ($U01$) = −0.061, ($U10$) = 0.077.

These results suggest that misclassification of workers by union status leads to a small downward bias in wage gap estimates derived from OLS, CS wage equations fitted to household survey data based on worker responses to the survey questions. My reasoning is this. Treat employer-worker disagreements in response to the union status question as though the truth were not known, i.e., as no response. On the other hand, treat response agreement as disclosing the truth. Then the "true" wage gap estimate, from the fifth equation, is 0.180. Compare this to the wage gap estimate (0.173) on the first line of the unnumbered table above.

Freeman [68] also fitted Micro, OLS, CS wage equations to the January 1977 CPS data. One equation (eq.1) covered only workers for whom there was no employer-worker disagreement regarding union status. The second equation (eq.2) covered only workers for whom the union status responses disagreed. In equation 2 the union status was based on worker responses. Other details of worker coverage were not reported, and the right-hand variables, in addition to union status, were described only as the "usual demographic and human capital controls." The resulting wage gap estimate from equation 2 was much smaller (indeed, it was not statistically different from zero on the usual tests) than that from equation 1. He repeated this exercise with the data from the May 1979 CPS with similar results. Unfortunately, one cannot derive from these results estimates of the magnitude of the bias in Micro, OLS, CS wage gap estimates caused by union status misclassification in household survey data.

My intuition tells me that the magnitude of such bias is small. The Mellow-Sider findings suggest that the bias may be downward and of the order of magnitude of 0.007. Yet before I accept and act upon this suggestion I would like to see more wage equations fitted to the January 1977 and May 1979 CPS data and replications of these CPS experiments.

6. Union Membership versus Collective Bargaining Coverage

In some of the Micro, OLS, CS wage equations surveyed in later chapters the union status dummy variable U is unity if the worker says that he is a union *member* (usually in the context of his current employment), while in other equations $U = 1$ if the worker says that in his current employment he is *covered by a collective bargaining agreement.* A worker can be covered by a collective bargaining agreement and yet not be a member of the covering union. A less likely possibility is that a worker can be a union member and not be covered by a collective bargaining agreement. That is, coverage does not imply membership or membership imply coverage.

In the *National Longitudinal Surveys* (NLS) the primary union status question pertained to coverage rather than membership, but each worker who responded affirmatively to the coverage question also was asked whether he was a member of the covering union. Workers who responded negatively to the coverage question were not asked whether they were union members. In the May 1979 *Current Population Survey* (CPS) the primary question pertained to membership (in connection with their primary job), but those who responded negatively also were asked whether in their primary job they were covered by a collective bargaining agreement. In what follows I assume that a negligible fraction of workers in the survey were union members but not covered by a bargaining agreement. With this assumption, these NLS and CPS data permit the estimation of matching wage gap estimates that differ only in the union status concept, coverage or membership, used.

Jones [103] and Mincer [136] provide such estimates from the NLS data and Katz[108] from the May 1979 CPS data. Jones fitted eight wage equations separately by color to the 1971 data for each of the four NLS panels by age group and sex. Each of her wage equations included two union status dummy variables separately identifying covered members and covered nonmembers. For each panel, farm, military, and private household workers were excluded along with those with missing data. Mincer fitted eight wage equations by year (1969, 1971), age group, and union status concept (coverage versus membership) to the NLS data for the two panels for white males. Students and workers with missing data were excluded. Katz's wage equations were fitted to the May 1979 CPS data for private workers in the mining, manufacturing, transportation, and service industries who were employed in States with a right-to-work law. Excluded were self-employed workers, sales workers, managers, farm workers, construction workers, and those with missing data. He fitted five equations separately by union status category: union members, not union members, covered (members plus covered nonmembers), not covered, and covered nonmembers. The two equations for not union members and for covered workers included a right-hand dummy variable for workers who were covered nonmembers.

Let *Mcov* and *Mmem* denote the wage gap estimates corresponding to the coverage and membership concepts respectively. Table 6.7 shows the values of *Mmem* – *Mcov* that I have calculated from these studies. Two things stand out in the table. First, except for black older men, *Mmem* exceeds *Mcov*. But second, the excess of Mmem over Mcov is less than 0.01 except for young workers in their later teens and early twenties. Although table 6.7 does suggest that Mmem exceeds Mcov (especially for young workers for whom the fraction of covered nonmembers is substantial), the evidence regarding the magnitude of the excess is rather thin. For this

Table 6.7 Wage Gap Estimates: Membership versus Coverage

Line No. (1)	Study No. (2)	Year (3)	Mmem − Mcov (4)	Worker coverage (5)
1	103	1971	.017	Young men, white
2	103	1971	.045	Young men, black
3	103	1971	.020	Young men, all
4	103	1971	.033	Young women, white
5	103	1971	.021	Young women, black
6	103	1971	.032	Young women, all
7	103	1971	.005	Older men, white
8	103	1971	−.004	Older men, black
9	103	1971	.004	Older men, all
10	103	1971	.005	Older women, white
11	103	1971	.002	Older women, black
12	103	1971	.005	Older women, all
13	136	1969	.017	Young men, white
14	136	1971	.008	Young men, white
15	136	1969	.004	Older men, white
16	136	1971	.009	Older men, white
17	108	1979	.005[a]	See text

[a]Three estimates.

reason, I do not attempt in later chapters to adjust wage gap estimates for differences in the underlying union status concept.

7. Nonrandomness by Design in the NLS, SEO, and PSID Data Sets

The *National Longitudinal Surveys* (NLS) and a portion (the so-called nonrandom half) of the *Survey of Economic Opportunity* (SEO) and the surveys of the *Panel Study of Income Dynamics* (PSID) were not random samples of the U.S. population they were designed to cover. (The nonrandomness of the SEO and PSID easily can be avoided by using only the "random half," but this was not always done in the SEO and PSID wage equations surveyed in this book.) In particular, in all of these surveys the relative frequency of black workers was much higher than in the corresponding U.S. population. This nonrandomness probably leads to a negligible problem of bias in Micro, OLS, CS wage gap estimates if the underlying wage equations are fitted separately by color to the data. Then the only problem is to use the appropriate *population* weights in averaging the black and white gap estimates, which I have uniformly attempted to do.

However, Micro, OLS, CS wage equations often were fitted to the combined data for both black and white workers (without a color*union status interaction variable). Then the resulting wage gap estimate is an average of underlying separate gap estimates by color in which the black gap estimate is heavily overweighted unless in fitting the wage equation each observation is weighted by the reciprocal of its sampling probability. Such weighting, however, seldom was done.

Of course, if the wage gap were the same for black workers as for others, overweighting of blacks in the NLS, SEO, and PSID would not matter. However, in Chapter 7 I show that wage gap estimates derived from these data tend to differ substantially by color. It is likely, therefore, that when Micro, OLS, CS wage equations are fitted to the combined data for blacks and nonblacks (without appropriate weights), overweighting of blacks may lead to bias in the combined wage gap estimates. In Chapter 8, section 3, I use data from Chapter 7 to derive adjustments for this bias.

8. Nonrandomness Produced by Missing Data

All of the commonly used, large micro-data sets such as the SEO, CPS, NLS, and PSID come from carefully designed sample surveys in which the sampling probability for each observation is known. Unfortunately, however, in all of these data files the sampling design is frustrated to a nonnegligible extent by failure of some observations to provide valid responses to some of the survey questions. For example, in the pooled data from the May CPS for 1973, 1974, and 1975 responses to the usual weekly earnings and usual weekly hours worked questions were missing for almost 28 percent of government and private workers, including the self-employed, who were working, with a job but not at work, or looking for work. (The 28 percent figure comes from my tabulations of these data.)

It is common practice in fitting wage equations to omit observations with missing data on the left-hand wage variable or on one or more of the right-hand variables. It is also common practice *not* to report the number of observations so excluded or their distribution by the variables for which data were missing. However, I judge from my tabulations of the 1973–75 May CPS data files that the chief culprit is the left-hand wage variable.

It is not surprising to me that earnings and hours questions frequently are not answered in household surveys. Earnings (before taxes and other deductions) and hours worked (rather than paid for) are somewhat complex questions whose truthful answering for many workers may require rather detailed record keeping. I, for example, could tell an interviewer my gross annual earnings in, say, 1983 at my principal job only after consulting my check stubs for 1983. And since I do not keep a time diary, I could give only a rough estimate of my hours and weeks worked in 1982.

Although my wife, acting as a proxy for me, could answer such questions about me as accurately as I could, there are, I daresay, many proxy respondents who really do not know the gross earnings of the workers for whom they are asked to respond. Furthermore, some respondents, no doubt, regard earnings questions as an improper invasion of privacy. And some respondents with high earnings may fear that truthful answering of earnings questions may lead to tax or other penalties.

Suppose that we were able to observe the wages of workers for whom no wage was reported (the excluded group) with as much precision as for workers for whom a wage was reported (the included group). Denote by e the wage residual calculated for a worker, included or excluded, from the Micro, OLS, CS wage equation fitted to the data for included workers. For included workers the residual e is uncorrelated with each of the right-hand variables in the wage equation, including the union status variable U. There is no guarantee, however, that this proposition will hold for the *excluded* workers. And if it does not, the exclusion of observations with missing data on the wage variable will affect the wage gap estimate.

One can only speculate regarding the sign and magnitude of the effect of excluding observations with missing wage data. It is not readily apparent to me that ignorance of the correct response, confusion resulting from the complexity of the wage concept, or affront to privacy should lead to upward rather than downward biasing nonresponse. In my judgment the most likely source of self-selection nonresponse bias is fear that disclosure of true earnings somehow or other may lead to subsequent penalties. Who are those with incentives not to disclose true earnings? Youngsters living at home who want to hide their earnings, perhaps partly from illegal or questionable activities, from their parents. Transfer payments recipients—from welfare programs, Social Security, Disability Insurance, and the like—who fear that disclosure of earnings will cost them their transfer benefits. Workers with high earnings they would like to hide and think they can hide from tax collectors. But here, too, even the direction of bias in the wage gap estimate is unclear to me.

Although the wage questions, I think, are the chief source of observations with missing data in fitting wage equations, missing data on right-hand variables occasionally may lead to sizable exclusions. For example, a special supplement to the May 1979 CPS contained questions on the size (employment) of the firm and establishment. A substantial number of workers either could not or did not answer the employer size questions.

Mellow [133] fitted wage equations to these data first excluding and then including workers with missing employer size data. The worker coverage was broad and the wage equations were identical except that the second equation included a right-hand dummy variable indicating the presence or absence of missing employer size data. The sample sizes and wage gap estimates for the two equations were (the first equation was reported in Mellow's paper as regression 4 in his table 2; the second equation was reported to me in correspondence with Mellow):

	Sample Size	*Wage Gap*
Excluding workers with missing employer size data	18,551	.075
Including these workers	22,538	.085

The number of workers excluded in the first equation was substantial, 3,987 or about 18 percent of 22,538, and the wage gap estimate was 0.01 lower when these workers were excluded than when they were included.

7 Micro, OLS, CS Estimates: Variations in the Wage Gap across the Labor Force

1. Introduction

This chapter is the first of three chapters that survey the union/nonunion wage gap estimates derived from the Micro, OLS, CS wage equations provided by a large number of empirical studies that have appeared since 1963. The focus of this chapter is on the question, Does the union/nonunion wage gap vary across the work force by characteristics of workers and their workplaces and, if so, by how much?

Consider first the following pair of Micro, OLS, CS wage equations fitted separately by sex:

$$W_i = a_i + a_{ix}x + M_iU + e_i;\ i = m,f; \tag{7.1}$$

where W is the natural logarithm of the wage variable, the x's are control variables (typically worker and workplace characteristics), U is the union status dummy variable, e is the residual, the a's are estimated coefficients, M is the wage gap estimate, and the subscript i denotes the sex (m = male, f = female) of a worker. Deriving the wage gap M's from the fitted equations involves no more than reading the equations and calculation of the gap difference $M_m - M_f$ by sex only a subtraction.

Notice that the pair of equations (7.1) may be written as a single equation

$$\begin{aligned} W = U[M_f + (M_m - M_f)D] + a_f + (a_m - a_f)D + a_{fx}x \\ + (a_{mx} - a_{fx})Dx + e_f + (e_m - e_f)D; \end{aligned} \tag{7.2}$$

where D is the sex variable equal to unity if $i = m$ and zero if $i = f$. In (7.2) the wage gap $M = M_f + (M_m - M_f)D$ depends upon sex D and the wage gap difference by sex $M_m - M_f$ is the partial derivative of the wage gap M with respect to D.

Alternatively, suppose that a single wage equation of the following form has been fitted to data:

$$W = a + a_x x + a_D D + U(b + b_D D) + e. \tag{7.3}$$

This equation, of course, is the simplified version of (7.2) that contains no interactions Dx. The estimated wage gap M is $b + b_D D$ whose partial derivative with respect to sex D is the estimated gap difference $M_m - M_f$ and is equal to the coefficient b_D of the interaction term UD in the wage equation.

For some studies the retrieval of estimated gap *differences* was as simple as the preceding paragraphs suggest. But in numerous other studies additional calculations were required. First, wage equations comparable to (7.1) often were fitted separately by sex and color (black workers versus white) yielding four wage gap estimates by sex and color. To obtain wage gap figures by sex for both colors combined, I calculated the employment-weighted mean of the wage gap estimates by color within each sex. (The employment weights almost always came from the sample data to which the equations were fitted with appropriate adjustments for oversampling of black workers in the NLS data files and in the nonrandom portion of the SEO and PSID surveys.) A similar procedure was followed in a few studies in which the wage equations were fitted separately by sex, color, and some other right-hand variables. Second, in the separate equations by sex (7.1) the union status variable U often was interacted with some or all of the x's as in (7.4):

$$W_i = a_i + a_{ix} x + U(b_i + b_{ix} x) + e_i; i = m,f. \tag{7.4}$$

The estimated wage gap M_i for $i = m,f$ then was calculated as $b_i + b_{ix}\bar{x}$ where $\bar{x}$ is the mean of x over the observations to which the equation was fitted. Third, in some wage equations the dependent wage variable was the wage e^W measured in its natural units rather than the wage W in logarithmic units. The required calculation then involves two steps. First proceed as though the dependent variable were W rather than e^W. Then divide the resulting wage gap or wage gap difference estimate by the mean of e^W over the covered observations.

The same procedure as for sex was followed for all of the qualitative or discrete variables describing workers and workplaces, such as color and region, and for continuous variables, such as years of school completed, treated as discrete variables. For continuous variables treated as continuous rather than discrete the procedure was essentially the same:

1. For each wage equation that includes the union status variable U on the right-hand side the estimated wage gap M is the partial derivative of $W = lne^W$ with respect to U. (When the wage equations are fitted separately by union status U, first write the pair of equations as a single equation that explicitly includes U on the right-hand side. If the left-hand wage

variable is e^W rather than W, divide the partial derivative of e^W with respect to U by the mean of e^W to obtain M.) In general, this partial derivative M will depend on some or all of the right-hand variables. I use years of school completed, denoted by S, as an example. That is, $M = M(S$, other variables).

2. The wage gap difference per year of school completed then is the partial derivative $\partial M/\partial S$ of M with respect to S. If this second derivative also depends on right-hand variables, evaluate it at the means of these variables over the observations covered in fitting the equation.

3. If S enters the wage equation as a quadratic, the curve relating M to S may be U-shaped or inverted U-shaped. If so, note the shape and calculate the value of S at which M is a minimum or maximum.

In summary, the estimates of wage gap *differences* presented in this chapter are second partial derivatives $\partial^2 W/\partial U \partial x$ calculated from Micro, OLS, CS wage equations where each x is a right-hand control variable in the equation.

I have emphasized in Chapters 4, 5, and 6 that union/nonunion wage gap estimates from Micro, OLS, CS wage equations are subject to several potentially serious biases, especially the left-out variables bias discussed in Chapters 4 and 5. Although this does not imply that the estimates of wage gap differences presented here also are seriously biased, I strongly suspect that some of them are. Thus I regard the estimates of wage gap differences presented in this chapter as quite tentative.

I turn now to these estimates. They are presented in the following order:

Section 2. By sex
Section 3. By color
Section 4. By marital status
Section 5. By major industry
Section 6. By major occupation
Section 7. By region and city size
Section 8. By years of school completed
Section 9. By age, experience, and seniority
Section 10. By extent of unionism
Section 11. By other worker and workplace characteristics
Section 12. Overview of findings

The studies from which the estimates were drawn are indicated by number in the list of references at the end of the book. In some studies the wage equations from which the estimates were calculated were incompletely reported and were obtained by correspondence with study authors. I have excluded studies in which the worker coverage was quite narrow, e.g., nurses and fire fighters. I have also excluded a substantial number of studies (1) containing information on the signs of gap differences but insufficient information to calculate the sizes of the differences, and (2) containing information that I suspected was erroneous.

2. Wage Gap Differences by Sex (Male/Female)

Table 7.1 reports estimates of wage gap differences by sex drawn from 41 studies. Column 2 of the table identifies each study by its number in the list of references. Column 3 shows the estimate (or range of estimates) of the excess of the male over the female wage gap. The date to which each estimate pertains is given in column 4, and column 5 briefly describes the worker coverage of the estimates. Several of the studies contain somewhat more detail on the sex gap difference than is shown in table 7.1. For example, study no. 17 provides estimates of the sex gap difference simultaneously by color, occupation, and industry.

Scan column 3. On 24 of the 48 lines of the table the gap difference figures are negative, on 23 lines positive, and on line 19 the sign is ambiguous. Replace each estimate *range* in column 3 by its midpoint. Then the mean of the 24 negative figures is −0.052, the mean of the 24 positive figures is 0.043, the overall mean of the 48 figures is −0.005, and the corresponding standard deviation is 0.068.

The worker coverage restrictions on lines 4, 7, 12, 14, 18–23, 28, 29, and 34 may be somewhat selective by sex. Hence ignore the figures on these 13 lines. On the remaining 35 lines there are 18 negative figures, 17 positive figures, the overall mean is −0.010, and the standard deviation is 0.046.

Nor is the story changed much when the figures are sorted by data source or by date:

	Positive	*Negative*	*Mean*	*Standard Deviation*
Panel A (SEO)	4	7	−.02	.04
Panel B (Michigan)	4	4	.01	.11
Panel D (CPS)	13	12	.00	.04
1967	4	8	−.02	.04
1969–71	5	3	.03	.10
1973–76	11	6	.01	.04
1976–79	5	6	.00	.04

In making these calculations I have ignored the extreme outlier on line 14.

I conclude from these 41 studies that in recent years (1967–79): (1) the sign of the mean male-minus-female wage gap difference is ambiguous, and (2) the numerical magnitude of the difference is close to zero.

The Micro, OLS, CS wage gap estimates that I have retrieved from recent studies are disproportionately for male workers who have comprised roughly 60 percent of the U.S. work force. Let M_m, M_f, and $\overline{M}$ denote the overall mean wage gap for male workers, female workers, and all workers, respectively. Then if the conclusion of the preceding paragraph is correct, the sign of $M_m - \overline{M} \simeq 0.4(M_m - M_f)$ is ambiguous and its numerical magnitude is close to zero.

3. Wage Gap Differences by Color (Black or Nonwhite minus White)

Table 7.2 presents estimates of the excess of the mean wage gap for black or nonwhite workers over the corresponding gap for white workers that I have calculated from Micro, OLS, CS wage equations in 48 studies. The format of the table is essentially the same as that of table 7.1. The gap difference estimates are in column 3.

Consider first the estimates of the gap difference on lines 1–25 from wage equations fitted to *Current Population Survey* (CPS) data. None of the figures in column 3 except that on line 9 for blue-collar construction workers is larger numerically than 0.05, and positive and negative figures occur with roughly equal frequency. Replace estimate ranges by their midpoints. Then the mean and standard deviation of the CPS gap estimates are as follows for various combinations of the estimates:

Line	*Mean*	*Standard Deviation*
1–25, except 7, 9, 11, 13	.01	.02
5, 8, 10, 18, (manufacturing)	−.01	.03
5, 6, 8, 10, 21, 25 (blue-collar)	.00	.02
5, 6, 12, 14, 25 (male)	.00	.02
3–6, 8, 14, 15, 20, 22, 23, 25 (1973–75)	.01	.03
1, 2, 12, 16–19, 24 (1976–79)	−.00	.02

Thus the estimates based on CPS data suggest that the overall mean black-white wage gap difference was approximately zero.

This suggestion, however, is not supported by the estimates on lines 26–43 from equations fitted to the Survey Research Center data or those on lines 44–53 fitted to the 1967 *Survey of Economic Opportunity* data. These estimates are disproportionately positive and their means and standard deviations (after replacing ranges by range midpoints) are:

Lines	*Mean*	*Standard Deviation*
26–43	.04	.08
26–43, except 28, 36, 40–42	.06	.07
44–53	.06	.06

Furthermore, the estimates on lines 54–67 for males based on *National Longitudinal Survey* data indicate marked variation in the black-white gap difference with age. The six figures on lines 54–59 for young (14–24 in 1966) males are all negative with a mean of −0.045 and standard deviation of 0.03, while the eight figures on lines 60–67 for older (45–59 in 1966) males are all positive with a mean of 0.12 and standard deviation of 0.04.

Thus the evidence on the overall mean black-white gap difference is somewhat murky. Estimates from CPS data suggest a negligible difference. But estimates from other data sources point rather strongly to a

Table 7.1 Wage Gap Differences by Sex (Male − Female)

Line No. (1)	Study No. (2)	Gap Difference (3)	Date (4)	Worker Coverage (5)
A. Studies Using 1967 Survey of Economic Opportunity Data				
1	17	.02	1967	Private, nonfarm, not private household, wage and salary
2	31	−.05	1967	⩾ 14 years of age
3	60	.02	1967	17–65 years of age
4	73	.01	1967	Private, operatives, nonstudent, ⩾ 14, selected industries
5	78	.02	1967	Private wage and salary (?)
6	79	−.03	1967	⩾ 14 years of age in 12 large SMSAs
7	114	−.00	1967	Full-time operatives, selected industries
8	127	−.02	1967	Private wage and salary (?)
9	146	−.02	1967	Private, urban, wage and salary, ⩾ 16 years of age
10	147	−.08	1967	Private, urban, wage and salary, ⩾ 16 years of age
11	180	−.08	1967	Private, full-time, wage and salary, 14–65 years of age
B. Studies Using Michigan Survey Research Center Data				
12	28	−.05	1967	Household heads, wage and salary, ⩾ 25 years of age
13	40	−.08	1969	Full-time, wage and salary, nonprofessionals, age 22–64
14	48	−.32/−.19	1976	Blue-collar with regular work schedules
15	59	.08	1977	Wage and salary, nonfarm, excluding construction and sales
16	82	−.12/−.12	1969	Full-time, 21–64 years of age
17	82	−.10/−.09	1973	Full-time, 21–64 years of age
18	141	.16	1970	Household heads, wage and salary, full-time, 17–65 years of age
19	169	−.04/.06	1969–71	Household heads, wage and salary, 18–65 years of age
20	169	.15	1969–71	Same as line 19, but only in manufacturing
C. Study Using National Longitudinal Survey Data				
21	103	.05/.06	1971	Nonfarm, not private household, young persons
D. Studies Using Current Population Survey Data				
22	5	.10	1973–75	Wage and salary, construction industry
23	12	−.08/−.05	1979	White-collar wage and salary

25	17	−.03	1973	Private, wage and salary, nonfarm, not private household
26	17	.00	1975	Private, wage and salary, nonfarm, not private household
27	33	−.03	1973–75	Private, nonfarm, wage and salary
28	71	−.02	1973–75	Private, blue-collar, wage and salary, manufacturing only
29	90	.09	1970	Blue-collar, wage and salary, nonstudent, manufacturing, 18–64
30	100	.00/.00	1973–76	Full-time, nonfarm, wage and salary, 34 large SMSAs, ages 17–72
31	110	.05	1973	Wage and salary, nonfarm, not private household, ages ⩾ 16
32	131	−.03	1977	Nonfarm, wage and salary, with data for both May 1977 and May 1978
33	133	−.04/−.01	1979	Wage and salary, ages 16–75
34	133	−.05	1979	Wage and salary, ages 16–75, manufacturing only
35	133	−.01	1978	Wage and salary, ages 16–75
36	150	−.05	1973	Private, full-time, wage and salary, in industries with injury data
37	160	−.05/−.04	1969	Private, full-time, blue-collar, nonfarm, ⩾ 14 years of age
38	177	.04	1973	Private, full-time, wage and salary, nonfarm, not private household
39	178	−.00/−.00	1973	Nonfarm, not private household, 29 large SMSAs
40	178	.01/.01	1978	Nonfarm, not private household, 29 large SMSAs
41	184	.02	1975	Nonfarm, not private household, wage and salary
42	186	.03	1973	Nonfarm, not private household, wage and salary, ages ⩾ 16
43	187	.02	1973	Nonfarm, not private household, wage and salary, ages ⩾ 16
44	188	.00	1975	Nonfarm, not private household, wage and salary, ages ⩾ 16
45	189	.03	1973	Nonfarm, not private household, wage and salary, ages ⩾ 16
46	190	−.01/−.01	1978	Wage and salary in 44 SMSAs
47	58	.02	1977	See line note
48	108	.05/.07	1979	See line note

Note:

Lines 3, 6. Government workers included and treated as nonunion.

Lines 4, 7. Included industries were mining, manufacturing, construction, transportation, communication, and utilities.

Lines 12, 18–20. Data source: *Panel Study of Income Dynamics* (PSID).

Lines 13, 16. Data source: *Survey of Working Conditions*.

Line 14. Data source: *Time Use Survey*. Estimate range covers 6 estimates.

Lines 15, 17. Data source: *Quality of Employment Survey*.

Lines 16, 17, 21, 30, 33, 37, 39, 40, 48. Estimate range covers 2 estimates.

Lines 19, 20. Farm, mining, finance, insurance, real estate, and government workers are excluded along with union workers who paid no union dues.

Line 19. Estimate range covers 5 estimates.

Line 21. Males 19–29, females 17–27.

Line 23. Estimate range covers 10 estimates.

Lines 24, 46. Estimate range covers 3 estimates.

Line 31. Coverage includes only Northeast and South regions.

Line 37. Wage and salary workers.

Line 47. Worker coverage excludes managers, sales workers, construction workers, and self-employed.

Line 48. Worker coverage includes private workers in mining, manufacturing, and service industries but excludes managers, sales workers, construction workers, farm workers, and self-employed.

Table 7.2 Wage Gap Differences by Color (Black − White)

Line No. (1)	Study No. (2)	Difference (3)	Date (4)	Worker Coverage (5)
				A. Studies Using Current Population Survey Data
1	12	−.02/−.01	1979	White-collar, wage and salary
2	13	.00	1976	Wage and salary
3	17	.04	1973	Nonfarm, not private household, wage and salary
4	17	.04	1975	Nonfarm, not private household, wage and salary
5	64	.01/.04	1973–75	Private, male, blue-collar, wage and salary, manufacturing
6	64	−.05/−.02	1973–75	Private, male, blue-collar, wage and salary, nonmanufacturing
7	64	−.02/.01	1973–75	Private, male, blue-collar, wage and salary, all industries
8	71	−.01	1973–75	Private, blue-collar, wage and salary, manufacturing
9	71	−.11	1973–75	Private, blue-collar, wage and salary, construction
10	90	.00	1970	Blue-collar, wage and salary, ages 18–64, manufacturing
11	94	.01/.04	1978	Male, nonfarm, nonstudent, wage and salary, ages 16–24
12	94	.01/.04	1978	Male, nonfarm, nonstudent, wage and salary, ages 16–64
13	94	−.03	1973–75	As on line 11, but see note
14	94	−.02	1973–75	As on line 12, but see note
15	110	.01	1973	Nonfarm, not private household, wage and salary, ages ≥ 16
16	131	.01	1977	Nonfarm, wage and salary with data for both 1977 and 1978
17	133	−.02/−.01	1979	Wage and salary, 16–75 years of age
18	133	−.04	1979	Wage and salary, 16–75 years of age, manufacturing
19	133	−.00	1978	Wage and salary, 16–75 years of age
20	150	.02	1973	Private, full-time, wage and salary, industries with injury data
21	160	.02/.02	1969	Private, blue-collar, full-time, full-year, nonfarm, wage and salary
22	177	.05	1973	Private, nonfarm, not private household, full-time, wage and salary
23	184	.03	1975	Nonfarm, not private household, wage and salary
24	58	−.00	1977	See line 47, table 7.1
25	157	.01	1973–75	Male craftsmen, construction
				B. Studies Using Michigan Survey Research Center Data
26	1	.07	1975	Male household heads, wage and salary, excluding construction
27	2	.10	1976	Male household heads, wage and salary, excluding construction

28	28	.14	1967	Household heads, wage and salary, ages ≥ 25
29	46	−.06	1970–71	Male household heads, 25–55 years of age in 1975
30	86	−.03	1968–74	Male household heads
31	86	−.01	1974	Male household heads
32	93	.18	1967	Male household heads, nonfarm, wage and salary, 20–62 in 1967
33	93	.11	1967–74	Male household heads, nonfarm, wage and salary, 20–57 in 1967
34	102	.08/.18	1972	Male household heads, wage and salary
35	125	.03	1973	Male household heads, ages ≥ 18
36	141	.01	1970	Full-time household heads, wage and salary, ages 17–65
37	143	.11/.13	1967–74	Male household heads, wage and salary, ≥ 65 years of age
38	145	.02/.09	1967–77	Male household heads, wage and salary, ages 18–65
39	144	.00/.02	1967–77	Male, nonfarm, household heads, ages 18–65
40	169	−.02/.02	1969–71	Household heads, wage and salary, ages 18–65, but see note
41	169	.01	1969–71	Household heads, wage and salary, ages 18–65, but see note
42	59	−.16	1977	Nonfarm wage and salary, excluding sales and construction workers
43	101	.04	1965–66	Male, blue-collar, household heads, nonstudent
		C. Studies Using 1967 Survey of Economic Opportunity Data		
44	16	.12	1967	Private, urban, male, wage and salary
45	17	.05	1967	Private, nonfarm, not private household, wage and salary
46	31	−.04	1967	Age ≥ 14
47	78	.04	1967	Private, wage and salary (?)
48	79	.03	1967	Ages ≥ 14 in 12 large SMSAs
49	114	.08	1967	Full-time, operatives, selected industries, private
50	127	.11	1967	Private wage and salary (?)
51	146	.02	1967	Private, urban, wage and salary, ≥ 16 years of age
52	147	.04	1967	Private, urban, wage and salary, ≥ 16 years of age
53	180	.17	1967	Private, full-time, wage and salary, 14–65 years of age
		D. Studies Using National Longitudinal Survey Data		
54	10	−.10	1969	Male, 14–24 in 1966, nonstudent, blue-collar
55	32	−.03	1966–71, 1973	Male, 14–24 in 1966, nonstudent, not college graduate
56	103	−.04/−.02	1971	Male, 14–24 in 1966, nonfarm, not private household
57	118	−.03	1969	Male, 14–24 in 1966, nonstudent, wage and salary
58	118	−.04	1971	Male, 14–24 in 1966, nonstudent, wage and salary
59	119	−.03	1971	Male, 14–24 in 1966, nonstudent, wage and salary

Table 7.2 (continued)

Line No. (1)	Study No. (2)	Difference (3)	Date (4)	Worker Coverage (5)
60	10	.07	1969	Male, 45–59 in 1966, blue-collar
61	103	.05/.06	1971	Male, 45–59 in 1966, nonfarm, not private household
62	118	.15	1969	Male, 45–59 in 1966, wage and salary
63	118	.13	1971	Male, 45–59 in 1966, wage and salary
64	117	.09/.13	1969	Male, 45–59 in 1966
65	119	.18	1969	Male, 45–59 in 1966, wage and salary
66	119	.17	1971	Male, 45–59 in 1966, wage and salary
67	182	.10/.15	1971	Male, 45–59 in 1966, wage and salary, nonfarm, not household
68	103	−.10/−.08	1971	Female, 14–24 in 1968, nonfarm, not private household
69	179	−.01	1973	Female, 14–24 in 1968, nonstudent
70	103	−.00/.00	1971	Female, 34–38 in 1971, nonfarm, not private household

Note:
Lines 1, 5–7, 34, 64. Estimate range covers 4 estimates.
Lines 11, 12, 17, 21, 37, 39, 56, 61, 67, 68, 70. Estimate range covers 2 estimates.
Lines 13, 14. Worker coverage is restricted to private, blue-collar in 98 largest SMSAs.
Line 15. Worker coverage restricted to Northeast and South regions.
Line 21. Age coverage is ≥ 14.
Lines 26–44. The data source is the *Panel Study of Income Dynamics* (PSID).
Line 29. Worker coverage is restricted to those who worked at least 500 hours each year 1970–74.
Line 37. Estimates available by year 1967–74 have a mean of 0.13 and a range of 0.06/0.19.
Line 38. Estimate range covers 3 estimates. Estimates by year 1967-77 have a mean of 0.09 and a range of 0.04/0.15.
Lines 40, 41. Exclude government, mining, finance, insurance, and real estate workers and union members with no union dues.
Line 40. Estimate range covers 5 estimates.
Line 41. Restricted to manufacturing workers.
Line 42. Data source is *Quality of Employment Survey*.
Line 43. Data source is *Survey of Consumer Finances*.
Line 48. Government workers were covered and treated as nonunion.
Line 49. Covered industries: mining, manufacturing, construction, transportation, communication, utilities.
Line 67. Sales workers are excluded.

positive difference of the order of magnitude of 0.05–0.10. Since black workers comprise about 10 percent of the male work force in the United States, a mean black-white gap difference for males of 0.10 implies that the mean wage gap for *all* males is about 0.01 larger than the mean wage gap for white males.

4. Wage Gap Differences by Marital Status

The wage gap difference discussed in this section is the excess of the mean wage gap for married workers (both spouse present and spouse absent) over that for workers in all other marital status categories. Eleven studies provide the estimates of this gap difference shown in table 7.3. In 10 of the 11 studies the gap difference estimate was negative, and the mean over the 11 studies was about −0.1.

5. Wage Gap Differences by Major Industry

All of the commonly used micro-data sets identify for each worker the industry in which, according to him or his proxy respondent, he was employed. The *Current Population Surveys* (CPS), for example, provide industry detail at the 1-digit, 2-digit, and 3-digit level. In a substantial number of the fitted Micro, OLS, CS wage equations the right-hand variables include industry dummy variables and their interactions with the union status variable U. Typically, however, the included industry detail is that of the 1-digit classification. I have not attempted to extract from these wage equations all of the detail that they provide on wage gap differences by industry even at the 1-digit level. My preliminary tabulations of wage gap differences by industry at the 1-digit level showed that the differences that were largest numerically and most stable in sign were between manufacturing and nonmanufacturing and within nonmanufacturing between construction and other nonmanufacturing. Columns 3, 4, and 5 of table 7.4 show estimates of the excess over the manufacturing wage gap of the wage gap in nonmanufacturing column 3, construction column 4, and other (than construction) nonmanufacturing column 5.

Consider first the figures in column 3, estimates of the excess of the nonmanufacturing over the manufacturing wage gap. Except for the slightly negative estimate on line 4, which is the only estimate for white-collar workers, all of the estimated gap differences in column 3 are positive, ranging from 0.08 to 0.24. Eleven of the column 3 figures cover both white-collar and blue-collar workers, and seven of the 11 fall in the range of 0.08–0.13. Thus these figures indicate that the excess of the nonmanufacturing over the manufacturing wage gap may be about 0.10. These data then strongly suggest that the mean wage gap for manufacturing workers is considerably lower than that for all workers.

Table 7.3 **Wage Gap Differences by Marital Status (Married − Other)**

Line No. (1)	Study No. (2)	Gap Difference (3)	Date and Source[a] (4)	Worker Coverage (5)
1	29	−.10	1973 CPS	Private, white, male, not Spanish surname, ages 25–64
2	29	−.06	1973 CPS	As on line 1, but manufacturing workers only
3	71	−.05	1973–75 CPS	Private, blue-collar, wage and salary, manufacturing
4	71	−.03	1973–75 CPS	Private, blue-collar, wage and salary, construction
5	90	−.13	1970 CPS	Blue-collar, wage and salary, manufacturing, ages 18–64
6	150	−.07	1973 CPS	Private, full-time, wage and salary, industries with injury data
7	133	.01	1979 CPS	Wage and salary, ages 16–75
8	133	.01	1979 CPS	Wage and salary, ages 16–75, manufacturing
9	133	.04	1978 CPS	Wage and salary, ages 16–75
10	49	−.18	1969 NLS	White males, ages 45–59 in 1966
11	49	−.17	1971 NLS	White males, ages 45–59 in 1966
12	119	−.05	1971 NLS	Males, ages 19–29, wage and salary, nonstudent
13	119	−.22	1969 NLS	Males, ages 45–59 in 1966, wage and salary
14	119	−.27	1971 NLS	Males, ages 45–59 in 1966, wage and salary
15	136	−.12	1968–78 PSID	White males ages ≤ 65, nonstudent
16	141	−.20	1970 PSID	Full-time, household head, wage and salary, ages 17–65
17	58	−.06	1977 CPS	Excludes managers, sales, construction
18	108	−.03/−.01	1979 CPS	Selected industries and States

[a]CPS = *Current Population Survey;* NLS = *National Longitudinal Survey;* PSID = *Panel Study of Income Dynamics*

Table 7.4 Wage Gap Differences by Industry (Excess over Manufacturing)

Line No. (1)	Study No. (2)	Gap Difference: Nonmfg. (3)	Gap Difference: Construction (4)	Gap Difference: Other (5)	Date and Source[a] (6)	Worker Coverage (7)
1	6	.13	—	—	1972–73 QES	Wage and salary
2	10	.20	.27	.16	1969 NLS	Male, blue-collar, nonstudent, ages 17–27
3	10	.24	.41	.17	1969 NLS	Male, blue-collar, ages 48–62
4	12	−.03/.00	—	—	1979 CPS	White-collar, wage and salary
5	13	.12	.24	.12	1976 CPS	Wage and salary
6	16	.16	.27	.11	1967 SEO	Private, white male, urban, BC, W + S
7	17	.12	.22	.09	1967 SEO	Private, nonfarm, nonhousehold, BC, W + S
8	17	.20	.29	.14	1973 CPS	Nonfarm, nonhousehold, BC, W + S
9	17	.15	.26	.11	1975 CPS	Nonfarm, nonhousehold, BC, W + S
10	29	.22	.36	.19	1973 CPS	Private, white, male, ages 25–64
11	33	.24	—	—	1973–75 CPS	Private, nonfarm, wage and salary
12	64	.19/.21	—	—	1973–75 CPS	Private, male, nonstudent, BC, W + S
13	64	.09	—	—	1967–72 EEC	Private, blue-collar, wage and salary
14	65	.11/.11	—	—	1967–72 EEC	Private, nonfarm, blue-collar, W + S
15	71	—	.31	—	1973–75 CPS	Private, blue-collar, wage and salary
16	94	.10	.24	.08	1978 CPS	Male, nonfarm, nonstudent, W + S, ages 16–64
17	114	—	.08	—	1967 SEO	Full-time operatives, selected industries
18	133	.12	.31	.10	1978 CPS	Wage and salary, ages 16–75
19	133	.08/.10	—	—	1979 CPS	Wage and salary, ages 16–75
20	136	.09/.13	.30/.31	.05/.10	1968–78 PSID	White, males, nonstudent, ages ≤ 65
21	141	.17	.18	.17	1970 PSID	Household heads, full-time, ages 17–65, W + S
22	143	.11	—	—	1967–74 PSID	Household heads, male, ages ≤ 65
23	145	.09/.15	.13/.24	.06/.15	1967–77 PSID	Household heads, male, ages 18–65
24	58	.19	—	—	1977 CPS	Excludes managers, sales, construction

Note:
Lines 4, 12. Estimate range covers 4 estimates.
Lines 6–9, 12, 14, 16, 21. BC = blue-collar; W + S = wage and salary.
Lines 14, 19, 20. Estimate range covers 2 estimates.
Line 17. Industries covered were mining, manufacturing, construction, transportation, communications, and utilities.
Line 23. Estimate range covers 5 estimates.

[a]QES = Michigan *Quality of Employment Survey;* NLS = *National Longitudinal Survey;* CPS = *Current Population Survey;* SEO = *Survey of Economic Opportunity;* PSID = *Panel Study of Income Dynamics;* EEC = *Expenditures for Employee Compensation Survey* (U.S. Bureau of Labor Statistics).

Now compare the figures in column 4 for construction workers with those in column 5 for other nonmanufacturing workers. In all of the 13 comparisons the figures for construction are higher, by amounts that exceed 0.10 in 11 of the 13 comparisons. Thus table 7.4 leaves little room for doubting that the mean wage gap in construction is exceptionally high compared to that in either manufacturing or nonmanufacturing.

6. Wage Gap Differences by Major Occupation

In a substantial number of Micro, OLS, CS wage equations the right-hand variables included occupation dummy variables at the 1-digit or less detailed level and their interactions with the union status variable *U*. The estimated wage gap differences by occupation that I have extracted from these equations are shown in table 7.5: column 3, the white-collar minus blue-collar difference; column 4, the craftsmen minus operatives difference; column 5, the laborers minus operatives difference; and column 6, the service workers minus operatives difference. The estimates in panel A are from equations in which both white-collar and blue-collar workers were covered without strong industry or age restrictions on coverage. The remaining estimates are in panel B.

Table 7.6 summarizes the wage gap differences given in table 7.5. In calculating 7.6 from 7.5, I have replaced estimate ranges in 7.5 by their midpoints.

Table 7.6 is divided into two parts. Part I considers all of the estimates in table 7.5. More than half of the estimates in table 7.5, however, are restricted to males or to household heads most of whom surely are male. Because there are marked differences between males and females in their occupational distributions, there is a danger that estimates of occupational wage gap differences for males will be biased estimates of the corresponding differences for both sexes combined. In part II the estimates for males and for household heads have been excluded. In my judgment the estimates in part II are superior to those in part I (in terms of evaluating gap differences for both sexes combined), though for the laborer/operative and service worker/operative comparisons the part I and part II figures differ very little. The following brief discussion deals only with part II of table 7.6.

All of the white-collar minus blue-collar gap difference estimates are negative. Their mean is −0.10 and their standard deviation is 0.03. Thus wage gap estimates for blue-collar workers will overstate the mean wage gap for both blue- and white-collar workers taken together. Since white-collar workers have recently comprised about half of the U.S. work force, this overstatement amounts to about 0.05.

Within the blue-collar category, the wage gap estimates for both craftsmen and service workers tend to be below corresponding gap estimates for

Table 7.5 Wage Gap Differences by Occupation

Line No. (1)	Study No. (2)	Gap Difference[a] WC − BC (3)	CR − OP (4)	LAB − OP (5)	SERV − OP (6)	Date (7)	Worker Coverage[b] (8)
				A.			
1	6	−.06	—	—	—	1972–73	Wage and salary
2	13	−.10	−.05	−.06	—	1976	Wage and salary
3	16	−.11	−.05	.09	−.08	1967	Private, urban, male W + S
4	17	−.12	−.04	.11	.07	1967	Private, nonfarm, nonhousehold, W + S
5	17	−.13	−.01	.05	−.05	1973	Nonfarm, nonhousehold, W + S
6	17	−.12	−.05	.03	−.07	1975	Nonfarm, nonhousehold, W + S
7	29	−.28/−.15	−.05/−.03	−.04/.18	−.14/−.05	1973	Private, white, male, ages 25–64
8	31	−.08/−.06	−.01	.12/.14	−.06/.01	1967	Ages ≥ 14
9	45	—	−.02	—	—	1970–71	Male household heads
10	94	−.22/−.17	−.08/−.07	−.02/−.02	−.10/−.05	1978	Male, nonfarm, nonstudent, 16–64, W + S
11	133	−.10/−.09	−.01/.05	−.02/−.00	−.05/−.03	1979	Ages 16–75, wage and salary
12	133	−.12	−.07	−.02	−.10	1978	Ages 16–75, wage and salary
13	141	−.23	−.04	.04	—	1970	Full-time, household head, ages 17–65, W + S
14	143	−.22/−.21	—	—	—	1967–74	Male, household head, ages ≤ 65, W + S
15	144	−.25/−.11	−.02/−.01	.05/.06	—	1967–77	Male, HH, nonfarm, ages 18–65, W + S
16	147	−.11/−.08	−.03/−.02	.14/.15	−.04/.05	1967	Private, urban, ages ≥ 16, W + S
17	150	−.10	.06	−.06	−.12	1973	Private, full-time, wage and salary
18	169	−.16/−.11	−.08/−.08	.01/.02	—	1969–71	Household heads, ages 18–65, W + S
19	177	−.14/−.12	.02/.02	.06/.07	−.08/−.07	1973	PVT, full-time, nonfarm, nonhousehold, W + S
20	192	−.25	−.01	.22	—	1966	Male, HH, nonfarm, nonstudent, W + S
				B.			
21	6	−.06	—	—	—	1973–75	Private, nonfarm, W + S, MFG
22	10	—	.04	−.03	—	1969	Male, nonstudent, ages 17–27, blue-collar
23	10	—	−.09	−.09	—	1969	Male, nonstudent, ages 48–62, blue-collar

Table 7.5 (continued)

Line No. (1)	Study No. (2)	Gap Difference[a] WC − BC (3)	CR − OP (4)	LAB − OP (5)	SERV − OP (6)	Date (7)	Worker Coverage[b] (8)
24	16	—	−.05	.08	—	1967	PVT, urban, white, male, BC, W + S
25	29	−.18	−.05	−.01	.05	1973	As on line 7, but manufacturing only
26	49	−.12	−.01	.16	−.03	1969	White, males, 48–62 years of age
27	49	−.20	−.13	.11	−.03	1971	White, males, 50–64 years of age
28	71	—	−.08	−.03	−.02	1973–75	Private, blue-collar, manufacturing, W + S
29	71	—	.09	.08	−.21	1973–75	Private, blue-collar, construction, W + S
30	73	—	−.03/−.01	.10/.18	—	1967	Male, PVT, BC, ages ⩾ 14, nonstudent
31	94	−.17/−.10	−.10/−.09	−.02/−.02	−.08/−.08	1978	As on line 10, but ages 16–24
32	94	—	−.07	−.05	−.11	1973–75	As on line 31, but see note
33	94	—	−.12	−.03	−.12	1973–75	As on line 10, but see note
34	117	−.29/−.27	−.02/−.00	.14/.14	.00/.04	1969	Males, 48–62 years of age
35	133	−.07	−.01	.02	−.01	1979	As on line 11, but manufacturing only
36	160	—	−.03/−.02	.03/.08	.02/.05	1970	PVT, BC, W + S, nonfarm, full-time, full-year
37	169	−.10	−.06	.04	—	1969–71	As on line 18, but manufacturing only
38	182	−.34	−.08	.07	−.06	1971	Males, ages 50–64, W + S, nonfarm, nonhousehold

Note:

Lines 7, 18. Estimate ranges cover 3 estimates.

Lines 8, 10, 11, 14, 15, 16, 19, 31, 34, 36. Estimate ranges cover 2 estimates.

Line 17. Worker coverage restricted to industries with injury data.

Line 18. Worker coverage additionally restricted to nonfarm, not mining, not finance, insurance, and real estate workers who paid union dues.

Line 20. Worker coverage excludes college graduates.

Line 30. Worker coverage additionally restricted to workers in mining, manufacturing, construction, transportation, communications, and utilities. Estimate ranges cover 7 estimates.

Lines 32, 33. Worker coverage additionally restricted to private, blue-collar workers in 98 largest SMSAs.

Line 38. Sales workers are not covered.

[a]Column headings: WC − BC = white-collar minus blue-collar; CR − OP = craftsmen minus operatives; LAB − OP = laborers minus operatives; SERV − OP = service workers minus operatives.

[b]Meaning of abbreviations used in this column: W + S = wage and salary; HH = household head; PVT = private; MFG = manufacturing; BC = blue-collar.

Table 7.6 A Summary of Table 7.5

Occupation Pair and Panel (1)	Gap Differences			
	Sign			
	Positive (2)	Negative (3)	Mean (4)	Standard Deviation (5)
I. All Estimates				
White-collar/blue-collar:				
Panel A	0	19	−.14	.06
Panels A and B	0	28	−.15	.07
Craftsmen/operatives:				
Panel A	3	15	−.03	.04
Panels A and B	5	30	−.04	.05
Laborers/operatives:				
Panel A	12	5	.05	.07
Panels A and B	22	12	.04	.07
Service/operatives:				
Panel A	2	10	−.05	.05
Panels A and B	5	19	−.05	.06
II. Estimates for Males and Household Heads Excluded				
White-collar/blue-collar[a]	0	13	−.10	.03
Craftsmen/operatives[a]	4	10	−.01	.05
Laborers/operatives[a]	9	5	.04	.07
Service/operatives[a]	3	10	−.05	.07

[a]Panels A and B.

operatives; for craftsmen, however, the mean difference is only −0.01 and for service workers the mean difference is −0.05. For laborers, on the other hand, the wage gap estimates tend to exceed those for operatives; the mean difference is 0.04.

7. Wage Gap Differences by Region and City Size

The estimates of wage gap differences by region come from Micro, OLS, CS wage equations containing regional dummy variables and their interactions with union status U. In the majority of such equations the regional detail was no finer than that of the four census geographic divisions, and in some instances the contrast was simply between the South and the non-South. Table 7.7 shows in columns 3, 4, 5 the estimated excess of the wage gap in a particular region over that in the South.

First consider lines 2, 3, 7, 19, 20, and 38 in which the regional contrast is between the South and all other areas of the United States. On four of these six lines the estimated gap differences are negative and their overall range is −0.08 to 0.02. These figures indicate that the wage gap is higher

Table 7.7 Wage Gap Differences by Region (Excess over South)

Line No. (1)	Study No. (2)	Gap Differences: N. East (3)	Gap Differences: N. Central (4)	Gap Differences: West (5)	Date (6)	Worker Coverage[a] (7)
A. Estimates without Strong Occupation, Industry, or City-Size Restrictions						
1	1	−.07	−.08	−.04	1975	Male, household heads, not construction, W + S
2	2		Non SO − SO = −.07		1976	Male, household heads, not construction, W + S
3	13		Non SO − SO = −.01		1976	Wage and salary
4	31	−.18/−.14	−.10/−.07	−.10/−.07	1967	Ages ⩾ 14
5	49	−.11	.00	.00	1969	White males, ages 48–62
6	59	−.12	−.07	−.05	1971	White males, ages 50–64
7	59		Non SO − SO = −.01		1977	Nonfarm, not construction, not sales worker, W + S
8	78	−.15	−.07	−.09	1967	Private, wage and salary (?)
9	86	−.16	−.07	−.01	1968–74	Male, household heads
10	86	−.08	.06	.33	1974	Male, household heads
11	94	−.11	−.09	−.13	1978	Male, nonfarm, nonstudent, ages 16–24, W + S
12	94	−.07	−.01	−.01	1978	Male, nonfarm, nonstudent, ages 16–64, W + S
13	110	−.15	—	—	1973	Nonfarm, nonhousehold ages ⩾ 16, W + S
14	119	−.15	−.01	−.01	1969	Males, ages 48–62, wage and salary
15	119	−.11	−.05	−.03	1971	Males, ages 50–64, wage and salary
16	133	−.06/−.05	.03/.03	.00/.01	1979	Wage and salary, ages 16–75
17	133	−.06	.01	.01	1978	Wage and salary, ages 16–75
18	141	−.05	−.00	−.06	1970	Full-time, household heads, ages 17–65, W + S
19	145		Non SO − SO = −.08/−.01		1967–77	Male, household heads, ages 18–65, W + S
20	144		Non SO − SO = .01/.02		1967–77	Male, household heads, ages 18–65, nonfarm, W + S
21	150	−.05	.01	−.01	1973	Private, full-time, wage and salary

22	169	−.09/−.05	−.09/−.02	−.04/.02	1969–71	Private, household heads, ages 18–65, but see note
23	177	−.12	−.03	−.06	1973	Private, full-time, nonfarm, nonhousehold, W + S
24	180	−.04	.09	.34	1967	Private, full-time, ages 14–65, W + S
				B. Other Estimates		
25	12	.00/.01	.05/.06	.03/.04	1979	White-collar, W + S
26	71	−.02	.00	.02	1973–75	Private, blue-collar, W + S, manufacturing
27	71	−.05	−.08	−.12	1973–75	Private, blue-collar, W + S, construction
28	90	−.13	−.02	−.02	1970	Nonstudent, blue-collar, ages 18–64, W + S, MFG
29	94	−.02	−.05	.01	1973–75	As on line 11, but private, BC, in 98 largest SMSAs
30	94	−.05	−.04	−.02	1973–75	As on line 12, but private, BC, in 98 largest SMSAs
31	114	−.07	−.04	−.04	1967	Full-time operatives, selected industries
32	133	−.10	−.01	−.00	1979	As on line 16, but manufacturing only
33	147	−.21/−.17	−.13/−.11	−.08/−.07	1967	Private, urban, ages ≥ 16, W + S
34	160	−.04/−.04	−.02/−.01	.01/.01	1970	Private, full-time, full-year, nonfarm, ages ≥ 14, W + S
35	169	−.15	−.06	−.02	1969–71	As on line 22, but manufacturing only
36	178	−.08/−.07	−.02/−.02	−.01/−.01	1973	Nonfarm, nonhousehold, 29 large SMSAs
37	178	−.02/−.01	.01/.01	.03/.03	1978	Nonfarm, nonhousehold, 29 large SMSAs
38	58		Non SO − SO = .01		1977	Excludes managers, sales, construction, self-employed
39	153	−.10	−.11	−.09	1973–75	White, male, blue-collar, manufacturing

Note:

Lines 2, 3, 7, 19, 20, 38. Estimate is for non-South minus South.

Lines 4, 16, 20, 33, 34, 36, 37. Estimate ranges cover 2 estimates.

Line 19. Estimate ranges cover 3 estimates.

Line 20. Coverage restricted to industries with injury data.

Line 22. Excludes mining and finance sectors and workers who paid no union dues. Estimate ranges cover 5 estimates.

Line 25. Estimate ranges cover 4 estimates.

Line 26. Selected industries are mining, manufacturing, construction, transportation, communications, and utilities.

[a]W + S = wage and salary; MFG = manufacturing; BC = blue-collar.

in the South than in the non-South but that the excess is probably not large.

Now turn to the other lines of the table in which the regions are a bit more detailed. In using these lines to arrive at consensus estimates of gap differences among the four regions, I have ignored lines 10 and 24 because of the extremely high estimates for the West. I have also ignored lines 11, 32, and 35 because the estimates on these lines pertain to workers who are covered on other lines for the same study. Table 7.8 summarizes table 7.7, excluding lines 2, 3, 7, 10, 11, 19, 20, 24, 32, 35, and 38. In calculating table 7.8 from table 7.7 I have replaced estimate ranges by their midpoints.

For each of the Northeast, North Central, and West regions the signs of the estimated gap differences (excess over South) are disproportionately negative and all of the means are negative. However, the table indicates little or no wage gap difference between the West and North Central regions, and for both of these regions the excess of the South wage gap is small, about 0.03. The outlier is the Northeast region whose estimated wage gap is well below that in other regions.

Table 7.8 A Summary of Table 7.7

Region Pair and Panel (1)	Gap Difference: Sign: Positive (2)	Gap Difference: Sign: Negative (3)	Gap Difference: Mean (4)	Gap Difference: Standard Deviation (5)
N. East–South, A	0	16	−.10	.04
N. East–South, A + B	1	27	−.09	.05
N. Central–South, A	4	11	−.03	.04
N. Central–South A + B	7	20	−.03	.04
West–South, A	3	12	−.03	.03
West–South, A + B	8	19	−.03	.04

The commonly used micro-data files do not permit the size (population) of the "city" in which a worker resides to be treated as a continuous rather than discrete variable. The May *Current Population Surveys,* for example, distinguish among (1) residence in the central city of a Standard Metropolitan Statistical Area (SMSA), (2) residence in an SMSA but not in the central city, and (3) residence outside an SMSA. (The CPS also identifies the 98 largest SMSAs so that among these SMSAs population distinctions can be made.) As a consequence most of the Micro, OLS, CS wage equations contain little detail on wage gap differences across communities of different size.

The estimates shown in column 3 of table 7.9, except on lines 3 and 8, are for the excess of the wage gap in SMSAs over that in other places. On lines 3 and 8 the contrast is urban minus rural. Only two of the 23 estimates are positive. Furthermore, except for the estimates on lines 3–5, 10,

Table 7.9 Wage Gap Differences by City Size

Line No. (1)	Study No. (2)	Gap Difference (3)	Date (4)	Worker Coverage (5)
1	12	−.04/−.04	1979	White-collar, wage and salary
2	13	−.06	1976	Wage and salary
3	31	−.13/−.08	1967	Ages ⩾ 14
4	49	−.16	1969	White males, ages 48–62
5	49	−.16	1971	White males, ages 50–64
6	71	−.07	1973–75	Private, blue-collar, wage and salary, construction
7	71	.01	1973–75	Private, blue-collar, wage and salary, manufacturing
8	78	−.09	1967	Private, wage and salary (?)
9	86	−.07	1968–74	Male, household heads
10	86	−.11	1974	Male, household heads
11	90	−.01	1970	Blue-collar, nonstudent, wage and salary, 18–64, manufacturing
12	94	.03	1978	Male, nonfarm, nonstudent, wage and salary, ages 16–24
13	94	−.03	1978	Male, nonfarm, nonstudent, wage and salary, ages 16–64
14	114	−.03	1967	Full-time operatives, selected industries
15	119	−.05	1971	Males, wage and salary, ages 19–29
16	119	−.16	1969	Males, wage and salary, ages 48–62
17	119	−.18	1971	Males, wage and salary, ages 50–64
18	133	−.05/−.04	1979	Wage and salary, ages 16–75
19	133	−.05	1979	Wage and salary, ages 16–75, manufacturing
20	133	−.03	1978	Wage and salary, ages 16–75
21	150	−.14	1973	Private, full-time, wage and salary, selected industries
22	160	−.07/−.07	1970	Blue-collar, nonstudent, wage and salary, 18–64, manufacturing
23	153	−.01	1973–75	White, male, blue-collar, manufacturing

Note:
Line 1. Estimate range covers 4 estimates.
Lines 3, 8. Gap difference is urban minus rural.
Lines 3, 18, 22. Estimate range covers 2 estimates.
Line 14. Selected industries: mining, manufacturing, construction, transportation, communications, utilities.
Line 21. Selected industries: those with injury data.

16–17, and 21, four of which are for older males, none of the estimates is as large as 0.10 numerically.

Ignore the estimates on lines 10, 12, and 19 which are included in broader coverage estimates from the same study and the estimates on lines 3 and 8 for the urban minus rural rather than SMSA minus not-SMSA comparison. I view the estimates for older males on lines 4–5 and 16–17 as misleading outliers and also ignore them. The mean of the remaining estimates is −0.05. About two-thirds of the U.S. work force reside in an

SMSA. Hence table 7.9 indicates that the mean wage gap for this urban work force will tend to understate the economy-wide mean wage gap by about 0.02.

8. Wage Gap Differences by Schooling

Almost all of the Micro, OLS, CS wage equations surveyed in this book included both years of school completed (*S*) and either years of age (*A*) or years of labor market experience (*E*) among the right-hand variables, and often these variables were interacted with the union status variable *U*. Typically the resulting wage gap *M* was a linear function of schooling *S* and a quadratic function of age *A* or experience *E*. From equations in which schooling *S* and age *A*, rather than experience *E*, were paired, both being treated as continuous rather than discrete variables, I calculated the partial derivative of the wage gap *M* with respect to schooling *S* (in years). These partial derivatives are shown in table 7.10 in column 3 headed "Est. *A*."

More frequently, however, it was experience *E* rather than age *A* that was entered in the wage equation together with schooling *S*. Usually experience *E* in these equations was defined as age *A* minus schooling *S* minus a constant. For all equations in which both *S* and *E* were treated as continuous variables I calculated two partial derivatives of *M* with respect to *S* as follows:

Est. *E:* the partial derivative of *M* with respect to *S* holding *E* constant. These derivatives are shown in table 7.10 in column 4 headed "Est. *E*."

Est. *A:* Est. *E* minus the partial derivative of *M* with respect to *E*, shown in table 7.10, column 3 headed Est. *A*. I interpret these as partial derivatives of *M* with respect to *S* holding age *A*, rather than experience *E*, constant.

Table 7.10 covers only wage equations in which schooling was treated as a continuous variable.

Much to my surprise, I discovered that the estimates of wage gap differences by schooling differed substantially according to the sources of the micro-data used in fitting the wage equation. In particular, the estimated derivatives of *M* with respect to *S* were considerably closer to zero in wage equations fitted to *Current Population Survey* (CPS) data than in other wage equations.

Consider first the CPS estimates on lines 1–22 of table 7.10. All of these estimates, except those on lines 10 and 12 for young males, are negative. Furthermore, on only three of the 22 lines are the estimates as high numerically as 0.03. Thus the CPS data indicate that the wage gap difference per year of schooling was about −0.02 to −0.01.

The estimates from wage equations fitted to data sources other than the CPS are on lines 23–39 of table 7.10. The data source for each line is given

Table 7.10 Wage Gap Differences by Schooling

Line No. (1)	Study No. (2)	Difference per Year: Est. *A* (3)	Difference per Year: Est. *E* (4)	Date (5)	Worker Coverage[a] (6)
		A. Estimates from Current Population Survey Data			
1	12	−.01/−.01	−.01/−.01	1979	White-collar, wage and salary
2	13	−.01	−.02	1976	Wage and salary
3	29	−.03	−.03	1973	Private, white, male, ages 25–64, not Spanish surname
4	29	−.04	−.04	1973	As on line 3 but manufacturing only
5	64	−.01/−.01	−.01/−.01	1973–75	Private, male, blue-collar, nonstudent, W + S, MFG
6	64	−.02/−.01	−.02/−.01	1973–75	As on line 5, but for nonmanufacturing
7	71	−.01	−.01	1973–75	Private, blue-collar, nonstudent, W + S, MFG
8	71	−.01	−.01	1973–75	Private, blue-collar, construction, W + S
9	90	−.01	−.01	1970	Blue-collar, nonstudent, ages 18–64, W + S, MFG
10	94	.00	—	1978	Male, nonfarm, nonstudent, ages 16–24, W + S
11	94	−.01	—	1978	As on line 10, but ages 16–64
12	94	.01	—	1973–75	As on line 10, but BC in 98 largest SMSAs
13	94	−.01	—	1973–75	As on line 11, but BC in 98 largest SMSAs
14	133	−.01/−.01	−.02/−.02	1979	Ages 16–75, wage and salary
15	133	−.01	−.00	1979	Ages 16–75, wage and salary, manufacturing
16	133	−.01	−.01	1978	Ages 16–75, wage and salary
17	150	−.03	−.03	1973	Private, full-time, W + S, industries with injury data
18	160	−.02/−.02	−.02/−.02	1969	Private, full-time, full-year, nonfarm, ages ⩾ 14, BC, W + S
19	58	−.01	−.01	1977	Excludes managers, sales, construction
20	108	−.01/−.01	−.01/−.01	1979	See note
21	153	−.00	—	1973–75	White, male, blue-collar, manufacturing
22	157	−.01	−.02	1973–75	Male craftsmen, construction industry

Table 7.10 (continued)

Line No. (1)	Study No. (2)	Difference per Year: Est. *A* (3)	Difference per Year: Est. *E* (4)	Date (5)	Worker Coverage[a] (6)
			B. Estimates from Other Data Sources		
23	1	−.04	−.05	1975	PSID, male, nonconstruction, wage and salary
24	2	−.04	−.04	1976	PSID, male, nonconstruction, wage and salary
25	86	−.03	−.03	1968–74	PSID, male
26	86	−.05	−.04	1974	PSID, male
27	136	−.04	−.05	1968–78	PSID, white, male, nonstudent, ages ≤ 65
28	144	−.03/−.02	−.03/−.03	1967–77	PSID, male, nonfarm, ages 18–65, wage and salary
29	161	−.03	−.04	1976	PSID, private, male, white, wage and salary
30	10	−.02	−.03	1969	NLS, blue-collar, nonstudent, ages 17–27, male
31	10	−.02	−.02	1969	NLS, blue-collar, ages 48–62, male
32	49	−.03	—	1969	NLS, white, ages 48–62, male
33	49	−.03	—	1971	NLS, white, ages 50–64, male
34	119	?	−.04	1971	NLS, ages 19–29, nonstudent, wage and salary, male
35	119	−.05	—	1969	NLS, ages 48–62, wage and salary, male
36	119	−.04	—	1971	NLS, ages 50–64, wage and salary, male
37	19	?	−.03	1967	SEO, white, male, urban, nonfarm, private, ages ≥ 16
38	180	−.05/−.04	−.06/−.05	1967	SEO, private, full-time, ages 14–65, W + S
39	101	−.02	—	1965–66	SCF, male, blue-collar, nonstudent, household head

Note:

Lines 1, 5, 6. Estimate ranges cover 4 estimates.

Lines 14, 18, 20, 28. Estimate ranges cover 2 estimates.

Line 20. Worker coverage: private, mining, manufacturing, transportation and service industries in right-to-work states; managers, sales, farm, and construction workers are excluded.

Lines 34, 37. Est. A cannot be calculated.

Line 38. Estimate ranges cover 3 estimates.

[a]W + S = wage and salary; MFG = manufacturing; BC = blue-collar; PSID, NLS, SEO, SCF, see text.

in column 6 where PSID is short for *Panel Study of Income Dynamics,* NLS for *National Longitudinal Surveys,* SEO for *Survey of Economic Opportunity,* and SCF is the Michigan *Survey of Consumer Finances.* All of the estimates on these 17 lines are negative, only four of 17 lines contain estimates as low numerically as 0.02, and most of the estimates are in the range -0.04 to -0.02.

Thus table 7.10 establishes a strong presumption that the wage gap falls as schooling rises, but the magnitude of the decline in the gap per year of schooling is indicated rather imprecisely. The CPS estimates suggest that the difference per year is about -0.015; other data sources put the difference at about -0.03, about twice as large numerically. In the U.S. work force the mean years of school completed is between 12 and 13 and the standard deviation is between 2.5 and 3.0. Hence a two standard deviation difference (say, 5.5) in years of schooling, centered about the mean, leads to a wage gap difference of about 0.08 according to the CPS estimate and about 0.16 according to the estimates from other data sources.

In nine studies [32, 59, 114, 127, 135, 141, 145, 169, and 172] not covered in table 7.10 schooling, interacted with union status U, was treated as a discrete rather than continuous variable. One used CPS data, three PSID, one NLS, three SEO, and one the Michigan *Quality of Employment Survey* data. It was not possible to calculate the mean wage gap difference per year of schooling from any of these studies. However, for each of these studies I did calculate the excess of the mean wage gap for workers with 12 or more years of schooling over that for workers with less than 12 years. In all of these studies this wage gap difference was negative.

9. Wage Gap Differences by Age, Experience, and Seniority

Table 7.11 summarizes estimates of wage gap differences by experience E. On lines 1, 10, and 11 of the table the experience variable was defined as age minus schooling minus seniority with current employer minus 6. On all of the other lines experience was defined either as actual labor market experience in years or much more frequently as age minus schooling minus a constant. On lines 28 and 29 the estimated wage gap function was a linear function of E, but on all of the other lines E entered the wage gap function quadratically. The estimates of the wage gap "difference per decade" given in columns 4 and 5 are partial derivatives of the wage gap M with respect to E (measured in decades) evaluated at $E=0$ in column 4 and at the sample mean of E in column 5. E^* in column 6 is the number of years of experience E at which the wage gap M reaches a maximum (on lines 21, 27, 30) or a minimum (on all other lines).

The estimates on lines 1–16 are derived from wage equations fitted to CPS data. On these lines $E=A-S-\text{constant}$ or $E=A-S-T-6$ on lines 1, 10, and 11 where T is tenure or seniority with current employer. Despite

Table 7.11 Wage Gap Differences by Experience

Line No. (1)	Study No. (2)	Date (3)	Difference per Decade: At $E = 0$ (4)	Difference per Decade: At Mean E (5)	E^* (Years) (6)	Worker Coverage[a] (7)
			A. Studies Using Current Population Survey Data			
1	12	1979	−.07/−.06	−.03/−.03	23	White-collar, wage and salary
2	13	1976	−.08	−.03	31	Wage and salary
3	29	1973	−.13	−.03	26	PVT, white, male, aged 25–64, W + S
4	29	1973	−.20	−.03	27	Line 3, manufacturing only
5	64	1973–75	−.14/−.11	−.03/−.03	27/29	PVT, male, nonstudent, BC, W + S, MFG
6	64	1973–75	−.12/−.06	−.03/−.02	26/30	Line 5, nonmanufacturing only
7	71	1973–75	−.09/−.09	−.01/−.01	26/26	PVT, BC, W + S, MFG
8	71	1973–75	−.06/−.06	−.02/−.02	29/29	PVT, BC, W + S, construction
9	90	1971	−.16	−.04	27	BC, W + S, nonstudent, nonfarm, aged 18–64, MFG
10	133	1979	−.03/−.02	−.02/−.01	30/84	Wage and salary, aged 16–75
11	133	1979	−.03	−.03	>100	Line 10, MFG only
12	133	1978	−.01	−.00	29	Line 10
13	160	1970	−.15/−.15	−.02/−.02	30/30	PVT, BC, W + S, nonfarm, full-time, full-year
14	58	1977	−.05	−.01	24	Excludes managers, sales, and construction
15	108	1979	−.04/−.04	−.01/−.00	21/22	See note
16	157	1973–75	−.14	−.05	32	Male craftsmen, construction industry

B. Studies Using Other Data Sources

17	1	1975	−.27	−.07	25	PSID, male, W + S, nonconstruction
18	2	1976	−.22	−.05	25	PSID, male, W + S, nonconstruction
19	86	1968–74	−.12	.02	20	PSID, male, household head
20	136	1968–78	−.20	−.04	25	PSID, white, male, aged ≤ 65, nonstudent
21	141	1970	.04	.02	22	PSID, full-time, W + S, aged 17–65, household head
22	144	1967–77	−.10/−.08	−.00/−.00	25/29	PSID, W + S, nonfarm, male, 18–65, HH
23	161	1976	−.20	−.06	25	PSID, PVT, white, male, household head
24	169	1969–71	−.10/−.06	.00/.01	21/22	PSID, PVT, W + S, HH, aged 18–65, nonfarm
25	169	1969–71	−.10	−.02	27	PSID, as on line 24, but MFG only
26	19	1967	−.12	?	32	SEO, PVT, white, male, urban, aged ≥ 16
27	114	1967	.00	.01	∞	SEO, full-time operatives, selected industries
28	180	1967	−.08	−.08	∞	SEO, PVT, full-time, W + S, aged 14–65
29	10	1969	−.14	−.14	∞	NLS, male BC, nonstudent, W + S, aged 17–27
30	59	1977	.24	.08	26	QES, W + S, not sales, construction, or managers

Note:

Lines 1, 5, 6. Estimate ranges cover 4 estimates.

Lines 1, 10, 11. Experience defined as age minus schooling minus seniority minus 6 in years.

Line 3. Workers with Spanish surnames excluded.

Lines 7, 8, 10, 13, 15, 22. Estimate ranges cover 2 estimates.

Line 15. Private sector, right-to-work States, mining, manufacturing, transportation, and service industries; excludes managers, sales, agricultural, and construction workers.

Line 24. Estimate ranges cover 5 estimates. Also excluded from coverage were workers in mining, finance, insurance, and real estate, and unionized workers who paid no union dues.

Line 27. Selected industries were mining, manufacturing, construction, transportation, communications, and utilities.

Lines 28, 29. Experience entered the wage gap function linearly.

[a]PVT = private; W + S = wage and salary; BC = blue-collar; MFG = manufacturing; PSID = *Panel Study of Income Dynamics;* HH = household head; SEO = *Survey of Economic Opportunity;* NLS = *National Longitudinal Survey;* QES = *Quality of Employment Survey* (Michigan).

differences in data, worker coverage, and other right-hand variables in the wage equations, these lines show much agreement on the way the wage gap M varies with experience E. In all cases the wage gap–experience profile is U-shaped. The minimum of the profile (except on lines 1, 10, and 11) occurs at a value of E^* ranging from 26–32 years with a mean of about 28 years. The sample means of E (except on lines 1, 10, and 11) range from 17 to 23 years with a mean of about 20 years, about eight years earlier than the value of E that minimizes M. The estimated gap difference per decade of E evaluated at sample mean E ranges from -0.05 to -0.00 with a mean of -0.02. The estimated gap difference per decade evaluated at $E=0$ not surprisingly has a much wider range, from -0.20 to -0.01, with a mean of roughly -0.09 or -0.08. Thus the picture of the wage gap–experience profile that emerges from the CPS data is U-shaped, with a minimum at about $E=28$ years, a slope per decade of -0.09 or -0.08 at $E=0$ and about -0.02 at sample mean E.

The story from lines 17–30 derived from wage equations fitted to other than CPS data differs in several respects. First, on lines 21 and 30 the estimated wage gap–experience profile has the shape of an *inverted* U. And on line 27 the profile is a slowly rising profile that is almost flat and close to zero at all reasonable values of E. These profiles are clearly outliers. Hence ignore lines 21, 27, and 30. Also ignore lines 28 and 29 where the estimated wage gap function was a linear rather than quadratic function of E. On the remaining nine lines the estimated profile is U-shaped with a minimum at values of E^* ranging from 20 to 32 years and averaging about 25 years. On these nine lines the wage gap difference per decade at $E=0$ ranges from -0.27 to -0.06 and averages about -0.16 and at the mean of E ranges from -0.07 to 0.02 and averages about -0.03. Thus there is less agreement on lines 17–30 than on lines 1–16 regarding the shape of the wage gap–experience profile. Furthermore, the U-shaped profile drawn by lines 17–20 and 22–26 is steeper, with a minimum at lower E than for the profile drawn by lines 1–16.

Embedded in the wage gap–*experience* profiles covered in table 7.11 are wage gap–*age* profiles for given years of schooling or, on lines 1, 10, and 11, given years of schooling plus years of seniority. Consider, for example, the experience profile on line 2. In this profile, experience = age minus schooling minus 6 with mean experience of 18 years and mean schooling of 12 years. Thus for workers with mean schooling, this profile converts to a wage gap–age profile with a slope (per decade) of -0.08 at 18 years of age, a slope of -0.03 at 36 years of age, and a minimum at 49 years of age.

Table 7.12 shows estimates of wage gap–*age* profiles drawn from five studies in which the wage gap was expressed as a quadratic function of age rather than experience. Column 4 shows the estimated slope (per decade) of the profile at age $A=18$ years, column 5 the corresponding slope at

Table 7.12 Wage Gap–Age Profiles

Line No. (1)	Study No. (2)	Date (3)	Difference per Decade At A = 18 (4)	Difference per Decade At A = 38 (5)	A* in Years (6)	Data Source[a] (7)
1	94	1978	−.06	.02	33	CPS
2	94	1978	−.02	−.03	∞	CPS
3	94	1973–75	−.04	.01	34	CPS
4	101	1965–66	−.12/−.11	.00/.01	37/37	SCF
5	145	1967–77	−.07/−.06	−.01/−.01	40/41	PSID
6	150	1973	−.10	−.03	48	CPS
7	153	1973–75	−.11	−.01	40	CPS

Note:

Line 1. Male, nonfarm, nonstudent, wage and salary, aged 16–64.
Line 2. As on line 1, but restricted to blue-collar in 98 largest SMSAs.
Line 3. As on line 2.
Line 4. Male household heads, blue-collar, nonstudents. Estimate ranges cover 2 estimates.
Line 5. Male household heads, wage and salary, aged 18–65. Estimate ranges cover 3 estimates.
Line 6. Private full-time workers in industries with injury data.
Line 7. White, male, blue-collar, manufacturing, aged 20–60 years.

[a]CPS = *Current Population Survey;* SCF = *Survey of Consumer Finances;* PSID = *Panel Study of Income Dynamics.*

$A = 38$ years, and column 6 the age A^* at which the wage gap was a minimum. In the data underlying these profiles mean age ranged from 36 to 39 years and averaged about 38 years.

Except for the profile on line 2, all of the wage gap–age profiles in table 7.12 are U-shaped with a slope per decade at age 18 (roughly zero years of experience on the average) averaging about −0.09. In these respects they resemble strongly the *age* profiles implied by the *experience* profiles on lines 1–16 of table 7.11. However, the U-shaped age profiles of table 7.12, except for that on line 6, reach a minimum at a considerably earlier age than is suggested by the experience profiles of table 7.11.

In several studies matching wage equations were fitted separately by age group permitting the separate estimation of the wage gap for each of the age groups. Table 7.13 reports the estimated wage gap differences between age groups drawn from these studies. The estimated gap difference is given in column 3.

The estimates in table 7.13 are broadly consistent with the picture of the wage gap–age profile that emerges from tables 7.11 and 7.12. And all three tables suggest rather strongly that wage gap estimates drawn from wage equations fitted to the NLS data for young males will tend to overstate the mean wage gap for males of all ages.

There is considerably less evidence on wage gap differences by seniority or tenure T on the current job or with the current employer than for the gap differences by age or experience. Table 7.14 summarizes estimates of wage gap differences by seniority that I have drawn from 13 studies. The

Table 7.13 Wage Gap Differences by Age Groups

Line No. (1)	Study No. (2)	Gap Difference (3)	Age Groups (4)	Date (5)	Data Source[a] (6)	Worker Coverage (7)
1	10	−.09	(48–62)–(17–27)	1969	NLS	Male, blue-collar, wage and salary, nonstudent
2	103	−.08/−.06	(50–64)–(19–29)	1971	NLS	Male, nonfarm, not private household
3	118	−.07	(48–62)–(17–27)	1969	NLS	Male, wage and salary, nonstudent
4	118	−.05	(50–64)–(19–29)	1971	NLS	Line 3
5	119	−.05	(50–64)–(19–29)	1971	NLS	Line 3
6	136	−.17/−.16	(48–62)–(17–27)	1969	NLS	White, male, nonstudent
7	136	−.14/−.14	(50–64)–(19–29)	1971	NLS	Line 6
8	103	−.07/−.03	(34–48)–(17–27)	1971	NLS	Female, nonfarm, not private household
9	142	.00/.01	(35–49)–(19–29)	1972	NLS	Female, full-time
10	93	.00	(40–62)–(20–36)	1967	PSID	White, male, nonfarm, wage and salary
11	93	.05	(40–62)–(30–46)	1967	PSID	Line 10
12	93	.03	(40–55)–(20–29)	1967–74	PSID	Line 10
13	93	.06	(40–55)–(30–39)	1967–74	PSID	Line 10
14	136	−.08/−.07	(≥30)–(<30)	1968–78	PSID	White, male, nonstudent, ages ≤ 65
15	94	−.15/−.15	(25–64)–(16–24)	1978	CPS	Male, nonfarm, nonstudent, wage and salary
16	94	−.10/−.10	(25–64)–(16–24)	1978	CPS	Line 15, but blue-collar in 98 largest SMSAs
17	94	−.09	(25–64)–(16–24)	1973–75	CPS	Line 16

Note:
Lines 2, 6–9, 14–16. Estimate ranges cover 2 estimates.
Lines 12, 13. Age is as of 1967.

[a]NLS = *National Longitudinal Survey;* PSID = *Panel Study of Income Dynamics;* CPS = *Current Population Survey.*

Table 7.14 Wage Gap Differences by Seniority

Line No. (1)	Study No. (2)	Date (3)	Difference per Decade: At $T = 0$ (4)	Difference per Decade: At $T = 1$ (5)	T^* (Years) (6)	Data Source[a] (7)	Worker Coverage[b] (8)
1	1	1975	−.10	−.08	48	PSID	Male, W + S, nonconstruction
2	2	1976	.03	−.01	9	PSID	Male, W + S, nonconstruction
3	136	1968–78	.09	.01	11	PSID	White, male, nonstudent, aged ≤ 65
4	141	1970	−.00	.03	1	PSID	Full-time, HH, W + S, aged 17–65
5	145	1967–77	−.13/−.12	−.03/−.03	13	PSID	Male, HH, W + S, aged 18–65
6	161	1976	−.06	−.07	∞	PSID	Private, white, male, HH, W + S
7	59	1977	−.11	−.07	31	QES	W + S, nonconstruction, not sales or managers
8	10	1969	−.01	−.01	∞	NLS	Male, blue-collar, nonstudent, W + S, 17–27
9	10	1969	−.08	−.08	∞	NLS	Male, blue-collar, W + S, aged 48–62
10	30	1971	−.12	−.12	∞	NLS	White, male, aged 50–64
11	30	1971	−.15	−.11	43	NLS	Line 10
12	117	1969	−.10	−.10	∞	NLS	Male, aged 48–62
13	12	1979	−.02/.01	.02/.03	5/∞	CPS	White-collar, W + S
14	133	1979	−.06	−.03	22	CPS	W + S, aged 16–75
15	133	1979	−.07	−.04	24	CPS	Line 14, but manufacturing only
16	108	1979	−.02/−.01	−.02/−.01	∞	CPS	See note

Note:

Line 5: Estimate ranges cover 3 estimates.

Lines 8–10, 12, 16: Wage gap was a linear function of seniority.

Line 13: Estimate ranges cover 4 estimates.

Line 16: Private sector in right-to-work States in mining, manufacturing, transportation, and service industries; managers, sales, farm, and construction workers are excluded.

[a]PSID = *Panel Study of Income Dynamics;* QES = *Quality of Employment Survey;* NLS = *National Longitudinal Survey;* CPS = *Current Population Survey.*

[b]W + S = wage and salary worker; HH = household head.

partial derivative of the estimated wage gap function with respect to seniority T in decades evaluated at $T=0$ appears in column 4 and at $T=1$ decade in column 5. Column 6 shows the estimated number of *years* of seniority at which the wage gap function peaks or troughs.

Consider first lines 1–7, all of which come from wage equations fitted to the University of Michigan Survey Research Center's PSID or QES data. The wage gap–seniority profiles on lines 1, 5, and 7 are U-shaped with a slope per decade at $T=0$ ranging from -0.13 to -0.10, corresponding slope at $T=1$ decade ranging from -0.08 to -0.03, and a minimum at values of T^* ranging from 13 to 48 years. The profiles on lines 2 and 3, on the other hand, have an inverted-U shape and peak at about 10 years of seniority. The profile on line 4 is positively inclined, except for the first year of seniority, and is rather flat. The profile on line 6 is negatively inclined and moderately steep at all values of T.

The NLS estimates appear on lines 8–12. All of them are for males with strong restrictions on age. Furthermore, except for line 11, the estimated wage gap functions were expressed as linear functions of seniority. These linear profiles are all negatively inclined and, except for that on line 8 for young males, decline at about 1 percent per year of seniority. The profile on line 11, though U-shaped, is negatively inclined until about 43 years of seniority. Thus the NLS data for older males (45–59 in 1966) indicate that the wage gap declines with seniority except, perhaps, at very high seniority.

The *Current Population Survey* (CPS) included a seniority question only in May 1979. As a consequence there are few CPS estimates of the wage gap–seniority profile. The estimates on line 13, for white-collar workers, picture an almost flat profile. The profiles on lines 14 and 15, which cover both white-collar and blue-collar workers, are U-shaped with a slope at $T=0$ of about $-0.07/-0.06$ per decade, at $T=1$ decade a slope of $-0.04/-0.03$ per decade, and trough at 22–24 years of seniority. The linear profile on line 16, though negatively inclined, is almost flat.

To avoid duplication of estimates from the same study, omit lines 10 and 15 of table 7.14. Then the mean wage gap difference per decade of seniority at $T=0$ (column 4) is -0.05 and the corresponding difference at $T=1$ (column 5) is -0.04.

10. Wage Gap Differences by Extent of Unionism

It is reasonable to suppose that in the presence of unionism in the economy, the relative wage of each worker depends not only on his union status, schooling, experience, and like variables, but also on the extent of unionism in the whole work force and the distribution of workers by union status among work force sectors (industries, occupations, areas, etc.). This argues for the presence of one or more extent of unionism variables on the right-hand side of estimated wage equations.

For present purposes I write the estimated wage equations as follows:

$$W = a_n + a_x x + a_{ny} y + U[a_u - a_n + (a_{uy} - a_{ny})y] + e, \tag{7.5}$$

where W is the wage (in logarithmic units), y is the extent of unionism variable, x is a set of other variables such as schooling, and e is the residual. The coefficient a_{ny} is an estimate of the partial derivative of W with respect to y for nonunion workers, a_{uy} that for union workers, and $a_{uy} - a_{ny}$ is the partial derivative of the wage gap M with respect to y. Several studies with at least moderately broad worker coverage have fitted such wage equations. The estimates of a_{ny} and $a_{uy} - a_{ny}$ that I have drawn from these equations are shown in table 7.15.

All of the studies covered in the table agree that the extent of unionism coefficients a_{uy} for union workers and a_{ny} for nonunion workers are positive. Furthermore, except for line 2, they agree that a_{uy} exceeds a_{ny}—i.e., that the wage gap M increases as extent of unionism increases. With these exceptions, however, there is not much agreement. The estimates of a_{ny} range from 0.00 to 0.43, of a_{uy} from 0.16 to 0.43, and of $a_{uy} - a_{ny}$ from -0.19 to 0.26 (though -0.19 is an outlier).

On lines 3–5, 13, and 14 the estimates are for blue-collar workers in manufacturing, and the estimates on line 7 are chiefly for manufacturing blue-collar workers. These five lines agree in putting the estimates of $a_{uy} - a_{ny}$ in the fairly narrow range 0.10 to 0.16, but disagree on the estimates of a_{ny} (range from 0.00 to 0.15) and a_{uy} (range from 0.15 to 0.31). The estimates on line 11 also are for manufacturing but cover both blue-collar and white-collar workers. The line 11 estimate 0.22 of $a_{uy} - a_{ny}$ is well above that suggested by lines 3–5, 7, and 13 for blue-collar workers.

Only two studies ([19] on line 2 and [133] on lines 10 and 12) provide estimates of a_{uy} and a_{ny} based on broad coverage by both industry and occupation. The estimates of a_{uy}, a_{ny}, and $a_{uy} - a_{ny}$ differ markedly across the three lines 2, 10, and 12. Another study (no. 12, line 1) with broad industry coverage but restricted to white-collar workers estimated both a_{uy} and a_{ny} at roughly 0.2. Study no. 94 (lines 8 and 9), with coverage restricted to blue-collar workers in the 98 largest SMSAs, differs from the other studies in including two extent of unionism variables in the fitted wage equation, one by 3-digit industry and the other by the 98 SMSAs. The two estimates of a_{ny} differed substantially (0.19 by industry and 0.06 by SMSA), but the two estimates of a_{uy} were almost equal (0.22 by industry and 0.19 by SMSA).

The sensitivity of estimates of a_{uy} and a_{ny} to wage equation specification and choice of the extent of unionism y variable is demonstrated in a study [11] by Antos. Because of its detail, this study is not included in table 7.15.

Antos fitted his wage equations, separately by union status, to the May–June 1979 CPS data for *white-collar* workers. In the equations covered in table 7.16 the dependent variable was the natural logarithmn of

Table 7.15 Wage Gap Differences by Extent of Unionism

Line No. (1)	Study No. (2)	Date (3)	y-Coefficients a_{ny} (4)	$a_{uy} - a_{ny}$ (5)	y-Variable (6)
1	12	1979	.17/.20	.02/.06	White-collar workers by 3-digit industry
2	19	1967	.43	−.19	See line note
3	43	1967–72	.01	.15	Blue-collar workers by 3-digit industry
4	71	1973–75	.00	.15	Blue-collar workers by 3-digit industry
5	71	1967–72	.04/.05	.13/.16	Blue-collar workers by 3-digit industry
6	71	1973–75	.06	.22	Blue-collar workers, construction, 29 State groups
7	73	1967	.14	.11	Blue-collar workers, 81 industries
8	94	1973–75	.19	.02	Blue-collar workers by 3-digit industry
9	94	1973–75	.06	.14	Blue-collar workers by 98 largest SMSAs
10	133	1979	.17/.20	.13/.26	Wage and salary workers by 3-digit industry
11	133	1979	.12	.22	Wage and salary workers by 3-digit industry
12	133	1978	.27	.09	Wage and salary workers by 3-digit industry
13	152	1973–75	.11/.15	.10/.16	White, full-time blue-collar by industry
14	153	1973–75	.12	.13	Line 13
15	157	1973–75	.16	.11	Male craftsmen, construction by SMSA or State

Note:

Line 1. White-collar wage and salary workers. Estimate ranges cover 2 estimates.

Line 2. y-variable: private, nonfarm, wage and salary workers by 64 industries and industry groups. Worker coverage: private, white males, nonfarm, urban wage and salary workers aged $\geqslant$ 16.

Line 3. Blue-collar wage and salary workers in manufacturing. Equation fitted to establishment data.

Line 4. Private blue-collar wage and salary workers in manufacturing.

Line 5. Blue-collar wage and salary workers in manufacturing. Equations fitted to establishment data. Estimate ranges cover 2 estimates.

Line 6. Private blue-collar wage and salary workers in construction.

Line 7. Private blue-collar, males, aged $\geqslant$ 14 in mining, manufacturing, construction, transportation, communications, and utilities.

Lines 8, 9. Private blue-collar wage and salary workers, nonfarm, aged 16–64 in 98 largest SMSAs. Wage equations included y by industry and y by SMSA.

Lines 10, 12. Wage and salary workers, aged 16–75.

Line 10. Estimate ranges cover 2 estimates.

Line 11. Wage and salary workers, aged 16–75, in manufacturing.

Lines 13, 14. White, male, full-time, blue-collar workers in manufacturing paid by the hour. Estimate ranges cover 2 estimates.

Line 15. Male craftsmen in construction industry.

"usual hourly earnings," and all of the equations, except those pertaining to lines 11 and 12 of table 7.16, included the following right-hand variables: years of school completed (S) and its square, seniority at current job (T) and its square, experience (age $- S - T - 6$) and its square, and dummy variables for sex, color, part-time work, marital status (four categories), establishment size (six categories), four regions, three city-size groups, four major occupations, and eight major industries. The equations underlying lines 11 and 12 omitted the establishment size and industry variables. In addition each equation, except those underlying lines 15 and 16, included one of the following 13 extent of unionism y variables:

ALL (3D ind)	All workers, both blue-collar (BC) and white-collar (WC), by 3-digit industry
WC (3D ind)	WC workers by 3-digit industry
BC (3D ind)	BC workers by 3-digit industry
ALL (2D ind)	As above, except by 2-digit industry
WC (2D ind)	
BC (2D ind)	
WC (3D occ)	WC workers by 3-digit occupation
WC (2D ind, 3D occ)	WC workers by 2-digit industry and 3-digit occupation
WC (3D ind, 1D occ)	WC workers by 3-digit industry and 1-digit occupation
WC (2D ind, 1D occ)	WC workers by 2-digit industry and 1-digit occupation

(Antos computed the above ten y variables from the May 1979 CPS data.)

ALL (3D ind) FM	The counterparts of ALL (3D ind), WC (3D ind), BC (3D ind), but taken from the Freeman and Medoff [69] estimates based on May CPS data for 1973–75.
WC (3D ind) FM	
BC (3D ind) FM	

First notice that in table 7.16 as in table 7.15 the estimates of $a_{uy} - a_{ny}$, though widely dispersed, are positive with only one exception. However, in sharp contrast to table 7.15, half of the estimates of a_{uy} and more than half of the estimates of a_{ny} are negative. Positive estimates of a_{uy} occur only when (1) the y variable pertains to or includes blue-collar (BC) workers (see lines 1, 2, 13, 14, 15b, 16b), or (2) the Freeman-Medoff y variable for white-collar (WC) workers in 1973–75 is used (see lines 5, 12), or (3) the wage equations omit the establishment size and industry variables (see line 11).

Table 7.16 Estimates of a_{uy} and a_{ny} from Antos Study [11]

Line No. (1)	a_{uy} (2)	a_{ny} (3)	$a_{uy} - a_{ny}$ (4)	y-Variable (5)
1	.01	−.05	.06	ALL (3D ind)
2	.28	.25	.04	ALL (3D ind) FM
3	−.00	−.14	.14	ALL (2D ind)
4	−.06	−.16	.10	WC (3D ind)
5	.22	.17	.05	WC (3D ind) FM
6	−.04	−.26	.22	WC (2D ind)
7	−.04	−.24	.20	WC (3D occ)
8	−.09	−.16	.07	WC (2D ind, 3D occ)
9	−.04	−.16	.12	WC (3D ind, 1D occ)
10	−.04	−.22	.18	WC (2d ind, 1D occ)
11	.04	−.07	.11	WC (3D ind)
12	.49	.36	.13	WC (3D ind) FM
13	.18	.14	.04	BC (3D ind)
14	.29	.37	−.08	BC (3D ind) FM
15a	−.24	−.30	.06	WC (3D ind)
15b	.37	.28	.09	BC (3D ind)
16a	−.42	−.35	.07	WC (3D ind) FM
16b	.56	.49	.06	BC (3D ind) FM

Table 7.17 presents the key results from an experiment I have made to discover the sensitivity of estimated extent of unionism coefficients a_{uy} and a_{ny} to the choice of the extent of unionism y variable and to the set of other variables included on the right-hand side of the wage equation. The table covers 20 Micro wage equations fitted by OLS to the May 1973 *Current Population Survey* (CPS) data. The workers covered are white male wage and salary workers employed in the private sector, at least 15 years of age, with needed data, but excluding farm and private household workers. Lines 1–5 also exclude workers in CPS detailed industries with fewer than 20 covered workers; lines 6–7 exclude workers in CPS detailed occupations with fewer than 20 covered workers, and lines 8–10 exclude workers not residing in an SMSA.

In all of the equations covered in the table the dependent variable is the natural logarithm of a worker's usual hourly earnings—his "usual weekly earnings" divided by his "usual weekly hours." All of the equations underlying columns 3 and 4 under the heading "Equation 7.5" follow the form of equation (7.5) above and include the following variables: an extent of unionism y variable that is different on each line of the table, the union status dummy variable U, the interaction Uy of U and y, years of school completed, age, one marital status dummy variable, two city-size dummy variables, a dummy variable for part-time work (usual weekly hours less than 35), five major occupation dummies, four major industry dummies, and three region dummies.

Table 7.17 Extent of Unionism Coefficients

Line No. (1)	Extent of Unionism (y) Variable (2)	Equation (7.5) a_{ny} (3)	$a_{uy} - a_{ny}$ (4)	Equation (7.6) a_{ny} (5)	$a_{uy} - a_{ny}$ (6)
1	U* by industry	.265	−.098	.240	−.056
2	BLS-PW by industry	.301	−.148	.195	−.112
3	BLS-AW by industry	.228	−.067	.164	−.023
4	CPS-PW by industry	.408	−.238	.305	−.176
5	CPS-AW by industry	.316	−.150	.289	−.105
6	U* by occupation	−.137	.263	−.307	.226
7	CPS by occupation	−.092	.254	−.308	.225
8	U* by SMSA	−.009	−.010	.250	−.023
9	CPS-PW by SMSA	.046	−.110	.244	−.118
10	CPS-AW by SMSA	−.006	−.095	.304	−.112

All of the equations underlying columns 5 and 6 headed "Equation 7.6" have the following form,

$$W = a_n + a_x x + a_x^* x^* + a_{ny} y + U[(a_u - a_n) + (a_{uy} - a_{ny})y] + e, \qquad (7.6)$$

which differs from (7.5) only in including x^* as well as x variables where each x^* is the mean of the corresponding x (among workers covered in the fitted equation) in the worker's detailed industry (on lines 1–5), or detailed occupation (lines 6–7), or SMSA (lines 8–10).

On lines 1–5 the y variable is by industry (154 CPS detailed industries), on lines 6–7 by occupation (91 CPS detailed headings), and on lines 8–10 by SMSA (98 listed SMSAs and one catchall category for all other SMSAs). U^* is the mean of U (among workers covered in the fitted wage equation) in each industry (line 1), or occupation (line 6), or SMSA (line 8), and pertains to union membership as reported in the May 1973 CPS. The remaining seven y variables were estimated by Freeman and Medoff [69] from U.S. Bureau of Labor Statistics (BLS) establishment data for 1968–72 on collective bargaining coverage separately for production workers (PW) and all workers (AW) by industry (lines 2 and 3), and from May 1973–75 CPS data on union membership by occupation (line 7), and separately for PW and AW by industry (lines 4 and 5), and by SMSA (lines 9 and 10).

First notice that the estimates in table 7.15 bear little resemblance to those in table 7.17. None of the estimates of a_{uy} and a_{ny} in table 7.15 are negative, while six (of 20) estimates of a_{ny} and five (of 20) estimates of a_{uy} are negative in table 7.17. Only one estimate of $a_{uy} - a_{ny}$ in table 7.15 is negative; 16 (of 20) such estimates are negative in table 7.17. The line 2 figures in table 7.15 are outliers in that table but not if they were in table 7.17.

Table 7.17 leaves no doubt that the estimates of a_{uy}, a_{ny}, and $a_{uy} - a_{ny}$ are quite sensitive to the choice of the extent of unionism y variable used in the wage equation. The range of the estimates of a_{ny} is -0.14 to 0.41 in column 3 and -0.31 to 0.30 in column 5. The estimates of a_{ny} by *industry* are all positive and average about 0.30 in column 3 and 0.24 in column 5; the corresponding estimates by *occupation* are all negative, averaging about -0.11 in column 3 and -0.31 in column 5; those by *SMSA* are close to zero in column 3 but average about 0.27 in column 5.

The estimates of a_{uy} from equation (7.5) range from -0.10 to 0.17 and those from equation (7.6) from -0.08 to 0.20. Those by *industry* are all positive and average about 0.15; those by *occupation* are positive and average about 0.14 from equation (7.5) but are both negative at about -0.08 from equation (7.6); those by *SMSA* are negative and average about -0.06 from equation (7.5), but are positive and average about 0.18 from equation (7.6).

Similarly the estimates of $a_{uy} - a_{ny}$ by industry and by SMSA are all negative, but the corresponding estimates by occupation are all positive. The figures by industry and SMSA range from -0.24 to -0.01, those by occupation from 0.22 to 0.26.

There can also be little doubt that for most of the 10 extent of unionismst variables in table 7.17 the estimates of their coefficients in wage equations are sensitive to the specification of the set of other right-hand variables. Equation (7.6) differs from equation (7.5) only in that (7.6) includes, but (7.5) does not, the means x^* (by industry or occupation or SMSA) of the x variables included in both equations. The listing below compares the (7.5) estimates with those from (7.6).

Coefficient	7.5 − 7.6 *Range*
Lines 1–5, by industry, a_{ny}	.02/.11
Lines 1–5, by industry, a_{uy}	−.02/.07
Lines 1–5, by industry, $a_{uy} - a_{ny}$	−.06/−.04
Lines 6–7, by occupation, a_{ny}	.17/.22
Lines 6–7, by occupation, a_{uy}	.21/.24
Lines 6–7, by occupation, $a_{uy} - a_{ny}$	.03/.04
Lines 8–10, by SMSA, a_{ny}	−.31/−.20
Lines 8–10, by SMSA, a_{uy}	−.29/−.19
Lines 8–10, by SMSA, $a_{uy} - a_{ny}$	.01/.02

The estimates of a_{ny} and a_{uy} on lines 6–10 (y variable by occupation or SMSA) are quite sensitive to the inclusion in (7.6) but not in (7.5) of the x^* variables. The corresponding estimates on lines 1–5 (y variable by industry) display considerably less, but not negligible, sensitivity to this difference in the specification of (7.5) and (7.6). Furthermore, the inclusion of x^* in (7.6) affected the estimates of a_{uy} and a_{ny} roughly equally, especially on lines 6–10, so that the estimates of $a_{uy} - a_{ny}$ were changed relatively little by the inclusion of x^*.

The sensitivity of the estimated a_y (a_{uy}, a_{ny}, $a_{uy} - a_{ny}$) coefficients to the specification of the extent of unionism variables would not matter to me if I knew the correct specification. Then I could ignore the estimates based on incorrect specifications. But I do not know it. (With the exception of the Freeman-Medoff study no. 71, the studies covered in table 7.15 had little or nothing to say on this issue.) Furthermore, I am not convinced that the wage effects picked up by the estimated a_y coefficients are mostly effects of unionism rather than mostly effects of omitted variables. I am reluctant, therefore, to give a unionism interpretation of the a_y coefficients in tables 7.15, 7.16, and 7.17.

11. Other Wage Gap Differences

This section reports estimates of wage gap differences by a miscellany of worker or workplace characteristics for each of which the number of pertinent studies was small (in no case exceeding eight, but for none less than three studies):

a) Private versus public employment
b) Establishment or firm size
c) Industry or locality unemployment rate
d) Industry concentration ratio
e) Workplace hazards
f) Worker health status
g) Worker veteran status

For each of these characteristics my reporting of findings will be quite brief. In particular, no mention will be made of dates, worker coverage, or data sources, unless such mention is especially relevant.

a) Private versus Public Employment

Here there are eight studies (nos. 81, 91, 100, 106, 182, 186, 188, 189, of which the last three have the same author), and all agree that the larger wage gap is for privately employed workers. The private minus public gap difference derived from [100] was 0.02, but in the other seven studies the difference ranged from 0.08 to 0.16 and averaged about 0.13. Since government workers recently have comprised about one-fifth of the U.S. work force, this gap difference implies that wage gap estimates confined to the private sector will overstate the all-employee mean wage gap by about 0.02–0.03.

b) Establishment or Firm Size

Seven studies (nos. 21, 29, 71, 90, 132, 133, 152) provide estimates of the partial derivative of the wage gap with respect to the size of the employing firm or establishment. Except in studies [21], [132], and [133], all of these estimates pertain to manufacturing workers. All of the estimated partial derivatives with respect to employer size that I have calculated from these studies (except those from study no. 21) were negative, indicating that the wage gap declines as firm or establishment size increases. Because of differences among the studies in the right-hand employer size variable or variables used in the fitted wage equations, it is difficult to compare numerically the estimated partial derivatives across the studies. However, the estimates from study no. 133 suggest that the decline in the wage gap with employer size is not numerically negligible: four estimates of the excess of the wage gap for small firms (less than 100 employees) over that for large firms (1,000 or more employees) ranged from 0.04 to 0.15.

c) Industry or Locality Unemployment Rate

In four studies (nos. 143, 145, 166, 170, with Raisian as the author or coauthor) the right-hand variables in the fitted wage equations included the *current* unemployment rate (in percent) in the *industry* in which a worker was employed, the interaction of this rate with the worker's union status *U, and the mean unemployment rate in the industry over a period of several years*. The coefficients of the interaction variable thus are estimates of the response of the wage gap to *cyclical* changes in industry unemployment rates. These four studies provide 13 estimates of the interaction coefficient ranging from 0.01 to 0.02, suggesting that the wage gap widens by 0.01/0.02 for each 1 percentage point cyclical increase in the industry unemployment rate.

In three other studies [94, 136, 141] the wage equations included the current unemployment rate (in %) in the locality (SMSA, county) in which a worker resided and the interaction of this rate with the worker's union status *U*, but did not include the mean over several years of the locality unemployment rate. Thus it is not clear that the coefficient of the interaction variable is reflecting effects on the wage gap of short-term changes in the locality unemployment rate, rather than long-term differences among localities in whatever it was that caused their unemployment rates to differ. The coefficient estimates from the three studies are:

[94], two estimates: −0.01, 0.02
[136], −0.01
[141], 0.00

d) Industry Concentration Ratio

Seven studies (nos. 29, 71, 90, 112, 126, 132, 133) provide estimates of the partial derivative of the wage gap with respect to the output concentration ratio in the industry in which a worker is employed. All of these estimates, except those in no. 126, pertain to manufacturing workers. The estimates from study nos. 29, 112, 126, 132, and 133 were all negative, from study no. 90 positive, and from study no. 71 two estimates were negative and two were positive.

e) Workplace Hazards

The wage equations in five studies (nos. 71, 150, 169, 193, 197) included one or another variable or variables indexing workplace hazards to life and limb and interactions of these variables with the union status variable U. In all of the equations fitted to observations on individual workers the estimated partial derivative of the wage gap with respect to the hazard variable was positive, indicating that the wage gap increased as workplace hazard rose. However, study [71] also fitted wage equations to establishment data and the estimates of the wage gap-hazard partial derivatives from these equations were negative, though probably not significantly different from zero in a statistical sense.

f) Worker Health Status

Five studies (nos. 10, 60, 90, 114, 136) reported wage equations that included a dummy variable for health status and its interaction with the union status dummy variable U. Except in study no. 90, the estimated wage gap was larger for workers reporting that poor health limited their work activities than for other workers. Study no. 90 found the opposite.

g) Worker Veteran Status

Study nos. 29, 141, and 160 provide separate estimates of the wage gap for war veterans and nonveterans. All three agree that the veteran-nonveteran gap difference was close to zero.

12. Overview of Findings

Let $\hat{W}_u(x)$ be the expected wage of a worker, conditional on his measured personal and workplace characteristics x, if he is in unionized status, and $\hat{W}_n(x)$ his corresponding wage if he is in nonunion status. His expected wage *gap* then is $M(x) \equiv \hat{W}_u(x) - \hat{W}_n(x)$. The findings of this chapter rather strongly reject the notion that the union/nonunion wage gap $M(x)$ does not depend upon the x's—i.e., that $M(x)$ is a constant.

Question: Can the variations in $M(x)$ with the x's described in this chapter be characterized in some simple way, simpler, that is, than reciting the findings of this chapter, x by x? For example, several authors of studies cited in this chapter have noted that if x is a "human capital" variable such as schooling, age, experience, and seniority, the union profile, $\hat{W}_u(x)$, of the wage related to x is flatter than the corresponding nonunion profile $\hat{W}_n(x)$—i.e., $\partial M(x)/\partial x$ has a sign that is opposite to that of $\partial \hat{W}_n(x)/\partial x$. This characterization of the variation in $M(x)$ is supported by the data presented in sections 8 and 9 for schooling and age, experience, and seniority. $\hat{W}_n(x)$ increases and $M(x)$ decreases as schooling rises. The nonunion profile $\hat{W}_n(x)$ for age, experience, or seniority is inverted-U shaped, but the corresponding wage gap profile $M(x)$ is U-shaped.

For ease of reference I term the hypothesis that the wage gap difference $\partial M(x)/\partial x$ has a sign opposite to that of the nonunion wage difference $\partial \hat{W}_n(x)/\partial x$ as the "F" (for flattening) hypothesis. This hypothesis holds for schooling and age, experience, and seniority. But does it hold in general for other right-hand x's in the wage equations?

I first consider other variables x for which the hypothesis holds—i.e., for which the hypothesis is an apt characterization of the way $M(x)$ varies. $\hat{W}_n(x)$ rises and $M(x)$ falls with both city size and firm or establishment size. $\hat{W}_n(x)$ is larger and $M(x)$ is smaller for married workers than for workers in other marital status, for workers in the West region than for workers in the South, for white-collar than for blue-collar, for craftsmen than for operatives, for operatives than for laborers, for government workers than for private, for workers in good health than for those in poor health.

However, there are several variables for which the hypothesis does not correctly describe the variation in $M(x)$. $\hat{W}_n(x)$ is markedly higher for males than for females, but the wage gap difference by sex is close to zero. $\hat{W}_n(x)$ is higher and so is $M(x)$ for construction workers than for nonmanufacturing workers, for operatives than for service workers, for more hazardous work than for less hazardous. $\hat{W}_n(x)$ differs little between the Northeast and North Central regions, but $M(x)$ is substantially lower in the Northeast. Indeed, in general the F-hypothesis does not perform very well in characterizing wage gap differences by region, industry, and occupation. $\hat{W}_n(x)$ is larger, but not by much, for white workers than for black or nonwhite workers. If the F-hypothesis is correct, then $M(x)$ should be smaller, but not by much, for white workers. This is close to the findings reported in section 3 from CPS data. However, if the CPS data are ignored, $M(x)$ is substantially lower for white workers.

Thus though the F-hypothesis performs better than its opposite in describing wage gap variations, I do not regard it as correctly describing some important components of these variations.

8 Micro, OLS, CS Estimates: Calculating and Adjusting Mean Wage Gap Estimates

1. Introduction

The focus now shifts from estimating variations in the union/nonunion wage gap across work force sectors in the United States to estimating the overall mean union/nonunion wage gap in the U.S. work force as a whole in recent years. As in Chapter 7, the basic estimation inputs are fitted Micro, OLS, CS wage equations and related numbers reported in (or obtained by correspondence with the authors of) a large number of empirical studies of wage differentials in the United States. Since the focus in this chapter and Chapter 9 is on the overall mean wage gap, I have ignored in this chapter and the next empirical studies in which the worker coverage was quite narrow—e.g., nurses, police, fire fighters, and even sectors as large as that of contract construction.

For each broad coverage Micro, OLS, CS wage equation I first calculate the unadjusted estimate of the mean wage gap. The calculation procedures are spelled out in section 2. These unadjusted estimates are then adjusted for nonrandomness in the underlying data files (section 3), differences in the left-hand wage variable (section 4), incomplete worker coverage (section 5), and finally for "incompleteness" in the set of right-hand variables (section 6). The resulting adjusted estimates are presented by data source and date in Chapter 9.

2. Calculating the Unadjusted Mean Wage Gap Estimates

Suppose, to begin with, that the fitted wage equation has the following simple form:

$$W = a + a_x + \overline{M}U, \qquad (8.1)$$

where W is the natural logarithm of a worker's wage, U is the union status dummy variable (equal to unity if the worker is unionized and zero otherwise), the x's are other right-hand variables describing the worker, his work, and his workplace; and the a's and $\overline{M}$ are estimated coefficients. Then $\overline{M}$ is the unadjusted estimate of the mean wage gap for the sample of workers covered in fitting the wage equation.

Notice that in (8.1) $\overline{M} = \partial W/\partial U$. What if the fitted wage equation has the following form as it did in several studies:

$$e^W = b + b_x x + b_U U, \tag{8.2}$$

where e^W of course is the worker's wage in its natural (rather than logarithmic) units and the b's are the estimated coefficients? Then $\partial W/\partial U = b_U/e^W$. For all such equations I calculated the unadjusted mean wage gap estimate $\overline{M}$ as b_U/(mean of e^W), where "mean of e^W" was that for the workers covered in fitting the wage equation.

The calculation procedure was not quite so simple when the wage equations contained interactions Ux of the union status dummy variable with other right-hand variables x, as in (8.3),

$$W = a_n + a_{nx}x + U[(a_u - a_n) + (a_{ux} - a_{nx})x], \tag{8.3}$$

or when a pair of wage equations, one for unionized workers and the other for nonunion workers, was fitted, as in (8.4):

$$W_i = a_i + a_i x;\ i = u \text{ if } U = 1;\ i = n \text{ if } U = 0. \tag{8.4}$$

For each such equation pair (8.4) I first rewrote the pair as the single equation (8.3). In equation (8.3) the estimated wage gap M depends upon the x's interacted with U:

$$M \equiv \frac{\partial W}{\partial U} = (a_u - a_n) + (a_{ux} - a_{nx})x. \tag{8.5}$$

The estimated mean wage gap $\overline{M}$ then is

$$\overline{M} = a_u - a_n + (a_{ux} - a_{nx})\bar{x}, \tag{8.6}$$

where $\bar{x}$ is the mean of x among workers covered in fitting the wage equation. That is, I calculated the mean wage gap $\overline{M}$ in (8.6) by setting each of the interacted x's in (8.5) equal to its mean value.

For those studies in which equation (8.3) was fitted separately for each of several mutually exclusive and exhaustive worker groups, I first calculated the estimated mean wage gap $\overline{M}_k$ for each of the groups by the procedures set out above and then calculated the all-group mean: $\overline{M} = \Sigma N_k \overline{M}_k / \Sigma N_k$, where N_k is the number of workers in the k-th group.

3. Adjusting for Nonrandomness in the SEO, NLS, and PSID Data Files

If the workers covered in the fitting of a Micro, OLS, CS wage equation (8.1) or (8.3) are a nonrandom sample of the whole U.S. work force, then for this reason alone the corresponding estimate of $\overline{M}$, the overall mean wage gap, drawn from the equation may be biased, perhaps seriously. Such nonrandomness may occur for several reasons:

a) Nonrandomness produced by missing data—i.e., by failure of a worker or his proxy respondent to respond to some questions in the underlying survey on right-hand or left-hand variables. It is common practice in fitting wage equations to screen out workers with such missing data. I discuss the problem such exclusions create in Chapter 6, section 8, and conclude that I know too little about the resulting bias to make an adjustment for it.

b) Nonrandomness by design: incomplete worker coverage. In the 1967 *Survey of Economic Opportunity* (SEO) the union status (membership) question was not asked of government workers. For this reason wage gap estimates derived from these SEO data necessarily are restricted to private sector workers. The four *National Longitudinal Surveys* (NLS) (Young Men, Mature Men, Young Women, Mature Women) were designed to cover only persons of specified ages at the initiation of each survey. For example, the surveys include only males who were 14–24 or 45–59 years old in 1966, excluding all males 25–44 or 60 and over in 1966.

In addition the authors of empirical wage equations often choose for various reasons to impose other worker coverage restrictions. Thus, for example, in one study coverage was restricted to white males 25–64 years old.

In all instances in which (a) the worker exclusions from coverage are clear and (b) I have a basis in the findings of Chapter 7 to adjust for an exclusion, I have made such an adjustment. The details of such adjustments are given below in section 5.

c) Nonrandomness by design: oversampling of black workers. In Chapter 6, section 7, I noted that in the *National Longitudinal Surveys* (NLS), and a portion (the so-called nonrandom half) of each of the 1967 *Survey of Economic Opportunity* (SEO) and the *Panel Study of Income Dynamics* (PSID) surveys, the proportion of black workers was much higher than in the U.S. population. Such nonrandomness, I judge, is not a serious problem if the wage equations provide separate wage gap estimates by color. Then the only problem is to use appropriate population weights (rather than the sample N_k's) in averaging the black and white wage gap estimates. The population weights that I used came from several sources, first of all from the study authors which I used to adjust both their wage gap estimates and other estimates from essentially the same data set. For most of the wage gap estimates based on the 1967 SEO, I obtained appropriate weights from the 1967 SEO data tape. When these sources failed me, I simply assigned a weight of 10 percent for blacks and 90 percent for whites.

However, in frequent instances wage equations were not fitted separately by color, and there were no union status∗color interactions. That is, the wage equation covered both black and white workers. Then the wage gap estimate is an average of underlying estimates by color in which the black estimate is heavily overweighted, unless in fitting the wage equation each observation is weighted by the reciprocal of its sampling probability, which seldom occurred.

Of course if the unobserved estimate for black workers were the same as that for white workers, the overweighting of blacks would not matter. But the wage gap estimates by color presented in Chapter 7, section 3, table 7.2, indicate that wage equations with broad worker coverage by age fitted to the SEO or PSID data typically have yielded gap estimates for blacks that exceed those for whites by about 0.06. The corresponding figure for estimates drawn from the NLS data for Mature Men is 0.12, for Young Men −0.045, but for the NLS female panels the black-white gap difference is unclear. These numbers suggest that when a single wage equation with no color∗union status interaction variable is fitted without population weights to the NLS data for both blacks and nonblacks or to the nonrandom portions of PSID or SEO data, the bias in the wage gap estimate from overweighting of blacks may not be negligible.

The amount of such bias could be estimated by fitting the wage equation both with and without population weights and comparing the two wage gap estimates. I know of no study, however, that has performed this experiment. Another way of evaluating the bias is to fit (without population weights) a pair of wage equations that differ only in that one includes and the other excludes a union status∗color interaction variable:

$$W = a + a_x x + a_b B + a_u U + a_{ub} UB + e; \qquad (8.7a)$$

$$W = A + A_x x + A_b B + A_u U + e'; \qquad (8.7b)$$

where $B = 1$ for a black worker and is zero otherwise, U is the union status dummy variable, the x's are other right-hand variables, and the a's and A's are the estimated coefficients. The first equation (8.7a) provides separate wage gap estimates by color: $\overline{M}_b = a_u + a_{ub}$, $\overline{M}_w = a_u$, so that $\overline{M}_b - \overline{M}_w = a_{ub}$ and the overall wage gap estimate is $\overline{M} = B^*\overline{M}_b + (1 - B^*)\overline{M}_w = a_u + a_{ub}B^*$, where B^* is the appropriate population weight for blacks. The second equation yields only an estimate A_u of the mean wage gap $\overline{M}$ for both blacks and nonblacks combined. This estimate A_u presumably overweights $\overline{M}_b$ relative to $\overline{M}_w$, and the overweighting bias is $A_u - (a_u + a_{ub}B^*)$. However, I know of no study that has performed this second experiment either.

Therefore I have taken a different and cruder approach to evaluating the bias. It follows from the left-out variable theorem applied to (8.7a) and (8.7b) that

$$A_u = a_u + a_{ub} b_{UB,U}, \tag{8.8}$$

where $b_{UB,U}$ is the coefficient of U in a regression of UB on U, B, and the x's. None of the studies surveyed in this book provides any estimates of this coefficient. I think it is likely, however, that $b_{UB,U}$ is approximated well by the coefficient $b'_{UB,U}$ of U in a regression of UB on U and B without the x's:

$$b'_{UB,U} = \bar{B}J; \; J \equiv \frac{\bar{U}_b(1 - \bar{U}_b)(1 - \bar{B})}{\bar{U}(1 - \bar{U})(1 - \bar{B}) - (\bar{B})(\bar{U}_b - \bar{U})^2}, \tag{8.9}$$

where $\bar{B}$ is the mean of B in the sample data, $\bar{U}_b$ is the mean of U among black workers in the sample, and $\bar{U}$ is the mean of U among all workers in the sample. Then the bias from overweighting of blacks is approximately

$$\text{Bias} = (\bar{B}J - B^*)a_{ub} = (\bar{B}J - B^*)(\bar{M}_b - \bar{M}_w). \tag{8.10}$$

Several of the studies covered in Chapter 7, table 7.2, panels *B, C,* and *D* (in particular, study nos. 10, 16, 17, 28, 46, 103, 114, 117–19, 144, 145, 169, 182) provide estimates of $\bar{B}$, $\bar{U}_b$, and $\bar{U}$ from which $\bar{B}J$ can be calculated. These estimates of $\bar{B}J$ (three from the SEO, four from the NLS Young Men panel, six from the NLS Mature Men panel, and five from the PSID) ranged from 0.27 to 0.37, averaged 0.31, and there were no systematic differences by data source. The population weight B^* for black wage and salary workers was close to 0.10 in all of the data sources. Hence I estimate that $\bar{B}J - B^*$ in (8.10) was approximately 0.21. The estimates of $\bar{M}_b - \bar{M}_w$ from Chapter 7, table 7.2, differ by data source: PSID and SEO, about 0.06; NLS Young Men, about −0.045, and NLS Mature Men, about 0.12. My adjustments for overweighting of blacks then are

Adjustment 1. Overweighting of blacks
- PSID and SEO: subtract 0.012 from wage gap estimate
- NLS Mature Men: subtract 0.024 from wage gap estimate
- NLS Young Men: add 0.009 to wage gap estimate

4. Adjusting for Differences in the Dependent Wage Variable

I take as my *standard* specification of the dependent variable in the wage equation the natural logarithm of a worker's real *compensation* (see Chapter 6, section 2) per hour worked. In almost all of the Micro, OLS, CS wage equations surveyed in Chapter 9, however, the dependent variable differed from this standard in one or more respects.

First, the wage concept typically was one that omitted most or all of the employer expenditures for fringe benefits. The findings presented in

Chapter 6, section 2 indicate that omissions of the fringe items biases mean wage gap estimates downward by about 0.028, unless the wage concept used was that of annual earnings or annual average hourly earnings for which the downward bias was a bit smaller, 0.020. Hence the adjustments for omission of fringe expenditures are:

Adjustment 2. Omission of fringes
a) Add 0.028, except when
b) wage concept is that of annual earnings or annual average hourly earnings; then add 0.020.

Second, in several studies weekly or annual earnings rather than an hourly wage measure were used. If unionism yields a union/nonunion gap in hours worked, then wage gap estimates based on weekly or annual earnings will differ from those based on hourly wages. The estimates given in Chapter 6, section 4, table 6.7 indicate that the hours *per week* gap was about −0.018 and the hours *per year* gap about −0.030. Hence in Chapter 9 I make hours gap adjustments as follows:

Adjustment 3. Hours gap adjustment
a) Wage gap estimates from weekly earnings: add 0.018
b) Wage gap estimates from annual earnings: add 0.030

Third, almost universally in the cross-section wage equations the dependent wage concept was that of a money rather than real wage—money wage deflated by a cross-section place of residence price index. I discuss this problem in Chapter 6, section 4. I conclude from the scanty evidence presented there that, if the wage equation includes place of residence variables on the right-hand side, there may be no significant bias from using a money rather than real wage. In any case I have too little evidence to make an adjustment for such bias.

Fourth, in a minority of wage equations the dependent wage variable was expressed in its natural units (e^W) rather than in logarithmic units (W). For each such equation I have calculated the wage gap estimate in logarithmic units by first calculating the gap estimate in the natural units of the wage variable e^W and then divided this estimate by the mean of e^W. Does this procedure itself produce biased estimates? Fortunately, in five studies (nos. 4, 160, 193, 196, 197) matching pairs of wage equations were fitted in which the equations differed only in the dependent variable, e^W (arithmetic) in one and W (logarithmic) in the other. In all five of these studies the wage gap estimates from the arithmetic (e^W) equations were lower than the corresponding gap estimates from the logarithmic (W) equations. The difference ranged from 0.012 to 0.030 and averaged 0.023. Therefore, in Chapter 9 I adjust the wage gap estimates from arithmetic equations upward by 0.023.

Adjustment 4. Arithmetic dependent variable
Add 0.023 to wage gap estimate

5. Adjusting for Incomplete Worker Coverage

The findings of Chapter 7 strongly suggest that incomplete coverage of the U.S. work force in fitted wage equations may lead to significantly biased estimates of the U.S. mean wage gap. The wage equations surveyed in this chapter and the next vary substantially in the categories of workers they cover. Many of them, e.g., pertain only to males, frequently only to white male wage and salary workers of specified ages, industries, occupations, etc. I have amassed too little information to adjust each wage gap estimate for incompleteness in all of its detail of the worker coverage in the underlying wage equation. On the other hand, Chapter 7 does provide a basis for making some adjustments for incomplete worker coverage. These adjustments are spelled out in this section.

a) Omission of one sex. See Chapter 7, section 2. The numerous estimates of the male minus female wage gap difference presented there indicate that the sign of this gap difference is ambiguous and that on the average this difference is close to zero. Accordingly I will make no adjustment for omitting workers of one sex, usually female, from coverage.

b) Omission of blacks or nonwhites. See Chapter 7, section 3. Panel A of table 7.2 indicates that wage equations fitted to CPS data yield wage gap estimates for blacks approximately equal to those for whites. Therefore, I will not adjust wage gap estimates derived from CPS data for omission of black or nonwhite workers. However, the other panels of table 7.2, which refer to data sources other than the CPS, suggest substantial black minus white wage gap differences averaging about 0.06 in the SEO and PSID data, 0.12 in the NLS data for Mature Men, and −0.045 for the NLS Young Men. Since blacks comprise about 10 percent of the U.S. work force, I make the following adjustments for omission of blacks in wage gap estimates from the SEO, PSID, and NLS data.

Adjustment 5. Omission of blacks
SEO and PSID data: add 0.006
NLS Mature Men: add 0.012
NLS Young Men: subtract 0.004

c) Omission of nonmanufacturing. See Chapter 7, section 5. Several of the wage gap estimates surveyed in Chapter 9 are from wage equations that cover only manufacturing workers. Because only about one-fourth to one-third of U.S. workers are employed in manufacturing and because the adjustment for the omission of nonmanufacturing is large and probably rather imprecise, these wage gap estimates for manufacturing will be given considerably less weight in evaluating the overall mean wage gap than gap estimates that pertain to both manufacturing and nonmanufacturing. Refer to column 3 of table 7.4. The figures in this column are estimates of the excess of the nonmanufacturing wage gap over that in manufacturing. Eleven of the column 3 figures cover both blue-collar and white-collar workers, and seven of the 11 fall in the range 0.08 to 0.13 with a mean of 0.11. Thus these figures suggest that the manufacturing wage gap is about 0.07 to 0.08 less than the overall mean wage gap.

Adjustment 6. Omission of nonmanufacturing
Add 0.07 to 0.08 to estimated gap for manufacturing

d) Omission of white-collar (blue-collar) workers. See Chapter 7, section 6 in which I estimated that the wage gap for blue-collar workers was about 0.05 *above* and that for white-collar workers about 0.05 *below* the all-worker wage gap. Hence in Chapter 9 I adjust estimates that pertain only to blue-collar or only to white-collar workers as follows:

Adjustment 7a. Subtract 0.05 from gap estimates for blue-collar workers
Adjustment 7b. Add 0.05 to gap estimates for white-collar workers

As for manufacturing, I will give estimates that pertain only to blue-collar or only to white-collar workers less weight than estimates that cover both occupation groups in evaluating the all-worker wage gap.

e) Omission of non-SMSA workers. See Chapter 7, section 7 in which I estimated that the wage gap for workers residing in an SMSA was about 0.02 below the all-worker mean wage gap. Hence the following adjustment:

Adjustment 8. Omission of non-SMSA workers
Add 0.02 to estimated wage gap

This adjustment, even if precise for the omission of workers not residing in an SMSA, is imprecise for gap estimates that pertain to "urban" workers or to workers residing in the 12 largest of 98 largest SMSAs. Nevertheless, even for such cases, it is better, I think, to make the adjustment than not to make it.

f) Omissions by age. As I noted earlier, the four NLS panels were designed to cover workers of specified ages. In particular, the NLS panel for Young Men covers only workers who were 14–24 years old in 1966, that for Mature Men only males who were 45–59 in 1966. Thus even when these panels are combined, males who were 25–44 or 60 and over in 1966 were omitted. There are numerous wage gap estimates based on wage equations fitted to these NLS data for men. Therefore, I am reluctant to ignore them in forming my judgment of the size of the all-worker mean wage gap. However, in the light of the findings reported in Chapter 7, section 9 with respect to variations in the wage gap with age, there is a considerable likelihood that these NLS-based estimates will be misleading unless they are adjusted for age omissions.

Consider first the Young Men 14–24 in 1966. The earliest estimates for this panel are for 1969 when these men were 17–27, the latest are for 1971 when they were 19–29. The findings of Chapter 7, section 9 strongly suggest that the wage gap for such young men was above the all-worker mean wage gap, but the amount of the excess cannot be estimated from the information given there. Fortunately, there are two studies, one by Holzer [94] and the other by Mincer [136] that contain useful information.

Holzer fitted wage equations separately by age, 16–24 and 25–64, to May 1978 CPS data for male wage and salary workers. The wage gap estimates I have calculated from his equations are:

	16–24	*25–64*	*16–64*
Estimate 1	.28	.13	.16
Estimate 2	.26	.11	.14

These figures indicate that the wage gap for 16–24-year-olds exceeded that for "all" ages (16–64) by about 0.12, while the wage gap for the 25–64-year-olds fell short of the all ages gap by about 0.03.

Mincer also fitted wage equations separately by age, less than 30 and 30 and over, to PSID data, 1968–78, for white males not over 65 years old. The wage gap estimates by age from his study are:

	<30	*≥30*	*≤65*
Estimate 1	.21	.15	.17
Estimate 2	.22	.15	.17

The gap estimates for young men (<30) exceed those for all ages (≤65) by 0.04 or 0.05, while the estimates for men 30 and over are about 0.02 lower than the all ages gap.

The major difference in the wage gap estimates from the two studies is in the figures for the young men. Mincer's young men (<30) probably average about five years older than Holzer's (16–24). At these ages the wage gap declines fairly rapidly with age. Thus a considerable part of the difference in gap estimates for the young may be the result of the five-year age difference. Furthermore, the two age groups, 16–24 and <30, span fairly closely the ages of the NLS Young Men in 1969–71. Hence to obtain the age adjustment for gap estimates based on the NLS data for Young Men I simply average the Holzer and Mincer estimates.

Adjustment 9. Age adjustment for NLS Young Men
Subtract 0.08 from wage gap estimate

One study covered in Chapter 9 restricted the age coverage in its fitted wage equations to workers 25–64 years old. The Holzer paper indicates that wage gap estimates from this study should be adjusted upward by about 0.03.

Adjustment 10. Omission of workers <25 years old
Add 0.03 to wage gap estimate

What about the wage gap estimates for the NLS Mature Men? Refer to table 7.13, column 3. The figures on the first seven lines are estimates of the excess of the wage gap for NLS Mature Men over the corresponding gap for NLS Young Men. On these lines replace estimate ranges by their midpoints and within each study average the estimates. Then the average over the five studies of the resulting column 3 figures is −0.08. This figure together with adjustment 9, the age adjustment for NLS Young Men, indicates that no age adjustment is required for the NLS Mature Men.

g) Omission of government workers. In many of the studies covered in Chapter 9, the fitted wage equations covered only workers in private employment. In Chapter 7, section 11, I estimated that exclusion of government workers would tend to increase the estimated all-worker mean wage gap by about 0.025. Hence:

Adjustment 11. Omission of government workers
Subtract 0.025 from wage gap estimates

I mentioned earlier that the 1967 SEO contains no information on the union status of government workers. Nevertheless, in a few studies wage equations covering both private and government workers were fitted to these data with all government workers being treated as nonunion. The fitted wage equations were of the form

$$W = a + a_x x + a_u U' + e, \qquad (8.11)$$

where $U' = 1$ for a unionized worker in the private sector and is zero otherwise. Thus $U' = 0$ both for nonunion private sector workers and for all government workers whether union or nonunion. Then the coefficient a_u of U' is an estimate of the wage differential between private union workers and all other workers. This differential has three components:

$$a_u = \overline{M} + (1 - \overline{P})(\overline{M}_p - \overline{M}_g) - (1 - \overline{P})G/(1 - \overline{U}_p\overline{P}), \qquad (8.12)$$

where $\overline{M}$ is the all-worker mean wage gap, $\overline{P}$ is the fraction of workers employed in the private sector, $\overline{M}_p$ is the mean wage gap in the private sector, $\overline{M}_g$ the corresponding wage gap of government workers, G is the wage differential of government workers over private nonunion workers, and $\overline{U}_p$ is the fraction of private workers who are unionized.

If government workers had been excluded in fitting (8.11), the third component, $-(1 - \overline{P})G/(1 - \overline{U}_p\overline{P})$, of a_u on the right-hand side of (8.12) would vanish. The second component, $(1 - \overline{P})(\overline{M}_p - \overline{M}_g)$, is the upward bias in a_u as an estimate of $\overline{M}$ that would result from such an exclusion. This bias, which I have roughly estimated at about 0.025, is the basis for adjustment 11 immediately above. The third component, $-(1 - \overline{P})G/(1 - \overline{U}_p\overline{P})$, is the result of including rather than excluding government workers but treating them all as nonunion.

Return to Chapter 7, section 11a, where I report estimates of the private minus public wage gap difference $\overline{M}_p - \overline{M}_g$. From six of the eight studies listed there (in particular, from nos. 81, 100, 182, 186, 188, 189) it was possible to estimate $a_u - \overline{M}$ in (8.12). The six estimates ranged from -0.012 to 0.006, three were positive, three negative, and their average was zero to two decimals. Therefore, I will make no adjustment to wage gap estimates based on 1967 SEO data that include government workers but treat them all as nonunion.

h) Other omissions from coverage. There were several other omissions from coverage, some common, some not, for which, because of lack of information, I have made no adjustments in the wage gap estimates reported in Chapter 9. These omissions include the self-employed, part-time workers, farm workers, and workers in private households, workers in other selected industries, the very young (e.g., less than 16) and very old (e.g., older than 65), and, in studies based on the PSID, workers who were not household heads. I know of no wage gap estimates for the self-employed, workers in private households, those less than 16 or over 65, workers who are not household heads. Omission of the self-employed was so common that the overall mean wage gap estimates of Chapter 9 should be characterized as pertaining to wage and salary workers. There are a few wage gap estimates for part-time workers and for farm workers, but too few and too dispersed to permit adjustment for their omission.

6. Adjusting for Differences in the Set of Right-Hand Variables

In part differences in wage gap estimates derived from wage equations stem from differences among the equations in their right-hand (RH) specifications. I distinguish here between two different aspects of RH specification. First, equations with the same list of wage-explanatory variables may differ in the extent to which they allow for interactions among the variables. Second, the equations may differ in the list of the RH variables included.

I consider first the effect on mean wage gap estimates of adding interactions among the right-hand variables. Interactions of the union status variable with other RH variables are essential, of course, for estimation of wage gap differences across sectors of the work force, as in Chapter 7. And in general I prefer wage equations with more interactions to those with fewer, mainly because they are likely to be more informative, rather than because the absence of interactions will lead to seriously biased estimates of the overall mean wage gap. Indeed, it is not obvious that their absence will cause such bias.

Turn then to table 8.1. The table does verify that adding interactions among the RH variables sometimes affects the wage gap estimates appreciably. And the table suggests that the addition of interactions is somewhat more likely to lower than to raise the wage gap estimate: on 20 of the 31 lines the sign of the effect in column 3 is negative. However, only five figures, all negative, exceed 0.025 numerically, and 13 of the figures are numerically smaller than 0.010.

Furthermore, two of the studies covered in the table, no. 29 (lines 8–10) and no. 133 (lines 15–17), indicate that the wage gap effect of adding interactions may be sensitive to equation specification. First consider the Bloch-Kuskin (B-K) study no. 29. B-K fitted four sets of wage equations to the May 1973 CPS data for white males (except those with Spanish surnames), 25–64 years of age, employed in the private sector:

Equation A: a single equation with the following RH variables: schooling, experience and its square, a price index by locality, three marital status dummies, a veteran status dummy, eight occupation dummies, 18 industry dummies, and a union status dummy.

Equations B: A pair of equations fitted separately by union status.

Equations C: nine equations fitted separately by occupation.

Equations D: 18 equations fitted separately by occupation and union status. RH variables in *B, C,* and *D* were the same as in *A*. Mean wage gap estimates from the four sets of equations were: $A = 0.147$, $B = 0.109$, $C = 0.128$, $D = 0.106$. Thus the B-K study provides two estimates of the wage gap effect of adding union status interactions and two for adding occupation interactions as follows:

Union status:
- −0.038 comparing *A* and *B,* line 8 of table 8.1
- −0.022 comparing *C* and *D,* line 10 minus line 9

Occupation:
- −0.019 comparing *A* and *C,* line 9
- −0.003 comparing *B* and *D,* line 10 minus line 8

Mellow in study no. 133 fitted four sets of wage equations to the May–June 1979 CPS data for wage and salary workers 16–75 years of age:

Equation A: A single equation with the following RH variables: a quadratic function of schooling, experience, and seniority; extent of unionism by 3-digit industry; and dummy variables for color, sex, marital status

Table 8.1 Wage Gap Effects of Adding Interactions

Line No. (1)	Study No. (2)	Estimated Effect (3)	Interactions Added (4)
1	1	−.013	Separate equations by union status (*U*)
2	2	−.024	Separate equations by union status (*U*)
3	12	.025	Separate equations by union status (*U*)
4	12	.004	Separate equations by sex
5	12	.007	Separate equations by occupation
6	13	−.001	Separate equations by sex and *U*
7	28	−.012	Separate equations by sex and color
8	29	−.038	Separate equations by *U*
9	29	−.019	Separate equations by occupation
10	29	−.041	Separate equations by occupation and *U*
11	101	−.010	*U**schooling, *U**age, *U**(age)^2
12	102	−.002	*U**color, color*schooling, color*experience, color*(experience)^2
13	117	−.031	See note
14	117	−.051	See note
15	133	.023	Separate equations by *U*
16	133	.021	Separate equations by firm size
17	133	.003	Separate equations by firm size and *U*
18	135	−.003	Separate equations by schooling (4 groups)
19	141	.011	Separate equations by *U*
20	145	−.002	*U**color
21	145	.005	*U**region (South vs. non-South)
22	145	−.023	*U**occupation (blue-collar vs. white-collar)
23	145	.001	*U**industry (3 headings)
24	145	−.021	*U**schooling (4 groups)
25	150	−.048	Separate equations by *U*
26	160	.023	Separate equations by *U*
27	177	−.000	Separate equations by sex and color
28	179	−.005	Separate equations by public vs. private
29	21	−.007	Separate equations by firm size
30	58	.002	Separate equations by *U*
31	108	−.015/−.012	Separate equations by *U*

Note:
Lines 3–5, 29. Coverage restricted to white-collar workers.
Line 5. Occupations were grouped into 4 headings.
Lines 9, 10. Occupations were grouped into 9 headings.
Lines 11, 26. Coverage restricted to blue-collar workers.
Lines 13, 14. Coverage restricted to males 45–59 in 1966.
Line 13. Interactions added: *U**occupation (3 white-collar), U_1*occupation (3 blue-collar), U_2*occupation (3 blue-collar) where *U* denotes union coverage, U_1 coverage by a craft union, U_2 coverage by other than a craft union.
Line 14. Interactions added: occupation (3 blue-collar)*industry (construction vs. other) and *U**occupation (3 blue-collar)*industry(construction vs. other).
Lines 16, 17, 29. Firms were grouped into 3 size categories.
Line 31. Range covers 2 estimates.

(3), region (3), city size (2), occupation (8), industry (8), firm size (4), part-time worker, and union status.

Equations B: two equations by union status.

Equations C: three equations by firm size category.

Equations D: six equations by firm size and union status. RH variables in *B, C,* and *D* were the same as in *A* and the four mean wage gap estimates were: $A = 0.0745$, $B = 0.0974$, $C = 0.0957$, $D = 0.0775$. Thus the estimates of the effects of adding union status or firm size interactions were:

Union status:
- 0.023 comparing *A* and *B,* line 15
- −0.018 comparing *C* and *D,* line 17 minus line 16

Firm size:
- 0.021 comparing *A* and *C,* line 16
- −0.020 comparing *B* and *D,* line 17 minus line 15.

This sensitivity to wage equation specification of the wage gap effects of adding interactions has dissuaded me from attempting to reconcile differences across studies in wage gap estimates stemming from differences in the interaction specifications of the wage equations.

I turn now to differences in gap estimates produced by differences in the list of RH variables. All of the commonly used data sets for individual workers contain information on the worker's union status, sex, color, schooling, labor market experience or age, and place of residence, and almost universally these variables were included on the right-hand side. In the sparsest of wage equation specifications these were the only right-hand variables. However, these data sources also identify the worker's industry and occupation, sometimes in considerable detail, marital status, worker class (public versus private employer, self-employed versus wage and salary worker), and distinguish between part-time and full-time workers. Moreover, some of the micro-data sources provide information on the worker's health status, veteran status, number of dependents, seniority, size of the employing firm or establishment, and on some nonpecuniary aspects of his work and workplace. Thus the wage equations underlying the wage gap estimates surveyed in the next chapter differ considerably in the list of RH variables, and undoubtedly some of the differences in the gap estimates are produced by differences in the list of wage-explanatory variables.

In Chapters 4 and 5 I stated that in my judgment left-out variables correlated with union status probably lead to nonnegligible upward bias in wage gap estimates from Micro, OLS, CS wage equations. I do not mean to imply that adding a right-hand variable, whatever it may be, will always lower rather than raise the wage gap estimate, but only that as the list of included and relevant wage-explanatory variables lengthens, the wage gap estimate will tend to fall. Fortunately several of the studies covered in Chapter 9 reported experiments on the wage gap effects of adding RH variables. Table 8.2 reports the results of these experiments. Column 4 lists the variables that were added and column 3 the effect on the wage gap estimate of the addition. For example, line 1, from study no. 33 by Brown and Medoff, states that the addition of eight occupation dummies ("8D") raised the wage gap estimate by 0.072. The line notes to the table explain that these occupation dummies were added to a sparse set of RH variables.

Notice that, except for lines 1–4, 13, and one of the two estimates on each of lines 5, 22, 24, and 33, all of the numbers in column 3 are negative, supporting my conjecture that lengthening the list of RH variables will tend to lower rather than raise wage gap estimates. Second, observe that all of the column 3 estimates that exceed 0.045 numerically, except that on line 20, occur when variables were added to a sparse set of RH variables. This observation indicates that the gap effect of adding a variable will tend to fall numerically as the list of variables to which it is added lengthens. Hence I will make what I think are conservative (numerically small) adjustments for the omission of RH variables, in order to avoid overadjusting when the list of RH variables is fairly long.

The first five lines of the table, drawn from five different studies, show the effect on wage gap estimates of adding dummy variables by major occupation group. Only one of the six estimates of the wage gap effect is negative. This is not surprising. Rank occupations by their mean wage and separately by their extent of unionism. The correlation between the two ranks is surely negative. Then the left-out variable theorem suggests that omitting the occupation variable will tend to lower the wage gap estimate.

The mean of lines 1–5, column 3, is 0.031. However, on lines 1 and 3 the occupation dummies were added to a quite short list of RH variables. Hence in order to avoid overadjustment for the omission of occupation, I will make a much smaller adjustment based largely on lines 2, 4, and 5.

Adjustment 12. Omission of occupation as a RH variable
Add 0.01 to wage gap estimate

Lines 6–13, from six different studies, show the wage gap effects of adding dummy variables for industry. All of the estimated effects are negative, except those on line 13 for white-collar workers. This, too, is not surprising, by reasoning analogous to that for occupation. On lines 10, 11, and 13 replace estimate ranges by their midpoints. Then the column 3 mean of lines 6, 7, 10–13 is −0.022, and the mean of lines 6, 9, 10–13 is −0.027. Here, too, to avoid overadjusting for the omission of industry, I will make a smaller adustment based mainly on lines 6, 10–12.

Adjustment 13. Omission of industry as a RH variable
Subtract 0.02 from wage gap estimate

Table 8.2 Wage Gap Effects of Adding Right-Hand Variables

Line No. (1)	Study No. (2)	Estimated Effect (3)	Variables Added (4)
1	33	.072	Occupation (8D)
2	55	.016	Occupation (8D)
3	81	.067	Occupation (5D)
4	98	.00	Occupation (8D)
5	11	−.003/.006	Occupation (3D)
6	33	−.017	Industry (22D)
7	70	−.08	Industry (20D)
8	70	−.10	Industry (45D)
9	70	−.11	Industry (200D)
10	102	−.024/−.021	Industry (5D) replacing Industry (2D)
11	196	−.015/−.004	Industry (25D), but see line note
12	55	−.019	Industry (11D)
13	11	.009/.019	Industry (7D)
14	13	−.011	Occupation (6D) and Industry (8D)
15	55	−.003	Occupation (8D) and Industry (11D)
16	100	−.002	Occupation (10D) and Industry (10D)
17	133	−.024/−.014	Occupation (9D) and Industry (10D)
18	64	−.025	Region (28D) and Industry (168D) replacing Region (3D) and Industry (45D)
19	12	−.011/−.008	Extent of unionism by industry
20	19	−.061	Extent of unionism by industry, but see note
21	133	−.023/−.017	Extent of unionism by industry
22	11	−.010/.019	Extent of unionism by industry
23	173	−.014/−.009	7 city amenity variables
24	173	−.009/.000	Region (3D)
25	133	−.039/−.028	Region (3D), city size (2D), marital status (3D), part-time worker (1D)
26	179	−.026	Seniority and its square
27	133	−.045/−.038	Seniority, its square, interactions of schooling with seniority and experience, firm size (4D)
28	133	−.019	Firm size (4D)
29	11	−.002/−.001	Firm size (5D)
30	112	−.015	Plant size and concentration ratio by industry
31	48	−.085/−.061	Work effort and 2 workplace dummies
32	48	−.037/−.013	Break time and training time
33	82	−.018/.002	5 or 6 working condition dummies

Note:

Lines 1, 3, 7–9, 14, 25, 31–33. Variables were added to a sparse set of RH variables.

Lines 1, 6, 30. Pertain to manufacturing workers only.

Lines 2, 3, 11, 12, 15, 16, 33. Pertain to full-time workers only.

Lines 4, 16, 23, 24. Pertain to urban workers only.

Line 4. Two estimates both 0.00.

Lines 5, 11, 13, 22, 24, 29, 32, 33. Range covers 2 estimates.

Lines 5, 13, 19, 22, 29. Pertain to white-collar workers only.

Lines 11, 18, 30–32. Pertain to blue-collar workers only.

Line 11. Twenty-five industry dummies and a dangerous work dummy replaced an injury rate variable by 3-digit industry.

Lines 17, 21, 25. Range covers 6 estimates.

Line 19. Range covers 8 estimates.

Line 20. In addition, numerous interactions of union status with other RH variables were added.

Lines 23, 27. Range covers 4 estimates.

Line 26. Pertains to women 14–24 years of age in 1968.

Line 31. Range covers 3 estimates.

Lines 14–17 verify that the effect of omitting industry is larger numerically, by about 0.01, than that of omitting occupation.

Lines 19–22 show the effect on wage gap estimates of adding an extent of unionism variable by industry (but see the note to line 20). On lines 19, 21, and 22 the extent of unionism variable was added to a set of variables that included major industry dummies. On the basis of lines 19–22, together with the results of several experiments I have performed, I will make the following adjustment:

Adjustment 14. Omission of extent of unionism by industry
Subtract 0.01 from wage gap estimate

Lines 23–33 deal with a rather diverse set of variables: line 23 with a set of city amenity variables; 24 with region; 25 with region, city size, marital status, and part-time work; 26 with seniority; 27 with seniority and firm size; 28–30 with firm size; 31–33 with various working conditions. The numbers in column 3 on these lines are almost all negative. However, the evidence provided by these lines is too slim to provide a basis for adjustments for the omission of the specific variables dealt with on these lines.

7. Summary of Adjustments

Table 8.3 summarizes the set of adjustments to wage gap estimates that will be made in Chapter 9.

Table 8.3 Adjustments to Wage Gap Estimates

Adj. No. (1)	Adjustment Amount (2)	Adjustment for (3)
1	−.012	Overweighting blacks in PSID and SEO
1	−.024	Overweighting blacks in NLS Mature Men
1	+.009	Overweighting blacks in NLS Young Men
2	+.028	Omission of fringes, except when wage concept is that of
2	+.020	annual earnings or annual average hourly earnings
3	+.018	Hours gap, weekly earnings dependent
3	+.030	Hours gap, annual earnings dependent
4	+.023	Arithmetic dependent variable
5	+.006	Omission of blacks, SEO and Michigan data
5	+.012	Omission of blacks, NLS Mature Men
5	−.004	Omission of blacks, NLS Young Men
6	+.07 to +.08	Omission of nonmanufacturing
7a	−.05	Omission of white-collar workers
7b	+.05	Omission of blue-collar workers
8	+.02	Omission of non-SMSA workers
9	−.08	Age exclusions, NLS Young Men
10	+.03	Omission of workers < 25 years of age
11	−.025	Omission of government workers
12	+.01	Omission of occupation variable
13	−.02	Omission of industry variable
14	−.01	Omission of extent of unionism by industry

9 The Adjusted Micro, OLS, CS Gap Estimates

1. Introduction

The goal of this chapter is to estimate the overall mean union/nonunion wage gap for the U.S. work force in recent years, especially the decade of the 1970s. Sections 2–7 present unadjusted and adjusted wage gap estimates by data source and years as follows:

Section 2: *Current Population Surveys* (CPS) for 1970–79
Section 3: *Survey of Economic Opportunity* (SEO) for 1967
Section 4: University of Michigan *Panel Study of Income Dynamics* (PSID) for 1967–78
Section 5: Other Michigan surveys (SRC) for various years
Section 6: *National Longitudinal Surveys* (NLS) for 1969–73
Section 7: Miscellaneous surveys for various years

Section 8 summarizes the wage gap estimates by year. This chapter covers Micro, OLS, CS wage gap estimates retrieved from 117 different studies.

The result of this survey is a set of numbers, one for each year in the period 1967–79. These numbers presumably are estimates of the mean union/nonunion wage gap in the whole U.S. work force. However, because I suspect that Micro, OLS, CS wage gap estimates tend to be upward biased, I present these numbers as *upper limit* estimates of the overall mean gap.

2. Adjusted Estimates from CPS Data

I consider first the wage gap estimates derived from Micro, OLS, CS wage equations fitted to *Current Population Survey* data, usually in May of each year, 1970–79. I have more gap estimates from this source than from any other. The CPS offered much larger sample sizes than the NLS and the University of Michigan surveys; in contrast to the SEO, the CPS provided union status information for government as well as private workers; in contrast to the NLS and the nonrandom portions of the SEO and the PSID, the CPS did not oversample blacks; the CPS was not restricted in coverage to particular age groups as in the NLS.

Table 9.1 reports unadjusted and adjusted mean wage gap estimates based on CPS data, 1970–79, from 35 different studies. I have excluded from this table and from other tables in this chapter numerous Micro, OLS, CS estimates that pertain to small sectors of the economy (construction workers, hospital employees, teachers, etc.). Moreover, for studies (or groups of similar studies involving the same author) providing more than one unadjusted mean gap estimate, I have chosen what I regarded as the single best estimate, sometimes a mean of several estimates. In making this choice I preferred broad to narrow coverage of workers, long to short lists of right-hand variables in the wage equation, and more to fewer interactions among the right-hand variables, especially interactions involving the union status variable. Furthermore, for some studies the wage gap estimates given in column 4 are based on wage equations supplied to me by the study author in correspondence rather than on equations reported in the author's study. The adjustments made in going from column 4 to column 5, which are listed by number in column 6, are those discussed in Chapter 8 and are shown in table 8.3.

Turn first to the estimates for 1973 on lines 25–35. The mean of the 11 adjusted estimates (after replacing ranges by their midpoints) is 0.158 and the median is 0.150. (The corresponding averages of the 11 unadjusted estimates are: mean 0.150, median 0.148.) However, the estimates on lines 30 and 32 are based on wage equations in which the worker coverage was restricted to those paid by the hour. On the basis of experiments reported to me in correspondence by Wesley Mellow I judge that the effect of such a coverage restriction is to bias wage gap estimates upward substantially. Hence discard the estimates on lines 30 and 32. The mean of the nine remaining adjusted estimates is 0.152, and the median is 0.146; the averages of the nine unadjusted estimates are: mean 0.149, median 0.148. The standard deviation of the nine adjusted estimates was 0.023, that for the unadjusted estimates was 0.038. This comparison of standard deviations indicates that the adjustments made to the unadjusted estimates have reduced the dispersion among the estimates substantially, at least for the 1973 CPS figures.

The best of the 1973 CPS estimates, in my judgment, are those based on the Ashenfelter study (no. 17 on line 25), the Bloch-Kuskin study (no. 29 on line 26), and the Sahling-Smith study (no. 178 on line 35). The mean of the adjusted estimates on these three lines is 0.147. Hence I tentatively fix 0.147 as the upper bound to the overall mean wage gap for 1973.

There are only three CPS-based wage gap estimates for 1974 (see lines 22–24) and one (line 24) of these is tainted for my purposes by restriction

Table 9.1 Estimates of the Mean Wage Gap from CPS Data

Line No. (1)	Year (2)	Study No. (3)	Wage Gap Estimate: Unadj. (4)	Wage Gap Estimate: Adj. (5)	Adjustments (6)
1	1979	11,12,14	.049	.127	2, 7b
2	1979	132,133	.077	.105	2
3	1979	108	.150	.168	2, 14
4	1978	94	.138	.156	2, 14
5	1978	131	.176	.194	2, 14
6	1978	132,133	.172	.200	2
7	1978	178	.175	.193	2, 14
8	1978	190	.174	.192	2, 8, 13, 14
9	1977	131	.188	.206	2, 14
10	1977	134	.150	.168	2, 14
11	1977	58	.195	.193	2, 13, 14
12	1976	13	.192	.210	2, 14
13	1976	70	.18	.18	2, 11
14	1976–78	94	.225	.168	2, 7a, 8, 9, 11
15	1975	17	.168	.186	2, 14
16	1975	64	.205	.158	2, 7a, 11
17	1975	71	.122	.145/.155	2, 6, 7a, 11
18	1975	130	.181	.194/.204	2, 6, 7a, 11, 14
19	1975	152,153	.118	.166/.176	2, 6, 7a
20	1975	184	.208	.206	2, 13, 14
21	1975	188	.190	.188	2, 13, 14
22	1974	64	.188	.141	2, 7a, 11
23	1974	71	.106	.129/.139	2, 6, 7a, 11
24	1974	152,153	.132	.180/.190	2, 6, 7a
25	1973	17	.148	.166	2, 14
26	1973	29	.106	.129	2, 10, 11, 14
27	1973	64	.197	.150	2, 7a, 11
28	1973	71	.110	.133/.143	2, 6, 7a, 11
29	1973	110,186–189	.21	.21	2, 13, 14
30	1973	130	.160	.173/.183	2, 6, 7a, 11, 14
31	1973	150	.155	.128	2, 11, 13, 14
32	1973	152,153	.142	.190/.200	2, 6, 7a
33	1973	173	.107	.145	2, 8, 14
34	1973	177	.182	.155	2, 11, 13, 14
35	1973	178	.128	.146	2, 14
36	1973–78	7	.243	.229	2, 3, 7a, 14
37	1973–76	100	.112	.150	2, 8, 14
38	1973–75	6	.112	.193/.203	2, 3, 6, 11, 14
39	1973–75	33	.103	.166/.176	2, 6, 11, 14
40	1973–75	94	.148	.121	2, 7a, 8, 11
41	1971	90	.112	.148/.158	2, 3, 6, 7a, 13, 14
42	1970	160	.140	.093	2, 7a, 11

Note:

Line 3. Pertains to workers in States with right-to-work laws employed in selected industries and occupations. No adjustments were made for the restrictions.

Line 5. Comparable unadjusted estimate for 1977 was 0.192.

Line 6. Comparable unadjusted estimate for 1979 was 0.126.

Line 9. Unadjusted estimate is based on employer responses to wage, industry, occupation, and union status questions. Corresponding estimate based on worker responses was 0.173.

Line 14. Pertains to 16–24-year-old males. Comparable unadjusted estimate for 1973–75 was 0.224.

Lines 18, 19, 24, 30, 32. Pertain to workers paid by the hour. No adjustment was made for this coverage restriction.

of coverage to workers paid by the hour. The mean of the other two adjusted gap estimates (after replacing the range on line 23 by its midpoint) is 0.138 or 0.009 below the tentative figure of 0.147 for 1973. What evidence is there in addition to this comparison that the mean wage gap fell by about 0.009 between 1973 and 1974? Six studies provide matching estimates for 1973 and 1974: nos. 64, 71, and 153 using CPS data (table 9.1) and nos. 136, 143, and 145 using PSID data (table 9.3). The excess of the 1973 estimate over the matching 1974 estimate for each of the six studies is:

no. 64: 0.009; no. 71: 0.004; no. 136: 0.009;
no. 143: −0.023; no. 145: 0.009; no. 153: 0.019.

The figure −0.023 from no. 143 is an outlier. The mean of the other five figures is 0.010. Thus I accept 0.138 tentatively as my upper-bound estimate for 1974.

Table 9.1 contains seven wage gap estimates for 1975 (lines 15–21), but two of these are made doubtful by coverage restricted to workers paid by the hour for which I made no adjustment. The mean of the other five adjusted estimates is 0.178. However, the three best studies for 1975, in my judgment, are nos. 17, 64, and 71 for which the mean of the adjusted estimates is 0.165 or 0.018 above my tentative bound for 1973. Seven studies, nos. 17, 64, 71, 130, and 153 using CPS data (table 9.1) and nos. 136 and 145 using PSID data (table 9.3), provide matching estimates for 1973 and 1975. The 1975 minus 1973 estimate differences from these studies are:

no. 17: 0.020; no. 64: 0.008; no. 71: 0.012; no. 130: 0.021;
no. 136: 0.024; no. 145: 0.015; no. 153: −0.024.

The last of these differences (−0.024) is clearly an outlier. The mean of the other six differences is 0.017. Hence I accept 0.165 tentatively as the upper-bound estimate for 1975.

The mean of the tentative upper-bound figures for 1973, 1974, and 1975 is 0.150. Three studies—see lines 38–40 in table 9.1—fitted wage equations to the pooled CPS data for 1973–75. The mean of the adjusted estimates on lines 38–40 is 0.163 or 0.013 above the mean (0.150) of the tentative upper bounds for 1973–75. Hence these three studies suggest that these bounds may be a bit too low.

There are no CPS-based estimates for 1972, one for each of 1970 and 1971, and none before 1970. Hence I first extrapolate my tentative upper-bound estimate for 1973 to the years 1970–72 with the help of studies 136, 143, and 145 based on PSID data (table 9.3) for 1970–73, and then check these extrapolations against the CPS-based estimates for 1970 and 1971 shown on lines 41 and 42 of table 9.1. The estimate differences from the three PSID studies are:

	1973 Minus 1972	*1973 Minus 1971*	*1973 Minus 1970*
no. 136	.007	.013	.039
no. 143	.021	−.006	.016
no. 145	.035	−.009	.022
Mean	.021	−.001	.026

Hence my extrapolations (1973 = 0.147) are: 1972 = 0.126, 1971 = 0.148, 1970 = 0.121. The CPS-based estimate on line 41 of table 9.1 for 1971 is 0.153, which is close to the extrapolation. On the other hand, the corresponding estimate for 1970 on line 42 is 0.093, which is almost 0.03 below the extrapolation for that year. Nevertheless, I tentatively fix the upper bound for 1972 at 0.13, for 1971 at 0.15, and for 1970 at 0.12.

The adjusted wage gap estimates on lines 4–14 indicate that the mean wage gap in 1976–78 was higher than that in 1973–75. The smaller and, I think, better of the two estimates for 1976 is 0.18 which is 0.03 above the upper bound I have set for 1973–75. This is quite consistent with the excess of the 1976 over the 1973–75 wage gap estimates shown in PSID-based studies 136 and 145 (see table 9.3). Hence I fix the tentative upper bound for 1976 at 0.180, which makes the average upper bound for 1973–76 equal to 0.158, a bit above the adjusted estimate for 1973–76 from study no. 100 on line 37 of table 9.1.

The three estimates for 1977 on lines 9–11 average 0.006 below the corresponding average for 1976, lines 12 and 13. A decline of this amount from 1976 to 1977 is consistent with the mean of the 1976–77 changes estimated in studies 136 and 145 (table 9.3). Therefore I put the tentative upper bound for 1977 at 0.174.

The mean of the five adjusted wage gap estimates for 1978 (lines 4–8, table 9.1) is 0.002 less than that for the three 1977 estimates (lines 9–11, table 9.1), which suggests an upper bound for 1978 of about 0.172. Other evidence on the change in the wage gap from 1977 to 1978 and from 1973 to 1978 is mixed. Study 131 (table 9.1, lines 5 and 9) shows a decline of 0.012 from 1977 to 1978. Study 136 (table 9.3) shows an even larger decline (0.043) from 1977 to 1978. But CPS-based study no. 178 (table 9.1, lines 7 and 35) shows a large increase 0.047 from 1973 to 1978. Thus with considerable uncertainty I put the upper bound for 1978 at 0.172. Notice that if the upper bounds are put at 0.174 in 1977 and 0.172 for 1978 and 0.180 in 1976, the mean 0.175 of these three bounds is above the wage gap estimate 0.168 from study 94 on line 14.

I regard the estimates on line 2 from the Mellow studies 132 and 133 as the best of the CPS-based wage gap estimates. The unadjusted estimate is derived from a wage equation (actually six wage equations fitted separately by union status and firm size) with no worker coverage restrictions other than the usual ones and, more important, the most complete (for CPS-based studies) list of right-hand variables. In particular, only this wage equation and that underlying the estimates on line 1 included both seniority and firm size as right-hand variables.

Notice that the estimates on line 2 are 0.095 lower than the corresponding estimates on line 6. About half of this difference is accounted for by the date difference, 1979 on line 2, 1978 on line 6. The rest of the difference is attributable to the inclusion of seniority and firm size as right-hand variables in the line 2, but not the line 6, equations. Thus if I were to accept the adjusted estimate 0.105 on line 2 as the 1979 upper bound, I would have to set the upper bounds for 1970–78 about 0.02 lower than I have put them. Instead, to be conservative in the upper-bound estimates, I put the 1979 upper bound at 0.126 as suggested by line 6 (see the line 6 note).

In summary: on the basis of the CPS-based estimates (with some help from PSID estimates) I have fixed the following upper bounds to the overall mean wage gap for 1970–79 (after rounding):

1970 = 0.12,	1971 = 0.15,	1972 = 0.12,	1973 = 0.15,	1974 = 0.14,
1975 = 0.16,	1976 = 0.18,	1977 = 0.17,	1978 = 0.17,	1979 = 0.13,

whose 10-year mean is 0.15. The mean excess of the adjusted estimates on lines 1–42 of table 9.1 over the corresponding upper bounds just listed is 0.012, and the standard deviation of these differences is 0.025.

3. Adjusted Estimates from 1967 SEO Data

Table 9.2 reports unadjusted and adjusted wage gap estimates derived from 16 different studies in which wage equations were fitted to 1967 *Survey of Economic Opportunity* data. The means and medians of the adjusted and unadjusted figures are all equal to 0.13. The standard deviation (0.027) of the adjusted estimates is about two-fifths lower than that (0.044) for the unadjusted estimates.

The best of the table 9.2 estimates, in my judgment, are those on lines 1, 2, 3, and 11 from three Ashenfelter studies and one by Oaxaca. The mean of these four estimates is 0.11. This mean is 0.04 below the tentative upper bound I have fixed for 1973 and thus is broadly consistent with estimates from Ashenfelter's study no. 17 (see line 2 and the line note) that the mean wage gap in 1967 was appreciably below that in 1973. Hence I put the tentative upper bound for 1967 at 0.11.

4. Adjusted Estimates from PSID Data

Table 9.3 reports unadjusted and adjusted wage gap estimates retrieved from 25 studies in which the underlying Micro, OLS, CS wage equations

Table 9.2 Estimates of the Mean Wage Gap from 1967 SEO Data

Line No. (1)	Study No. (2)	Wage Gap Estimate Unadj. (3)	Adj. (4)	Adjustments (5)
1	16	.107	.100	2, 11, 14
2	17	.118	.111	2, 11, 14
3	19	.067	.096	2, 5, 8, 11
4	31	.195	.168	2, 11, 13, 14
5	60	.138	.144	1, 2, 14
6	73	.133	.091	2, 7a, 13
7	78	.189	.162	2, 11, 13, 14
8	79	.103	.131	2, 8, 12–14
9	114	.137	.105	2, 7a, 14
10	127	.201	.174	2, 11, 13, 14
11	146	.128	.141	2, 8, 11, 14
12	147	.166	.159	2, 8, 11, 13, 14
13	180	.060	.088	2–4, 11–14
14	181	.103	.131	2–4, 11–14
15	185	.098	.122	2, 5, 14
16	193	.198	.141	2, 7a, 11, 14

Note:
Line 2. Comparable CPS estimates (adjusted) for 1973 = 0.166, for 1975 = 0.186.

were fitted to the University of Michigan *Panel Study of Income Dynamics* data for one or another year or period during 1967–78. The primary purpose of this tabulation is to check the upper bounds I have tentatively fixed in sections 2 and 3. Column 6 shows for each year or period the values of these bounds.

Since I have not yet fixed bounds for 1968 and 1969 I first attend to that task. I estimate the bound for 1969 by extrapolation of that (0.15) for 1971 with the help of eight studies (136, 143, 145, and 169 in table 9.3 based on PSID data; and 49, 118, 119, and 136 in table 9.5 based on NLS data for Mature Men) that provided comparable estimates for both 1969 and 1971. In these eight studies the excess of the 1971 over 1969 estimate is:

Table 9.3	*Table 9.5*
136 = .041	49 = .039
143 = .037	118 = .032
145 = .052	119 = .032
169 = .010	136 = .030

The figure from study 169 is an outlier. The mean of the other seven figures is 0.038. Hence I put the 1969 upper bound at 0.11.

There are only three studies (136, 143, and 145 in table 9.3) that provide estimates for 1968 along with comparable estimates for 1967 or 1969–71, and they disagree sharply with respect to placing the 1968 gap relative to

Table 9.3 Estimates of the Mean Wage Gap from PSID Data

Line No. (1)	Study No. (2)	Year (3)	Gap Estimate: Unadj. (4)	Gap Estimate: Adj. (5)	Bound (6)	Adjustments (7)
1	28	1967	.251	.271	.11	2, 10, 13, 14
2	93	1967	.157	.177	.11	2, 12, 14
3	141	1970	.190	.188	.12	1, 2, 14
4	66	1971	.150	.190	.15	2, 10, 14
5	102	1972	.134	.144	.12	2, 14
6	201	1972	.198	.204	.12	2, 5, 12–14
7	109	1973	.106	.106	.15	2, 12–14
8	125	1973	.208	.208	.15	2, 12–14
9	137	1973	.133	.139	.15	2, 5, 12–14
10	86	1974	.107	.137	.14	2, 3, 12–14
11	1	1975	.073	.073	.16	2, 12–14
12	42	1975	.19	.20	.16	2, 5, 12–14
13	2	1976	.076	.076	.18	2, 12–14
14	161	1976	.191	.172	.18	2, 5, 11–14
15	123	1967–73	.11	.13	.12	2, 3, 14
16	143	1967–74	.180	.170	.13	2, 13, 14
17	165	1967–74	.163	.159	.13	1, 2, 3, 13, 14
18	166	1967–74	.236	.214	.13	1, 2, 13, 14
19	144	1967–77	.204	.194	.14	2, 13, 14
20	145	1967–77	.204	.204	.14	1, 2, 14
21	170	1967–77	.219	.207	.14	1, 2, 12–14
22	136	1968–78	.134	.150	.14	2, 5, 14
23	169	1969–71	.177	.142	.13	2, 11, 13, 14
24	45	1970–71	.050	.071	.13	1, 2, 4, 14
25	46	1970–71	.209	.229	.13	2, 10, 13, 14

Note:

Line 16. Unadjusted estimate in column 4 is the mean of separate yearly estimates as follows: 1967 = 0.199, 1968 = 0.235, 1969 = 0.143, 1970 = 0.158, 1971 = 0.180, 1972 = 0.153, 1973 = 0.174, 1974 = 0.197.

Line 18. Estimate in column 4 is the mean of 4 separate estimates.

Line 20. Unadjusted estimate in column 4 is the mean of yearly figures as follows: 1967 = 0.207, 1968 = 0.204, 1969 = 0.165, 1970 = 0.186, 1971 = 0.217, 1972 = 0.173, 1973 = 0.208, 1974 = 0.199, 1975 = 0.223, 1976 = 0.242, 1977 = 0.220.

Line 22. Estimate in column 4 is the mean of 3 estimates from 3 different wage equations fitted to pooled 1968–78 data. Quite different estimates by year from a fourth wage equation are: 1968 = 0.026, 1969 = 0.040, 1970 = 0.055, 1971 = 0.081, 1972 = 0.087, 1973 = 0.094, 1974 = 0.085, 1975 = 0.118, 1976 = 0.125, 1977 = 0.130, 1978 = 0.087.

Line 23. Estimate in column 4 is the mean of yearly figures as follows: 1969 = 0.174, 1970 = 0.173, 1971 = 0.184.

that in 1967 or in 1969–71. Hence I arbitrarily fix the gap for 1968 at 0.11 as in 1967 and 1969.

The mean excess of the adjusted estimates in column 5 over the bound in column 6 is 0.028 over the 25 lines of the table. The corresponding standard deviation is 0.059. Notice, however, that seven lines, 16–21 and 23, have an author (Raisian) in common. When these seven lines are combined and treated as one line, the mean excess (over 19 lines now) is 0.021

and the standard deviation is 0.064. The corresponding figures for the CPS data in table 9.1 are 0.012 for the mean and 0.025 for the standard deviation, and for the 1967 SEO data in table 9.2 the mean excess is 0.019 and the standard deviation is 0.027. The best of the estimates in table 9.3, in my opinion, is that on line 22 from the Mincer study. The adjusted figure 0.150 from the Mincer study for the period 1968–78 is 0.01 above the corresponding bound. Thus I do not regard the PSID-based estimates in table 9.3 as seriously challenging the upper bounds I have tentatively set. There is a suggestion that the upper bounds perhaps are about 0.01 too low.

5. Adjusted Estimates from other Michigan Survey Research Center (SRC) Data

Table 9.4 summarizes the unadjusted and adjusted wage gap estimates I have calculated from wage equations in 15 studies that were fitted to Survey Research Center survey data other than the PSID. The survey used on lines 1–6 of the table was the 1972–73 *Quality of Employment Survey* about which there is some ambiguity evidenced in the studies with respect to the date of the dependent wage variable. Some of the studies report the date as 1972, others 1973, and still others do not report the date. I have put the date at 1973 on the basis of correspondence with one of the authors.

The mean excess of the adjusted estimates in column 5 over the bound in column 6 on the 14 lines of the table for which I have estimated the column 6 bound is 0.008, and the standard deviation of these differences is 0.039. The estimate on line 8, I think, is an unacceptable outlier. When it is discarded, the mean excess is 0.001 and the standard deviation is 0.030. The best of the adjusted estimates in table 9.4, I judge, is that on line 6, which is 0.025 below the corresponding upper bound. Thus table 9.4 suggests to me that perhaps I have set the upper bounds a bit too high.

6. Adjusted Estimates from National Longitudinal Surveys

I have unadjusted and adjusted wage gap estimates from 22 studies in which wage equations were fitted to data from the *National Longitudinal Surveys*. These estimates are presented in table 9.5.

From the point of view of estimating the overall mean wage gap in the U.S. work force, all four of the NLS panels suffer from strong age restrictions on worker coverage and from oversampling of black workers. Furthermore, I have been able to adjust for the age restriction only for the panel of Young Men and crudely at that.

Nevertheless, the adjusted estimates in column 5 of table 9.5 offer no more serious a challenge to the upper bounds (column 6) than the adjusted

Table 9.4 Estimates of the Mean Wage Gap from Other SRC Data

Line No. (1)	Study No. (2)	Year (3)	Gap Estimates Unadj. (4)	Adj. (5)	Bound (6)	Adjustment (7)
			A. Quality of Employment Survey			
1	4	1973	.20	.14	.15	2, 5, 7a, 12–14
2	6	1973	.101	.119	.15	2, 14
3	82	1973	.145	.179	.15	2, 5, 10, 13, 14
4	98	1973	.109	.133	.15	2, 3, 8, 13, 14
5	135	1973	.120	.146	.15	2, 3, 5, 13, 14
6	199	1973	.115	.125	.15	2, 14
7	55	1977	.202	.220	.17	2, 14
8	59	1977	.264	.272	.17	2, 12–14
9	112	1977	.171	.189/.199	.17	2, 6, 7a, 13, 14
			B. Survey of Working Conditions			
10	40	1969	.110	.133	.11	2, 4, 12–14
11	82	1969	.070	.104	.11	2, 5, 10, 13, 14
12	196,197	1969	.108	.098	.11	2, 3, 7a, 14
			C. Survey of Consumer Finances			
13	81	1968	.153	.151	.11	2, 13, 14
14	101	1965–66	.285	.243	n.a.	2, 7a, 12–14
15	192	1966	.152	.185	n.a.	2, 4, 14
			D. Time Use Survey			
16	48	1976	.174	.132	.18	2, 7a, 12–14

Note:
Line 5 is the mean of 6 estimates. n.a. = not available.

estimates based on CPS data in table 9.1. The mean excess of the adjusted estimates over the corresponding bounds across the 34 lines of table 9.5 is 0.002 and the standard deviation of the differences is 0.045. The corresponding figures for table 9.1 are 0.012 for the mean and 0.025 for the standard deviation. Furthermore when the outliers on lines 4, 14, 21, 23, 26, and 28 of table 9.5 are ignored, the mean excess is 0.009 and the standard deviation drops to 0.023.

7. Adjusted Estimates from Other Sources

There remain eight studies in which the wage gap estimates are based on data sources other than those already covered in previous sections. The estimates from these studies are shown in table 9.6. The mean excess of the adjusted estimates over the previously set upper bounds is −0.021 and the

Table 9.5 Estimates of the Mean Wage Gap from NLS Data

Line No. (1)	Study No. (2)	Year (3)	Gap Estimates Unadj. (4)	Adj. (5)	Bound (6)	Adjustments (7)
			A. Young Men			
1	10	1969	.259	.170	.11	2, 4, 7a, 9, 14
2	36	1969	.193	.130	.11	1, 2, 9, 12–14
3	74	1969	.203	.140	.11	1, 2, 9, 12–14
4	113	1969	.287	.224	.11	1, 2, 9, 12–14
5	118	1969	.214	.142	.11	2, 9, 12–14
6	136	1969	.21	.13	.11	2, 5, 9, 12–14
7	137	1969	.167	.091	.11	2, 5, 9, 12–14
8	36	1970	.188	.125	.12	1, 2, 9, 12–14
9	75	1970	.163	.100	.12	1, 2, 9, 12–14
10	35,36	1971	.190	.127	.15	1, 2, 9, 12–14
11	103	1971	.209	.127	.15	2, 9, 13, 14
12	118,119	1971	.224	.152	.15	2, 9, 12–14
13	136	1971	.22	.14	.15	2, 5, 9, 12–14
14	57	1970–71	.279	.216	.13	1, 2, 9, 12–14
15	32	1966–71, 1973	.177	.104	.125	1, 2, 9, 13, 14
			B. Mature Men			
16	10	1969	.165	.156	.11	2, 4, 7a, 14
17	49	1969	.129	.133	.11	2, 5, 13, 14
18	106	1969	.122	.116	.11	1, 2, 14
19	118,119	1969	.129	.137	.11	2, 12–14
20	117	1969	.123	.141	.11	2, 14
21	136	1969	.05	.07	.11	2, 5, 12–14
22	49	1971	.168	.172	.15	2, 5, 13, 14
23	91	1971	.061	.056	.15	1, 2, 12, 13
24	103	1971	.149	.147	.15	2, 13, 14
25	118,119	1971	.161	.169	.15	2, 12–14
26	136	1971	.08	.10	.15	2, 5, 12–14
27	182	1971	.142	.140	.15	2, 13, 14
28	126	1971	−.073	.011/.021	.15	1, 2, 6, 12
			C. Young Women			
29	103	1971	.151	.149	.15	2, 13, 14
30	142	1972	.124	.132	.12	2, 12–14
31	179	1973	.160	.168	.15	2, 12–14
			D. Mature Women			
32	103	1971	.111	.109	.15	2, 13, 14
33	142	1972	.126	.134	.12	2, 12–14
34	158	1971	.14	.17	.15	2, 12–14

Note:

Lines 2, 8. Column 4 is the mean of 3 estimates.

Lines 10, 15. Column 4 is the mean of 4 estimates.

Lines 12, 18, 19, 25. Column 4 is the mean of 2 estimates.

Line 15. Column 6 is the mean of bounds for 1967–71 and 1973.

Table 9.6 Estimates of the Mean Wage Gap from Other Sources

Line No. (1)	Study No. (2)	Year (3)	Gap Estimates: Unadj. (4)	Gap Estimates: Adj. (5)	Bounds (6)	Adjustments (7)
1	43	1967–72	.116	.101/.111	.12	6, 7a, 11–13
2	64	1967–72	.160	.085	.12	7a, 11, 12, 14
3	65	1967–72	.173	.108	.12	7a, 11, 12
4	71	1967–72	.119	.124/.134	.12	6, 7a, 11, 12
5	12	1977	.053	.131	.17	2, 7b
6	20,21	1977	.102	.162	.17	7b, 8, 14
7	116	1978	.13	.14	.17	2, 12–14

Source:

Lines 1–4. U.S. Bureau of Labor Statistics: *Employer Expenditures for Employee Compensation* (EEEC) surveys. In these surveys the observations are for establishments rather than individual workers.

Lines 5–6. A sample of 95 large establishments in 13 large SMSAs appearing in both the Bureau of Labor Statistics EEEC surveys and their *Area Wage Surveys*.

Line 7. Rand *Health Insurance Study*.

Note:

Line 4. Figure in column 4 is the mean of 2 estimates.

Line 7. The survey covered only 6 locations (cities or counties). No adjustment was made for this coverage restriction.

standard deviation is 0.013. Thus these studies suggest that I may have set the upper bounds a bit too high.

8. Summary of Estimates

In the preceding pages of this chapter I have set a tentative upper bound on the overall mean wage gap for each of the years 1967–79, a period that covers almost all of the years for which Micro, OLS, CS wage gap estimates are available. In fixing these bounds I have given preference to estimates (1) based on CPS data and (2) derived from wage equations with long lists of right-hand variables including interactions of union status with other right-hand variables. Furthermore, I have taken account of the information provided by several studies on date to date changes in the mean wage gap.

As a last check on these upper bounds I have sorted the adjusted gap estimates in tables 9.1–9.6 by year instead of data source, and for each year I have calculated the mean, standard deviation, and range. In making these calculations I have not excluded any of the estimates for 1967–79 reported in these tables and have given equal weight to each of the estimates. The results of these calculations appear in table 9.7. Column 3 reports the number of estimates, column 4 the mean, column 5 the standard deviation, column 6 the range of the adjusted estimates, and column 7 the upper bound I have tentatively fixed for each year.

Table 9.7 Adjusted Mean Wage Gap Estimates by Year

Line No. (1)	Year (2)	No. of Ests. (3)	Mean Est. (4)	Est. S.D. (5)	Est. Range (6)	Tent. Bound (7)	Period Mean (8)
1	1967	20	.14	.04	.09/.27	.11	
2	1968	4	.15	.07	.03/.22	.11	
3	1969	20	.13	.04	.05/.22	.11	
4	1970	8	.13	.05	.06/.19	.12	
5	1971	20	.14	.05	.02/.22	.15	
6	1972	7	.14	.03	.09/.20	.12	
7	1973	24	.15	.03	.10/.21	.15	
8	1974	7	.15	.04	.09/.20	.14	
9	1975	11	.17	.04	.07/.22	.16	
10	1976	7	.16	.05	.08/.24	.18	
11	1977	10	.19	.04	.13/.27	.17	
12	1978	7	.17	.04	.09/.20	.17	
13	1979	3	.13	.03	.11/.17	.13	
14	1967–79	148	.15	—	—	.14	
15	1967–72	4	.11	.02	.08/.13	.12	.14
16	1967–74	2	.18	—	.16/.21	.13	.14
17	1967–77	1	.21	—	—	.14	.15
18	1968–78	1	.15	—	—	.14	.15
19	1970–71	3	.17	—	.07/.22	.14	.14
20	1973–75	3	.16	—	.12/.20	.15	.16
21	1973–76	1	.15	—	—	.16	.16
22	1973–78	1	.23	—	—	.16	.17
23	1976–78	1	.17	—	—	.16	.17

Note:

Line 14 is the 1967–79 mean (or total in column 3) of the yearly figures on lines 1–13.

Lines 15–23. The estimates in columns 4, 5, and 6 come from wage equations fitted to pooled data for several years without union status*year interactions. (There is no duplication between lines 1–13 and lines 15–23.) The figures in column 7 are appropriately dated means of the yearly bounds on lines 1–13. The figures in column 8 similarly are appropriately dated means of yearly means given in column 4 of lines 1–13.

Refer especially to line 14 which shows unweighted means across lines 1–13 of the 13 yearly figures for 1967–79. Notice that the 13-year mean of the adjusted estimates in column 4 is only 0.01 above the corresponding mean of the bounds in column 7. (That this column 4 mean 0.15 is a bit higher than that 0.14 for column 7 is not surprising given that in deriving column 7 from the underlying adjusted estimates I gave much greater weight to some estimates than to others.) Furthermore, the simple correlation across lines 1–13 between columns 4 and 7 is 0.76.

In my judgment tables 9.1–9.7 strongly support my estimates of the mean wage gap in column 7 of table 9.7. Hence I now drop the adjective "tentative" I have used to describe these figures. I have much more confidence, of course, in their 1967–79 average 0.14 than in the individual yearly figures which range from 0.11 to 0.18.

I describe these estimates of the U.S. mean wage gap, all derived from Micro, OLS, CS wage equations, as "upper bounds" because I believe that in general such estimates suffer from upward bias resulting from the omission of right-hand variables correlated with the union status variable. I do not rule out the possibility that during 1967–79 the U.S. mean wage gap averaged as high as 0.14, but I suspect that the average was lower.

10 Unions and Relative Wage Inequality

1. Introduction

Up to this point the focus of this book has been on the question: In the United States in recent years has there been a difference—a union/nonunion gap—between the wage a worker could expect to be paid if he were unionized and the corresponding wage if he were nonunion, and, if so, how large was the average gap and how did the gap vary across the U.S. work force by characteristics of workers and their employments? In this question the wage contrast is between unionized and nonunion status in the presence of the existing unionism.

The following question sounds much like the one just asked, but it is really quite different: Has there also been a difference—a "presence/absence" gain—between the wage a worker could expect to be paid in the presence of the existing unionism and the corresponding wage in the absence of monopoly unionism and, if so, how large was the average gain separately by union status, and how did the gains by union status vary across the work force? The contrast in this second question is between the presence of the existing unionism and the absence of monopoly unionism. In section 5 of Chapter 2, I argued that estimates of such presence/absence gains could not be derived from the cross-section wage equations from which I derived the union/nonunion wage gap estimates presented in Chapters 3–9.

The focus now shifts to questions about the effects of unionism on wage inequality. For example, has unionism raised the relative wage position of black workers, and, if so, by how much? As it now stands, this question is ambiguous because it is unclear whether the effect of unionism is a gap effect in which the contrast is by union status in the presence of unionism or a gain effect in which the comparison is between the existing unionism and its "absence."

First consider the gap effect of unionism on the black/white wage differential. Define the wage gap by color in a manner similar to that for the union/nonunion wage gap: the excess of the wage a worker could expect to receive if he were black over the corresponding wage if he were white. This color gap may depend on union status. Hence the question: Is the color gap for a worker in unionized status typically different from the corresponding gap if he were nonunion? This is a union/nonunion gap question, and estimates of the union/nonunion difference in the color gap may be derived from the same wage equations from which I have obtained estimates of the union/nonunion wage gap M. Indeed, in section 6 of Chapter 2—see especially equation (2.21)—I showed that the union/nonunion difference in the color gap is exactly the same as the color difference in the union/nonunion wage gap:

$$C_u - C_n = M_1 - M_2, \qquad (2.21)$$

where C_u is the black/white or color gap for unionized status, C_n that for nonunion status, M_1 is the union/nonunion gap for black color, and M_2 that for white color. Such differences in the union/nonunion wage gap are the subject of Chapter 7. In particular, in section 2 of Chapter 7, I estimated that the union/nonunion wage gap differed little by sex and in section 3 that the union/nonunion wage gap for black color was perhaps 0.05–0.10 higher than for white color except that studies using *Current Population Survey* (CPS) data showed a negligible black/white difference.

Chapter 7, however, has nothing whatsoever to say about the relative wage *gains*—in the presence of unionism versus "absence" of unionism sense—of black workers or of female workers. Denote by W_1^q and W_2^q the mean wages of black and white workers, respectively, in the presence of unionism, and V_1^q and V_2^q the corresponding means in the "absence" of unionism. Then $A_1^q \equiv W_1^q - V_1^q$ and $A_2^q \equiv W_2^q - V_2^q$ are the mean wage gains induced by unionism for black and white workers, and $F \equiv A_1^q - A_2^q$ is the excess of the black gain over the white gain. Since wages V in the absence of unionism cannot be observed directly in recent data nor inferred from cross-section wage equations fitted to these data, the A's and hence F cannot be estimated from these data.

Yet three recent studies purport to estimate black/white or female/male differences in relative wage gains. These studies are the subject of the next section. I show there that the "gain" estimates consist only of a gap component that can be estimated and omit a gain component of unknown size and sign.

Now consider a second and rather different question regarding the effect of unionism on wage inequality: What has been the effect of unionism on the dispersion of relative wages among individual workers? Here, too, it is important to distinguish sharply between the *gap* effect of unionism in which the contrast is between unionized status and nonunion status in the presence of the existing unionism and the *gain* effect in which the contrast is between the existing unionism and its "absence."

Let wage dispersion be measured by the standard deviation σ or variance σ^2 of wages and denote by $\sigma(W_u)$ and $\sigma(W_n)$ the standard deviations, across all workers irrespective of their actual union status, of W_u and W_n, respectively, where W_n is the wage (in natural logarithmic units) a worker would be paid if he were nonunion and W_u the corresponding wage if he were unionized. Then $g \equiv \sigma(W_u) - \sigma(W_n)$ is the union/nonunion wage standard deviation gap and $G \equiv \sigma^2(W_u) - \sigma^2(W_n)$ is the corresponding wage variance gap.

In actual cross-section data at any specified date, W_u can be observed only for unionized workers and W_n only for nonunion. Therefore, $\sigma(W_u)$ and $\sigma(W_n)$ cannot be calculated directly from these wage data. In section 6 of Chapter 2, I showed, however, that these standard deviations can be estimated by fitting wage equations separately by actual union status to cross-section data for individual workers. (If the wage equations are fitted by ordinary least squares, however, the resulting estimates of g and G, like those for the union/nonunion wage gap M, probably are somewhat tainted by union status selection bias [see Chapter 2, section 6].) Many of the wage studies surveyed in this book reported cross-section wage equation pairs fitted separately by actual union status. Yet none reported either estimates of g or G or the underlying data in enough detail that I could calculate the estimates from their data.

Now consider the *gain* counterparts of the *gap* concepts g and G. Denote by $\sigma(W)^a$ the standard deviation of actual wages (W_u for union workers and W_n for nonunion) across all workers in the presence of the actual unionism and by $\sigma(V)^a$ the corresponding standard deviation in the absence of monopoly unionism. Then the counterpart of g is $h \equiv \sigma(W)^a - \sigma(V)^a$, the "presence/absence" or gain effect of unionism on the standard deviation of wages, and the counterpart of G is $H \equiv \sigma^2(W)^a - \sigma^2(V)^a$, the gain effect on wage variance. There is, of course, no problem in estimating $\sigma(W)^a$; one needs only the cross-section data on actual wages W. However, as I have stated in Chapter 2, section 5, wages V in the "absence" of unionism cannot be observed directly and cannot be inferred from wage equations fitted to recent data in the presence of unionism. Yet several recent papers report numbers that are described as estimates in the gain sense of the impact of unionism on wage dispersion. I review these papers in section 3.

2. Unions and Relative Wage Gains by Color and Sex

In Chapter 2 (see eqq. [2.22]–[2.25] and associated text) I showed that the excess $F \equiv A_1^a - A_2^a$ of the black mean relative wage gain over that for white can be decomposed into two components as follows:

$$F \equiv A_1^a - A_2^a = F^* + (\bar{A}_{1n} - \bar{A}_{2n}); \\ F^* \equiv \overline{U}_1 M_1^u - \overline{U}_2 M_2^u; \qquad (2.25)$$

where $\overline{U}_1$ and $\overline{U}_2$ are the fractions unionized of black and white workers, respectively, M_1^u and M_2^u are the mean union/nonunion wage gaps averaged over unionized workers, and $\bar{A}_{1n}$ and $\bar{A}_{2n}$ are the mean wage gains averaged over all workers and evaluated at nonunion status. (Recall that for each worker A_n would be his wage gain if he were in nonunion status.) F^*, the gap component of F, involves only data in the presence of unionism and can be estimated from cross-section wage equations fitted to such data. $\bar{A}_{1n} - \bar{A}_{2n}$, the gain component of F, however, cannot be estimated from these wage equations even with respect to sign. Hence F and F^* may differ even in sign.

Indeed, $F \equiv A_1^a - A_2^a$ and $F^* \equiv \overline{U}_1 M_1^u - \overline{U}_2 M_2^u$ are rather different concepts. $A_j^a \equiv W_j^a - V_j^a (j = 1,2)$ is the excess of the mean wage W_j^a in the presence of unionism over the corresponding mean wage V_j^a in the "absence" of unionism for color group j. On the other hand, $\overline{U}_j M_j^u$ is the excess of the mean wage W_j^a in the presence of unionism over the mean wage $\overline{W}_{jn}$ also in the presence of unionism evaluated at nonunion status (see Chapter 2, especially eq. [2.23] and associated text). I think that it is very unlikely that $V_j^a = \overline{W}_{jn}$.

Ashenfelter [16] was the first to state the decomposition (2.25) of F into its gain component $\bar{A}_{1n} - \bar{A}_{2n}$ and corresponding gap component $F^* \equiv \overline{U}_1 M_1^u - \overline{U}_2 M_2^u$. (However, he assumed implicitly that $M_j^u = \overline{M}_j$ where $\overline{M}_j$ is the mean wage gap among all j workers both union and nonunion.) Furthermore, he explicitly recognized that the $\bar{A}_n$'s could not be estimated from the wage equations and underlying data he used to estimate the $\overline{U}_j \overline{M}_j$'s. Accordingly, he set for himself the "more modest task" of estimating only the gap component F^* of F.

Ashenfelter used the 1967 *Survey of Economic Opportunity* data for private urban wage and salary workers to estimate F^* by color (black/white) and sex (female/male). His estimates of F^* were: black/white, 0.02; female/male for white workers, −0.02; female/male for black workers, −0.06. Oaxaca [146] used essentially the same data set to estimate $\overline{U}_1 \overline{M}_1 - \overline{U}_2 \overline{M}_2$ by sex (female/male) for white workers, −0.01; for black workers, −0.06. Leigh [117] based his estimates of $\overline{U}_1 \overline{M}_1 - \overline{U}_2 \overline{M}_2$ by color (black/white) on the 1969 *National Longitudinal Survey* data for male wage and salary workers 48–62 years of age. His estimates by color (black/white) and type of unionism (craft versus industrial) were: craft, −0.02; industrial, 0.04. All three of these authors characterized their estimates of $\overline{U}_1 \overline{M}_1 - \overline{U}_2 \overline{M}_2$ as though they were estimates of $F \equiv A_1^a - A_2^a$.

In my 1963 book [121, pp. 8, 283–84] I presented what I said was an estimate of the gain concept F for the female/male wage differential. In making the estimate I assumed that $M_1^u = M_2^u = \overline{M}$ and that $\bar{A}_{1n} = \bar{A}_{2n}$. I would not now make these assumptions. I also presented figures [121, chapter 9] that purported to be estimates of the effect of unionism in the gain sense on the dispersion of relative wages among 2-digit industries. In calculating these estimates I made assumptions similar to those for the sex differential.

In addition to the studies by Ashenfelter, Oaxaca, and Leigh there are numerous other studies that provide estimates of the union/nonunion wage gap $\overline{M}$ and matching figures for the fraction unionized $\overline{U}$ by sex and by color (see sections 2 and 3 of Chapter 7). The wage gap $\overline{M}$ estimates by sex indicate that in recent years there was a negligible gap difference between males and females, i.e., $\overline{M}_1 \simeq \overline{M}_2 \simeq \overline{M}$. The matching figures for the fraction unionized $\overline{U}$, not shown in Chapter 7, indicate that recently $\overline{U}_2 - \overline{U}_1$ (female = 1, male = 2) did not exceed 0.2. If $\overline{M}_1 = \overline{M}_2 = \overline{M}$ and $\overline{U}_2 - \overline{U}_1 \leq 0.2$, then $\overline{U}_2\overline{M}_2 - \overline{U}_1\overline{M}_1 = (\overline{U}_2 - \overline{U}_1)\overline{M} \leq 0.2\overline{M}$. In Chapter 9 I estimated that $\overline{M}$ for the whole U.S. work force in recent years at most was 0.11–0.18 depending on the date. Hence recently $\overline{U}_2\overline{M}_2 - \overline{U}_1\overline{M}_1$ at most was in the range 0.02–0.04.

The corresponding figures by color (black = 1, white = 2) from the studies surveyed in section 3 of Chapter 7 are: $0 \leq \overline{M}_1 - \overline{M} \leq 0.09$; $0 \leq \overline{M} - \overline{M}_2 \leq 0.01$; $0 \leq \overline{U}_1 - \overline{U} \leq 0.05$; $0 \leq \overline{U} - \overline{U}_2 \leq 0.01$; $\overline{U} \simeq 0.23$; and from Chapter 9 $\overline{M}$ at most was 0.11–0.18 depending on the year. Hence $\overline{U}_1\overline{M}_1 - \overline{U}_2\overline{M}_2$ may have been negligible and at most was 0.04.

3. Unions and Wage Dispersion among Individual Workers

The key paper here is that by Freeman [64] on the effects of unionism on wage dispersion among individual private male wage and salary workers. As his measure of wage dispersion among a specified group of workers—blue-collar workers in manufacturing, e.g.—he used the standard deviation or the variance of the natural logarithm of the wages of the individual workers in the group. In the presence of unionism the overall variance of actual wages is $\sigma^2(W)^a$. Its counterpart in the "absence" of unionism is $\sigma^2(V)^a$. I presume that what Freeman wanted to estimate was either $h = \sigma(W)^a - \sigma(V)^a$ or $H = \sigma^2(W)^a - \sigma^2(V)^a$.

There is no problem, other than that of measurement error, in estimating $\sigma(W)^a$. On the other hand, since wages V in the "absence" of unionism cannot be directly observed in the presence of unionism and cannot be inferred from cross-section wage equations fitted to data in the presence of unionism, $\sigma(V)^a$ cannot be estimated from such data. Therefore what Freeman estimated were not h and H but the rather different concepts h^* and H^* which I discussed in section 6 of Chapter 2 (see especially equations [2.34] and the related text).

Because Freeman erred in calculating his estimates of H^* (at line 1 in his table 9) and did not calculate h^* completely, I set out here in somewhat tedious detail my calculations of h^* and H^* from numbers reported in his paper. His most complete estimates are for private male blue-collar wage and salary workers. For these workers he fitted OLS cross-section wage equations separately by union status and industry group (manufacturing, nonmanufacturing) to pooled data for 1973–75 from the May *Current Population Survey.* The estimates of h^* and H^* derive from these wage equations and the data underlying them.

The dispersion concepts H^* and h^* are defined in equations (2.34) and the associated text of Chapter 2:

$$\begin{aligned} H^* &\equiv \sigma^2(W)^a - \sigma^2(W_n); \\ h^* &\equiv \sigma(W)^a - \sigma(W_n); \end{aligned} \quad (2.34)$$

where $\sigma(W_n)$ is the standard deviation of W_n among all workers.

I estimated $\sigma(W)^a$ from Freeman's numbers with the help of this equation:

$$\sigma^2(W)^a = \overline{U}\sigma^2(W_u)^u + (1 - \overline{U})\sigma^2(W_n)^n + \overline{U}(1 - \overline{U})(W_u^u - W_n^n)^2, \quad (10.1)$$

where $\overline{U}$ is the fraction of workers who are unionized, $\sigma^2(W_u)^u$ is the variance of actual wages W among unionized workers, $\sigma^2(W_n)^n$ the corresponding variance for nonunion workers, W_u^u is the mean actual wage W among unionized workers and W_n^n the similar mean for nonunion workers. Table 10.1 shows the details of the calculations from Freeman's numbers.

The calculation of $\sigma^2(W_n)$ is almost as straightforward. First return to section 6 of Chapter 2 and notice that equations (2.32) and (2.33) and the associated text imply that

$$\begin{aligned} \sigma^2(W_n) = {} & \overline{U}[a_{nx}^2\sigma^2(x)^u + \sigma^2(e_n)^n] + (1 - \overline{U})\sigma^2(W_n)^n \\ & + \overline{U}(1 - \overline{U})(W_u^u - W_n^n - M^u)^2. \end{aligned} \quad (10.2)$$

All of the terms on the right-hand side of (10.2) may be estimated from numbers reported by Freeman. Table 10.2 shows my calculations of the right-hand-side estimates together with the estimates of H^* and h^*.

Table 10.1 Calculation of $\sigma(W)^a$ for Private Male Blue-Collar Wage and Salary Workers, Freeman Data

Estimate of	MFG	Non-MFG	Source in Freeman
$\overline{U}$	.550	.404	Table 1
$\sigma(W_u)^u$	.288	.350	Table 1
$\sigma(W_n)^n$	.398	.451	Table 1
$W_u^u - W_n^n$	.19	.51	Table 9, line 2b note
$\sigma^2(W)^a$	.126	.233	My calculation
$\sigma(W)^a$	.355	.483	My calculation

Table 10.2 Calculation of H^* and h^* for Private Male Blue-Collar Wage and Salary Workers, Freeman Data

Line	Estimate of	MFG	Non-MFG	Source
1	$\overline{U}$	.550	.404	Freeman, table 1
2	$W_u^u - W_n^n$	.19	.51	Freeman, table 9 line 2b note
3	M^u	.12	.32	Freeman, p. 21, but see note below
4	$\overline{U}(1 - \overline{U})(W_u^u - W_n^n - M^u)^2$	.001	.009	My calculation
5	$\sigma(W_n)^n$	.398	.451	Freeman, table 1
6	$(1 - \overline{U})\sigma^2(W_n)^n$	.071	.121	My calculation
7	$\sigma(W_u)^u$	.288	.350	Freeman, table 1
8	$[a^2_{nx}\sigma^2(x)^u + \sigma^2(e_n)^n]^{1/2} - \sigma(W_u)^u$	.088	.082	Freeman, table 4, line 2b
9	Line 7 + line 8	.376	.432	My calculation
10	Square of line 9 × line 1	.078	.075	My calculation
11	$\sigma^2(W_n)$	.150	.205	Sum of lines 4, 6, and 10
12	Square root of line 11	.388	.453	My calculation
13	$\sigma^2(W)^a$	.126	.233	Table 10.1
14	H^* = line 13 − line 11	−.024	.028	My calculation
15	h^* = (Line 13)$^{1/2}$ − line 12	−.033	.030	My calculation

Note: Freeman's figures are for $\overline{M}$, the all-worker mean wage gap, rather than M^u, the mean wage gap among union workers.

The corresponding estimates of H^* by Freeman appear on line 3b of his table 9 where he refers to them as "All male workers" estimates: Manufacturing, −0.040; nonmanufacturing, 0.021. These figures are lower than mine on line 14 of table 10.2 because of an error by Freeman on line 1 of his table 9 where he entered incorrect figures. (He discovered the error after his paper had been published.)

On line 3a of his table 9, Freeman presented a second pair of estimates of H^* that he termed "Comparable workers" estimates. In these "Comparable workers" estimates he assumed that $W_u^u - W_n^n = \overline{M}$. I regard this assumption as unacceptable, and in what follows I ignore the "Comparable workers" estimates.

Turn back to table 10.2. It is simple to combine the separate estimates (of H^* or h^*) for manufacturing and nonmanufacturing into a single estimate for both sectors taken together. Denote the two sectors by subscripts 1 and 2. Then

$$\sigma^2(W)^a = p\sigma_1^2(W)^a + (1-p)\sigma_2^2(W)^a + p(1-p)(W_1^a - W_2^a)^2, \quad (10.3)$$

where p is the fraction of private male blue-collar wage and salary workers employed in manufacturing (subscript 1), and W_i^a $(i = 1{,}2)$ is the mean of actual wages W in sector i. In Freeman's data p was 0.495 (from his table 1) and $W_1^a - W_2^a$ was 0.013 (from computer printouts supplied to me by

Freeman). The estimates of $\sigma_i^2(W)^a$ are on line 13 of table 10.2. When these numbers are inserted into (10.3), the resulting estimate of $\sigma^2(W)^a$ is 0.180 and $\sigma(W)^a$ is 0.424.

Similarly,

$$\sigma^2(W_n) = p\sigma_1^2(W_n) + (1 - p)\sigma_2^2(W_n) + p(1 - p)(\overline{W}_{n1} - \overline{W}_{n2})^2, \quad (10.4)$$

where $\overline{W}_{ni}$ $(i = 1,2)$ is the mean of W_n in sector i over all workers in that sector. From equations (2.23) in Chapter 2 it follows that $\overline{W}_{n1} - \overline{W}_{n2} = (W_1^a - W_2^a) - (\overline{U}_1 M_1^u - \overline{U}_2 M_2^u)$. Hence (10.4) becomes

$$\sigma^2(W_n) = p\sigma_1^2(W_n) + (1 - p)\sigma_2^2(W_n) + p(1 - p)(W_1^a - W_2^a - \overline{U}_1 M_1^u + \overline{U}_2 M_2^u)^2 \quad (10.5)$$

The estimates of $\sigma_i^2(W_n)$ appear on line 11 of table 10.2, p is 0.495, $W_1^a - W_2^a$ is 0.013, the $\overline{U}$'s are on line 1, and the M^u's on line 3 of table 10.2. Hence the overall estimate of $\sigma^2(W_n)$ is 0.180 and of $\sigma(W_n)$ is 0.424. Then the estimate of H^* for both sectors taken together is 0.000 and the corresponding estimate of h^* also is 0.000.

Freeman's treatment of male white-collar workers was far less detailed. In his table 9 he assumed for them that $H^* = h^* = 0$ and that $W^a - \overline{W}_n = \overline{U}M^u = 0$. Let the subscript 1 in equations (10.3)–(10.5) now denote white-collar workers and the subscript 2 blue-collar workers. Then it follows from equations (10.3) and (10.5) and the definition of H^* that:

$$H^* = p(1-p)[(W_1^a - W_2^a)^2 - \{(W_1^a - W_2^a) - (\overline{U}_1 M_1^u - \overline{U}_2 M_2^u)\}^2] + pH_1^* + (1-p)H_2^*, \quad (10.6)$$

where $H_1^* = 0$ and $\overline{U}_1 M_1^u = 0$ by assumption and $H_2^* = 0$ from the preceding paragraph. In the *Current Population Survey* data used by Freeman p was 0.378 (from his table 1 and note to line 5 of table 8), $W_1^a - W_2^a$ was 0.288 (from his table 1, line 5 note of table 8, line 4 note of table 9, and his computer printouts), and $\overline{U}_2 M_2^u = \overline{U_2 M_2}$ was 0.097 (from his table 1 and p. 21). Insert these numbers into (10.6) to obtain $H^* = -0.015$.

In order "to minimize problems of comparability" Freeman's study dealt only with male workers. In equation (10.6) let the subscript 1 denote female workers and 2 male workers, and let p be the fraction of workers who are female. Suppose that Freeman had treated female workers in the same way he treated male white-collar workers, by assuming that $H_1^* = 0$ and $\overline{U}_1 M_1^u = 0$. From the pooled May *Current Population Survey* data for 1973–75 I have estimated that p was 0.420, $W_1^a - W_2^a$ was -0.397, and $\overline{U}_2$ was 0.310. (These three figures include government as well as private workers.) In Chapter 9, I estimated that in 1973–75 $\overline{M}_2$ was 0.15. Hence in (10.6) let $p = 0.420$, $W_1^a - W_2^a = -0.397$, $\overline{U}_2 M_2^u = 0.046$, and $H_2^* = -0.015$. Then $H^* = 0.000$. This figure does not support Freeman's finding that "on net unionism reduces inequality."

In a later paper [67] focused on wage dispersion within establishments, Freeman claims to have presented estimates in the gain sense of the effects of unionism on wage inequality *within* each of nine manufacturing industries in which time rates were the usual method of wage payment. For each industry the estimates covered both sexes and both blue-collar and white-collar workers. The nine industries were paints and varnishes, textile dyeing and finishing, cotton and man-made fiber textiles, wool textiles, industrial chemicals, wood household furniture, miscellaneous plastic products, fabricated structural steel, and nonferrous foundries. His procedures differed only in their details from those of his 1980 paper [64]. (One difference should be mentioned. In [67] he assumed that, in equations [10.1] and [10.2], $W^u_u - W^n_n = \overline{M}$. The likely effect of this assumption is to underestimate H^*.) His estimates of H^* within industry ranged from -0.059 to -0.001 over the nine industries, and the employment-weighted mean of the nine estimates was -0.008.

Denote the nine industries by subscripts 1 to 9. For these nine industries taken together equation (10.6) becomes

$$H^* = \sum_{i=1}^{9} p_i H^*_i + \sigma^2(W^a) - \sigma^2(W^a - \overline{U}M^u), \tag{10.7}$$

where p_i is the fraction of workers employed in industry i, $\sigma^2(W^a)$ is the p-weighted variance of industry mean wages W^a, and $\sigma^2(W^a - \overline{U}M^u)$ is the p-weighted variance across the industries of $W^a - \overline{U}M^u$. From the preceding paragraph $\Sigma p_i H^*_i = -0.008$. However, Freeman does not report the between-industry component, $\sigma^2(W^a) - \sigma^2(W^a - \overline{U}M^u)$ of H^* in (10.7).

Feldman, Lee, and Hoffbeck [61] followed a procedure similar to but differing in one important respect from that of Freeman [64] to estimate the effect of unionism on hospital wage inequality. In particular, their estimates held constant (at their mean values) the right-hand control variable (x's) in their wage equations. When the x's are held constant at their mean values, it follows from equations (2.26) in Chapter 2, equations (10.1) and (10.2), and the definition of H^*, that

$$H^* = \overline{U}[\sigma^2(e_u)^u - \sigma^2(e_n)^n] + \overline{U}(1 - \overline{U})\overline{M}^2 . \tag{10.8}$$

They made separate estimates of the right-hand side of (10.8) for three hospital occupations: nurses, -0.001; health aides, 0.009; and technical workers, 0.000. These estimates, of course, ignore any effects of unionism on *between-x* wage dispersion.

Podgursky [160] estimated frequency distributions of wages (annual earnings in 1969) both in the presence of unionism and also, he claimed, in its "absence" for private full-time year-round blue-collar wage and salary workers. He based his estimates on individual-worker data from the March 1970 *Current Population Survey*. To these data he fitted separate wage equations by actual union status U. I write these equations for present purposes as

$$\hat{W}_i = a_i + a_{ix}x + a_{iy}y; \; i = u \text{ if } U = 1; \; i = n \text{ if } U = 0; \qquad (10.9)$$

where $\hat{W}_i$ is the expected wage conditional on worker and employment characteristics x and fraction unionized y by industry. He assumed without discussion that in the "absence" of unionism the corresponding wage $\hat{V}$ would be equal to $\hat{W}_n$ at $y = 0$. That is, he assumed that

$$\hat{V} = \hat{W}_n(y = 0) = a_n + a_{nx}x. \qquad (10.10)$$

I regard this assumption as incorrect (see section 5 of Chapter 2).

Podgursky calculated frequency distributions of both the actual value of $\hat{W}$ given each worker's union status and the predicted $\hat{W}_n(y = 0)$ over all of the workers covered in his fitting of equations (10.9). He measured wage inequality by the Gini coefficient and, alternatively, by three Atkinson indexes. The two Gini coefficients were the same for the presence of unionism as for its "absence," and the Atkinson indexes were slightly higher for presence than for "absence" of unionism.

Hale and Main [77], Hirsch [89], Hyclak [95, 96, and 97], and Plotnick [159] estimated wage dispersion effects of unionism from wage *dispersion* equations fitted to macro-data. In these equations the left-hand variable was a measure of wage dispersion and the unionism variable on the right-hand side (along with other dispersion-explaining variables) was an extent of unionism (fraction unionized) variable rather than the union status variable U. In Chapter 3, section 3, I showed that when wage (*level*, not *dispersion*) equations are fitted to macro-data, the coefficient of the extent of unionism variable estimates a mixture in uncertain ratio of the union/nonunion wage gap $\overline{M}$ and an "extent of unionism" effect. The same problem arises when wage *dispersion* equations are fitted to macro-data.

Assume that data on wage dispersion and right-hand explanatory variables are available by industry and within industry by union status and for simplicity measure wage dispersion by the variance of wages W in logarithmic units. Let the fitted wage dispersion equation have the following form:

$$\sigma^2(W) = g + g_x x + g^* U^* + GU + r, \qquad (10.11)$$

where $\sigma^2(W)$ is the within-union status and within-industry variance of W, U is the union status dummy variable, U^* is the fraction unionized (mean of U) in the industry, the x's are other right-hand variables such as the mean and variance of schooling by industry and union status, and r is the residual. If the residuals r are well-behaved, the coefficients of (10.11) may be estimated without bias by fitting the equation by ordinary least squares. In particular the fitted coefficient of the union status variable U is an estimate of the within-industry union/nonunion wage *variance* gap G discussed earlier in this chapter and in Chapter 2. Similarly the coefficient of the extent of unionism variable U^* estimates an extent of unionism effect g^* on within-industry wage variance.

Now aggregate (10.11) within industry to obtain:

$$\sigma^2(W)^* = g + g_x x^* + (g^* + G)\, U^* + U^*(1 - U^*)(W_u^* - W_n^*)^2 + r^*, \tag{10.12}$$

where $\sigma^2(W)^*$ is the overall within-industry variance of W, x^* is the industry mean of x, W_u^* the industry mean of W among unionized workers, W_n^* the corresponding mean for nonunion workers, and r^* is the industry mean of r. Even if r is well-behaved in (10.11), there is no assurance that r^* in (10.12) also will be. This is especially likely if the term $U^*(1 - U^*)(W_u^* - W_n^*)^2$ is incorporated into the residual r^*. But even apart from such problems, the estimated coefficient of the extent of unionism variable U^* in (10.12) is an estimate of $g^* + G$, a mixture of the union/nonunion variance gap G and an extent of unionism effect g^*. Furthermore, on the basis of the experiments reported in section 4 of Chapter 3 I strongly suspect that the estimate of $g^* + G$ will be quite sensitive to the specification of right-hand x variables in the dispersion equation, the choice of the extent of unionism variable, and the type of aggregation (industry, locality, occupation, etc.). The aggregation problem discussed in this and the preceding paragraph is not peculiar, of course, to the wage *variance* as the measure of wage dispersion. Similar problems arise with other measures of wage dispersion.

In the Hale and Main paper [77] separate dispersion equations were fitted for the years 1963 and 1967 across 98 Standard Metropolitan Statistical Areas (SMSAs). In both equations the dependent variable was the coefficient of variation of the "adjusted gross income" reported on personal income tax returns (both joint and separate) from grouped data by SMSA of the U.S. Internal Revenue Service. The estimated coefficients of the extent of unionism variable (fraction of production workers in the SMSA or State who were unionized) were: 1963 = − 14.2; 1967 = − 17.0. The 1963 coefficient was 13 percent of the 1963 dependent variable, the 1967 coefficient 14 percent of the 1967 dependent variable.

In the first Hyclak paper [95], the observations were for 87 Standard Metropolitan Statistical Areas (SMSAs). The dependent variable in the wage dispersion equation was either the fraction of families with 1969 family income below the poverty line or the Gini coefficient measured from the 1969 distribution of family income for the SMSA. In the equation in which the Gini coefficient was dependent, the estimated coefficient of the extent of unionism variable U^* was −0.021 (t-ratio was 2.73), which was about 6 percent of the mean Gini coefficient. In his equation with the fraction of families below the poverty line as dependent variable, the U^* coefficient was -0.019 ($t=2.10$).

The observations in the second Hyclak paper [96] also were for SMSAs (77 for all workers, 58 for black workers), and the dependent variable in the wage dispersion equations was the Gini coefficient for the distribution of 1969 annual earnings among individual workers in the SMSA. He fitted dispersion equations separately by sex for all workers and separately for black workers. The estimated U^* coefficients (t-ratios in parentheses) were: all men, -0.038 (3.8); black men, -0.038 (2.9); all women, -0.011 (0.92); black women, 0.036 (1.4). For both "all men" and "black men" Hyclak reported that the elasticity of the Gini coefficient with respect to U^* (evaluated at means) was about -0.06.

In the third Hyclak paper [97] the data were by State and year (1949, 1959, and 1969). Separate equations were fitted for each of the three years. Hyclak used two alternative dependent variables in his dispersion equations: *A*, the Gini coefficient of the distribution of family income by State, and *B*, the percent of families with annual family income below $2,000 in 1949, and $3,000 in 1959 and 1969. The U^* variable was the ratio of union membership to total nonagricultural employment by State. The estimated U^* coefficients were:

Dependent	*1949*	*1959*	*1969*
A	−.116	−.030	−.072
B	−.260	−.114	−.148

The corresponding elasticities of dependent variables with respect to U^* were:

Dependent	*1949*	*1959*	*1969*
A	−.078	...	−.046
B	−.22	...	−.30

The Hirsch paper [89] was more detailed. The observations were for 3-digit *Census of Population* industries with separate equations for the manufacturing and nonmanufacturing sectors. Two alternative measures of wage dispersion among male workers were used: the Gini coefficient of the distribution of 1969 annual earnings, and the variance $\sigma^2(W)^*$ of 1969 log-earnings. He also used two alternative measures of U^*, one (U^*COV) based on U.S. Bureau of Labor Statistics estimates of collective bargaining coverage by industry, and the second (U^*MEM) based on *Current Population Survey* data of union membership by industry. The wage dispersion equation was one of three simultaneous equations fitted by ordinary least squares (OLS), two-stage least squares (2SLS), and three-stage least squares (3SLS). Thus there were 24 different estimates of the U^* coefficient in the wage dispersion equation. Table (10.3) reports these 24 co-

Table 10.3 U^* Coefficients, Hirsch Study [89]

	Dependent Variable[a]					
	$\sigma^2(W)^*$			Gini Coefficient		
U^* Variable	OLS	2SLS	3SLS	OLS	2SLS	3SLS
	Manufacturing					
U^* COV	−.004	−.007	.013	−.043	−.065	−.079
U^* MEM	−.155	−.167	−.147	−.099	−.117	−.150
	Nonmanufacturing					
U^* COV	−.120	−.405	−.552	−.099	−.180	−.239
U^* MEM	−.167	−.468	−.716	−.135	−.268	−.383

[a]Mean of $\sigma^2(W)^*$: manufacturing, 0.532; nonmanufacturing, 0.933. Mean of Gini: manufacturing, 0.322; nonmanufacturing, 0.416

efficients together with the corresponding means of the Gini coefficient and of $\sigma^2(W)^*$.

The ratio of the estimated U^* coefficient to the mean of the dependent dispersion variable ranged from −0.47 to 0.02 among the 12 estimates for manufacturing and from −0.92 to −0.13 for nonmanufacturing. The lower ends of both of these ranges are for 3SLS estimates with the Gini coefficient dependent and U^*MEM as the right-hand extent of unionism variable.

I am very skeptical that unionism in 1969 produced an average within-industry union/nonunion wage dispersion gap nearly half as large as the overall mean within-industry wage dispersion.

Plotnick [159] based his estimates of the effect of unionism on male earnings inequality on annual time series data for the years 1958–64, 1966–77. The observations for each year covered all males in the U.S. work force. In the wage dispersion equations with the fullest set of right-hand variables (reported in his table 1) the dependent variable was an estimate of the variance of the natural logarithm of annual earnings. His right-hand extent of unionism U^* variable was an estimate of the ratio of male union members to the male labor force. The wage dispersion equations were fitted by OLS. In the wage dispersion equation that included U^* (fraction unionized) the estimated coefficient of U^* was −6.48, (t = 2.4), about minus 4.5 times the mean (1.43) of the dependent variable. This is an incredible result. Furthermore, it is not the result of a computing error. Plotnick supplied his time series data to me and I have replicated his coefficient estimate.

It may be the result, at least in part, however, of errors in measuring U^*. The union membership data used by Plotnick are by no means free of measurement problems. Accordingly, I decided to experiment with a new time series on U^* recently prepared by Pencavel and Hartsog [156]. The numerator of the Pencavel-Hartsog series is an estimate of the number of U.S. workers, both male and female, represented by trade unions; the denominator is an estimate of full-time equivalent employment. When this series is substituted for that used by Plotnick, the estimated coefficient for U^* is $+0.48$ with a t-ratio of 0.20.

In summary of this section:

1. Wage dispersion gap estimates cannot be inferred from wage dispersion equations fitted to macro- (aggregated) data.

2. There are fairly strong suggestions in the two papers by Freeman that the union/nonunion wage dispersion gap G or g is considerably negative for male blue-collar workers in manufacturing, i.e., that for these workers unionism has made wage dispersion smaller for unionized status than for nonunion status.

3. None of the 10 studies surveyed in this section has provided estimates of the dispersion gap in either the G or H^* sense for the whole U.S. work force, though both the Freeman [64] and Podgursky [160] studies hint that H^* is close to zero.

4. Nor have any of these studies succeeded in estimating the effects of unionism in the gain (presence/"absence") sense on either the overall wage inequality in the U.S. work force as a whole or in any of its parts.

References

1. Abowd, John M., and Farber, Henry S. "Relative Wages, Union Membership, and Job Queues: Econometric Evidence Based on Panel Data." Mimeographed. Cambridge: Massachusetts Institute of Technology, July 1978.
2. ______. "Job Queues and the Union Status of Workers." *Industrial and Labor Relations Review* 35 (1982):354–67.
3. Adamache, Killard W., and Sloan, Frank A. "Unions and Hospitals: Some Unresolved Issues." *Journal of Health Economics* 1 (1982):81–108.
4. Allen, Steven G. "Work Attendance and Earnings." Mimeographed. Raleigh: North Carolina State University, Department of Economics, November 1978.
5. ______. "Unionized Construction Workers Are More Productive." *Quarterly Journal of Economics* 99 (1984):251–74.
6. ______. "How Much Does Absenteeism Cost?" *Journal of Human Resources* 18 (1983):379–93.
7. ______. "Trade Unions, Absenteeism, and Exit-Voice." *Industrial and Labor Relations Review* 37 (1984):331–45.
8. Alpert, William T. "Unions and Private Wage Supplements." *Journal of Labor Research* 3 (1982):179–99.
9. ______. "Manufacturing Workers Private Wage Supplements: A Simultaneous Equations Approach." *Applied Economics* 15 (1983):363–78.
10. Andrisani, Paul J., and Kohen, Andrew I. "The Effects of Collective Bargaining as Measured for Men in Blue-Collar Jobs." *Monthly Labor Review* 100 (1977):46–49.
11. Antos, Joseph R. "Union Spillovers and Bargaining Strength Effects on White-Collar Pay: Fact or Artifact?" Mimeographed. Washington, D.C.: Bureau of Labor Statistics, March 1982.

12. ______. "Union Effects on White-Collar Compensation." *Industrial and Labor Relations Review* 36 (1983):461–79.

13. Antos, Joseph R.; Chandler, Mark; and Mellow, Wesley. "Sex Differences in Union Membership." *Industrial and Labor Relations Review* 33 (1980):162–69.

14. Antos, Joseph R., and McDonald, Richard J. "A New Strategy for the Analysis of Employee Compensation." Mimeographed. Washington, D.C.: Bureau of Labor Statistics, December 1982.

15. Ashenfelter, Orley. "The Effect of Unionization on Wages in the Public Sector: The Case of Fire Fighters." *Industrial and Labor Relations Review* 24 (1971):191–202.

16. ______. "Racial Discrimination and Trade Unionism." *Journal of Political Economy* 80 (1972):435–64.

17. ______. "Union Relative Wage Effects: New Evidence and a Survey of Their Implications for Wage Inflation." In *Econometric Contributions to Public Policy,* edited by R. Stone and W. Peterson. New York: St. Martin's Press, 1978.

18. Ashenfelter, Orley, and Johnson, George E. "Unionism, Relative Wages, and Labor Quality in U.S. Manufacturing Industries." *International Economic Review* 13 (1972):488–508.

19. Ashenfelter, Orley, and Taussig, Michael K. "Notes on Documentation of 'Alternative Estimates of Union-Nonunion Wage Differentials.'" Mimeographed. Princeton: Princeton University, Industrial Relations Section, May 1971.

20. Atrostic, B. K. "Alternative Compensation Measures: Effects on Estimates of Wage and Compensation Differentials." Mimeographed. Washington, D.C.: Bureau of Labor Statistics, November 1981.

21. ______. "Establishment Size, Aggregation, and Pay Differentials." Mimeographed. Washington, D.C.: Bureau of Labor Statistics, January 1983.

22. ______. "Alternative Pay Measures and Labor Market Differentials." Working Paper no. 127, revised. Mimeographed. Washington, D.C.: Bureau of Labor Statistics, March 1983.

23. Bailey, William R., and Schwenk, Albert E. "Employer Expenditures for Private Retirement and Insurance Plans." *Monthly Labor Review* 95 (1972):15–19.

24. Bartel, Ann, and Lewin, David. "Wages and Unionism in the Public Sector: The Case of Police." *Review of Economics and Statistics* 63 (1981):53–59.

25. Baugh, William H., and Stone, Joe A. "Teachers, Unions, and Wages in the 1970's: Unionism Now Pays." *Industrial and Labor Relations Review* 35 (1982):368–76.

26. Becker, Brian E. "Union Impact on Wages and Fringe Benefits of Hospital Nonprofessionals." *Quarterly Review of Economics and Business* 19 (1979):27–44.
27. Blau, Francine D., and Kahn, Lawrence M. "Job Search and Unionized Employment." *Economic Inquiry* 21 (1983):412–30.
28. Blinder, Alan S. "Wage Discrimination: Reduced Form and Structural Estimates." *Journal of Human Resources* 8 (1973):436–55.
29. Bloch, Farrell E., and Kuskin, Mark S. "Wage Determination in the Union and Nonunion Sectors." *Industrial and Labor Relations Review* 31 (1978):183–92.
30. Borjas, George J. "Job Satisfaction, Wages, and Unions." *Journal of Human Resources* 14 (1979):21–40.
31. Boskin, Michael J. "Unions and Relative Real Wages." *American Economic Review* 62 (1972):466–72.
32. Brown, Charles. "Equalizing Differences in the Labor Market." *Quarterly Journal of Economics* 94 (1980):113–34.
33. Brown, Charles, and Medoff, James. "Trade Unions in the Production Process." *Journal of Political Economy* 86 (1978):355–78.
34. Cain, Glen, G.; Becker, Brian E.; McLaughlin, Catherine G.; and Schwenk, Albert E. "The Effect of Unions on Wages in Hospitals." *Research in Labor Economics* 4 (1981):191-320.
35. Chamberlain, Gary. "On the Use of Panel Data." Mimeographed. Madison: University of Wisconsin, Department of Economics, 1978.
36. ______. "Multivariate Regression Models for Panel Data." *Journal of Econometrics* 18 (1982):5–46.
37. Chambers, Jay G. "The Impact of Collective Bargaining for Teachers on Resource Allocation in Public School Districts." *Journal of Urban Economics* 4 (1977):324–39.
38. Chowdhury, Gopa, and Nickell, Stephen. "Individual Earnings in the U.S.: Another Look at Unionization, Schooling, Sickness, and Unemployment Using Panel Data." Discussion Paper no. 141. Mimeographed. London: London School of Economics, Center for Labour Economics, November 1982.
39. Christensen, Sandra, and Maki, Dennis. "The Wage Effect of Compulsory Union Membership." *Industrial and Labor Relations Review* 36 (1983):230–37.
40. Cohen, Malcolm S. "Sex Differences in Compensation." *Journal of Human Resources* 6 (1971):434–47.
41. Dalton, James A., and Ford, E. J., Jr. "Concentration and Labor Earnings in Manufacturing and Utilities." *Industrial and Labor Relations Review* 31 (1977):45–60.

42. Da Vanzo, Julie, and Hosek, James R. "Does Migration Increase Wage Rates?—An Analysis of Alternative Techniques for Measuring Wage Gains to Migration." Working Draft no. WD-566-2-NICHD. Santa Monica: Rand Corporation, November 1980.
43. Donsimoni, Marie-Paule. "Union Power and the American Labor Movement." *Applied Economics* 13 (1981):449–64.
44. Donsimoni, Marie-Paule, and Shakotko, Robert. "Employment Compensation Packages: Is There a Union Effect?" Discussion Paper no. 113. Mimeographed. New York: Columbia University, Department of Economics, April 1981.
45. Duncan, Greg J. "Nonpecuniary Work Rewards." In *Five Thousand American Families: Patterns of Economic Progress,* vol. 2, edited by James N. Morgan. Ann Arbor: University of Michigan, Institute for Social Research, 1974.
46. ______. "Paths to Economic Well-Being." In *Five Thousand American Families: Patterns of Economic Progress,* vol. 5, edited by Greg J. Duncan and James N. Morgan. Ann Arbor: University of Michigan, Institute for Social Research, 1977.
47. ______. "An Empirical Model of Wage Growth." In *Five Thousand American Families: Patterns of Economic Progress,* vol. 7, edited by Greg J. Duncan and James N. Morgan. Ann Arbor: Institute for Social Research, 1979.
48. Duncan, Greg J., and Stafford, Frank P. "Do Union Members Receive Compensating Wage Differentials?" *American Economic Review* 70 (1980):355–71.
49. Duncan, Gregory M., and Leigh, Duane E. "Wage Determination in the Union and Nonunion Sectors: A Sample Selectivity Approach." *Industrial and Labor Relations Review* 34 (1980):24–34.
50. ______. "The Endogeneity of Union Status: An Empirical Test." Mimeographed. Pullman: Washington State University, Department of Economics, January 1984.
51. Edwards, Linda N., and Edwards, Franklin R. "Public Unions, Local Government Structure, and the Compensation of Municipal Sanitation Workers." *Economic Inquiry* 20 (1982):405–25.
52. Ehrenberg, Ronald G. "Municipal Government Structure, Unionization and the Wages of Fire Fighters." *Industrial and Labor Relations Review* 27 (1973):36–48.
53. ______. "An Economic Analysis of Local Government Employment and Wages." Final Report DL 91-25-73-09-1, Department of Labor, Washington, D.C., 1973, chapter 4.
54. Ehrenberg, Ronald G., and Goldstein, Gerald S. "A Model of Public Sector Wage Determination." *Journal of Urban Economics* 2 (1975):223–45.
55. Ehrenberg, Ronald G., and Schumann, Paul L. "Compensating Wage Differentials for Mandatory Overtime." Working Paper no.

805. Mimeographed. Cambridge, Mass.: National Bureau of Economic Research, November 1981.

56. Ehrenberg, Ronald G.; Sherman, Daniel R.; and Schwarz, Joshua L. "Unions and Productivity in the Public Sector: A Study of Municipal Libraries." *Industrial and Labor Relations Review* 36 (1983):199–213.

57. Farber, Henry S. "Unionism, Labor Turnover, and Wages of Young Men." *Research in Labor Economics* 3 (1980):33–53.

58. ______. "Right-to-Work Laws and the Extent of Unionization." *Journal of Labor Economics* 2 (1984):319–52.

59. ______. "Worker Preferences for Union Representation." *Research in Labor Economics,* Supplement 2 (1983):171–205.

60. Fechter, Alan E., and Thorpe, Charles O., Jr. "Labor Market Discrimination against the Handicapped: An Initial Inquiry." Working Paper no. 3610-1. Mimeographed. Washington, D.C.: Urban Institute, January 1977.

61. Feldman, Roger; Lee, Lung-Fei; and Hoffbeck, Richard. "Hospital Employees' Wages and Labor Union Organization." Final Report, Grant no. 1-R03-HS03649-01, National Center for Health Services Research, OASH, Washington, D.C., November 1980.

62. ______. "An Empirical Study of Irreversible Choices: Unionism and Wages Revisited." Mimeographed. Minneapolis: University of Minnesota, Department of Economics, November 1981.

63. Fottler, Myron D. "The Union Impact on Hospital Wages." *Industrial and Labor Relations Review* 30 (1977):342–55.

64. Freeman, Richard B. "Unionism and the Dispersion of Wages." *Industrial and Labor Relations Review* 34 (1980):3–23.

65. ______. "The Effect of Trade Unionism on Fringe Benefits." *Industrial and Labor Relations Review* 34 (1981):489–509.

66. ______. "Troubled Workers in the Labor Market." Working Paper no. 816. Mimeographed. Cambridge, Mass.: National Bureau of Economic Research, December 1981.

67. ______. "Union Wage Practices and Wage Dispersion within Establishments." *Industrial and Labor Relations Review* 36 (1982):3–21.

68. ______. "Longitudinal Analyses of the Effects of Trade Unions." *Journal of Labor Economics* 2 (1984):1–26.

69. Freeman, Richard B., and Medoff, James L. "New Estimates of Private Sector Unionism in the United States." *Industrial and Labor Relations Review* 32 (1979):143–74.

70. ______. "The Impact of Collective Bargaining: Illusion or Reality." In *U.S. Industrial Relations 1950–1980: A Critical Assessment,* edited by Jack Stieber, Robert B. McKersie, and D. Quinn Mills. Madison, Wis.: Industrial Relations Research Association, 1981.

71. ______. "The Impact of the Percentage Organized on Union and Nonunion Wages." *Review of Economics and Statistics* 63 (1981):561–72.
72. Fuchs, Victor R. *The Service Economy.* New York: Columbia University Press (for NBER), 1968.
73. Gay, Robert S. "The Impact of Unions on Relative Real Wages: New Evidence on Effects within Industries and Threat Effects." Ph.D. dissertation, University of Wisconsin–Madison, 1975.
74. Griliches, Zvi. "Wages of Very Young Men." *Journal of Political Economy* 84 (1976):569–85.
75. ______. "Earnings of Very Young Men." In *Income Distribution and Economic Inequality,* edited by Zvi Griliches, Wilhelm Krelle, Hans-Jürgen Krupp, and Oldrich Kyn. Frankfurt: Campus Verlag, 1978.
76. Gustman, Alan L., and Clement, M. O. "Teachers' Salary Differentials and Equality of Educational Opportunity." *Industrial and Labor Relations Review* 31 (1977):61–70.
77. Hale, Carl W., and Main, Robert. "Size Distributions of Individual Income in United States Standard Metropolitan Statistical Areas—1963 and 1967." *Journal of Regional Science* 17 (1977):255–70.
78. Hall, Robert E. "Prospects for Shifting the Phillips Curve through Manpower Policy." *Brookings Papers* 3 (1971):659–701.
79. ______. "Wages, Income, and Hours of Work in the U.S. Labor Force." In *Income Maintenance and Labor Supply,* edited by Glen G. Cain and Harold W. Watts. Chicago: Markham, 1973.
80. Hamermesh, Daniel S. "White-Collar Unions, Blue-Collar Unions, and Wages in Manufacturing." *Industrial and Labor Relations Review* 24 (1971):159–70.
81. ______. "The Effects of Government Ownership on Union Wages." In *Labor in the Public and Nonprofit Sectors,* edited by Daniel S. Hamermesh. Princeton: Princeton University Press, 1975.
82. ______. "Economic Aspects of Job Satisfaction." In *Essays in Labor Market Analysis: In Memory of Yochanan Peter Comay,* edited by Orley C. Ashenfelter and Wallace E. Oates. New York: Wiley, 1977.
83. Hausman, Jerry A., and Taylor, William E. "Panel Data and Unobservable Individual Effects." *Econometrica* 49 (1981):1377–98.
84. Haworth, C. T., and Rasmussen, D. W. "Human Capital and Inter-Industry Wages in Manufacturing." *Review of Economics and Statistics* 53 (1971):376–80.
85. Haworth, C. T., and Reuther, Carol Jean. "Industrial Concentration and Inter-Industry Wage Determination." *Review of Economics and Statistics* 60 (1978):85–95.

86. Heckman, James J., and Neumann, George R. "Union Wage Differentials and the Decision to Join Unions." Mimeographed. Chicago: University of Chicago, Department of Economics, March 1977.
87. Hendricks, Wallace. "Regulation and Labor Earnings." *Bell Journal of Economics* 8 (1977):483–96.
88. Hirsch, Barry T. "The Interindustry Structure of Earnings and Unionization." Mimeographed. Greensboro: University of North Carolina at Greensboro, Department of Economics, July 1981.
89. ______. "The Inter-Industry Structure of Unionism, Earnings, and Earnings Dispersion." *Industrial and Labor Relations Review* 36 (1982):22–39.
90. Hirsch, Barry T., and Berger, Mark C. "Union Membership Determination and Industry Characteristics." *Southern Economic Journal* 50 (1984):665–79.
91. Hirsch, Werner Z., and Rufolo, Anthony M. "Determinants of Municipal Wages: Some Tests of the Competitive Wage Hypothesis." *Research in Urban Economics* 2 (1982):309–27.
92. ______. "Effects of Prevailing Wage Laws on Municipal Government Wages." *Journal of Urban Economics* 13 (1983):112–26.
93. Hoffman, Saul D. "Discrimination over the Life Cycle: A Longitudinal Analysis of Black-White Experience-Earnings Profiles." Ph.D. dissertation, University of Michigan, 1977.
94. Holzer, Harry J. "Unions and the Labor Market Status of White and Minority Youth." *Industrial and Labor Relations Review* 35 (1982):392–405.
95. Hyclak, Thomas J. "Unionization and Urban Differentials in Income Inequality." *Journal of Economics* 3 (1977):205–8.
96. ______. "The Effect of Unions on Earnings Inequality in Local Labor Markets." *Industrial and Labor Relations Review* 33 (1979):77–84.
97. ______. "Unions and Income Inequality: Some Cross-State Evidence." *Industrial Relations* 19 (1980):212–15.
98. Hyman, David N., and Fearn, Robert M. "The Influence of City Size on Labor Incomes." *Quarterly Review of Economics and Business* 18 (1978):63–73.
99. Ichniowski, Casey. "Economic Effects of the Firefighters' Union." *Industrial and Labor Relations Review* 33 (1980): 198–211.
100. Johnson, George E. "Inter-Metropolitan Wage Differentials in the U.S." In *The Measurement of Labor Cost*, edited by Jack E. Triplett. Chicago: University of Chicago Press (for NBER), 1983.
101. Johnson, George E., and Youmans, Kenwood C. "Union Relative Wage Effects by Age and Education." *Industrial and Labor Relations Review* 24 (1971): 171–79.

102. Johnson, William R. "Racial Wage Discrimination and Industrial Structure." *Bell Journal of Economics* 9 (1978): 70–81.

103. Jones, Ethel B. "Union/Nonunion Differentials: Membership or Coverage?" *Journal of Human Resources* 17 (1982): 276–85.

104. Kahn, Lawrence M. "Union Impact: A Reduced Form Approach." *Review of Economics and Statistics* 59 (1977): 503–7.

105. ______. "Unionism and Relative Wages: Direct and Indirect Effects." *Industrial and Labor Relations Review* 32 (1979): 520–32.

106. Kalachek, Edward, and Raines, Fredric. "The Structure of Wage Differences among Mature Male Workers." *Journal of Human Resources* 11 (1976): 484–506.

107. Kasper, Hirschel. "The Effects of Collective Bargaining on Public School Teachers' Salaries." *Industrial and Labor Relations Review* 24 (1970): 57–72.

108. Katz, Lawrence. "Union Status, Union Wages, and the Free Rider Problem: The Issue of Membership *vs.* Coverage." Mimeographed. Cambridge: Massachusetts Institute of Technology, Department of Economics, July 1983.

109. Kenny, Lawrence W. "Male Wage Rates and Marital Status." Mimeographed. Gainesville: University of Florida, Department of Economics, July 1978.

110. Kiefer, Nicholas M., and Smith, Sharon P. "Union Impact and Wage Discrimination by Region." *Journal of Human Resources* 12 (1977): 521–34.

111. Killingsworth, Mark R. "Union-Nonunion Wage Gaps and Wage Gains: New Estimates from an Industry Cross-Section." *Review of Economics and Statistics* 65 (1983):332–36.

112. Kwoka, John E., Jr. "Monopoly, Plant, and Union Effects on Worker Wages." *Industrial and Labor Relations Review* 36 (1983):251–57.

113. Lazear, Edward. "Age, Experience, and Wage Growth." *American Economic Review* 66 (1976):548–58.

114. Lee, Lung-Fei. "Unionism and Wage Rates: A Simultaneous Equations Model with Qualitative and Limited Dependent Variables." *International Economic Review* 19 (1978):415–33.

115. ______. "Some Approaches to the Correction of Selectivity Bias." *Review of Economic Studies* 49 (1982):355–72.

116. Leibowitz, Arleen. "Fringe Benefits in Employee Compensation." In *The Measurement of Labor Cost*, edited by Jack E. Triplett. Chicago: University of Chicago Press (for NBER), 1983.

117. Leigh, Duane E. "Racial Discrimination and Labor Unions: Evidence from the NLS Sample of Middle-Aged Men." *Journal of Human Resources* 13 (1978):568–77.

118. ______. "An Analysis of the Interrelation between Unions, Race, and Wage and Nonwage Compensation." Final Report under Re-

search and Development Grant no. 91-53-77-06, Employment and Training Administration, Department of Labor, Washington, D.C., April 1978.

119. ______. "Racial Differentials in Union Relative Wage Effects: A Simultaneous Equations Approach." *Journal of Labor Research* 1 (1980):95–114.

120. ______. "Do Union Members Receive Compensating Wage Differentials? Note." *American Economic Review* 71 (1981):1049–55.

121. Lewis, H. Gregg. *Unionism and Relative Wages in the United States.* Chicago: University of Chicago Press, 1963.

122. ______. "Union Relative Wage Effects: A Survey of Macro Estimates." *Journal of Labor Economics* 1 (1983):1–27.

123. Lillard, Lee A., and Willis, Robert J. "Dynamic Aspects of Earnings Mobility." *Econometrica* 46 (1978):985–1012.

124. Link, Charles R., and Settle, Russell F. "Hospitals as Monopsonists in the Market for Professional Nurses." Mimeographed. Newark: University of Delaware, Department of Economics, 1977.

125. Linneman, Peter. "The Economic Impacts of Minimum Wage Laws: A New Look at an Old Question." *Journal of Political Economy* 90 (1982):443–69.

126. Long, James E., and Link, Albert N. "The Impact of Market Structure on Wages, Fringe Benefits, and Turnover." *Industrial and Labor Relations Review* 36 (1983):239–50.

127. Lucas, R. E. B. "Hedonic Wage Equations and Psychic Wages in the Returns to Schooling." *American Economic Review* 67 (1977):549–58.

128. Masters, Stanley H. "An Interindustry Analysis of Wages and Plant Size." *Review of Economics and Statistics* 51 (1969):341–45.

129. McLaughlin, Catherine G. "The Impact of Unions on Hospital Wages." Ph.D. dissertation, University of Wisconsin–Madison, 1980.

130. Medoff, James L. "Layoffs and Alternatives under Trade Unions in U.S. Manufacturing." *American Economic Review* 69 (1979):380–95.

131. Mellow, Wesley. "Unionism and Wages: A Longitudinal Analysis." *Review of Economics and Statistics* 63 (1981):43–52.

132. ______. "Employer Size and Wages." *Review of Economics and Statistics* 64 (1982):495–501.

133. ______. "Employer Size, Unionism, and Wages." *Research in Labor Economics,* Supplement 2 (1983):253–82.

134. Mellow, Wesley, and Sider, Hal. "Accuracy of Response in Labor Market Surveys: Evidence and Implications." *Journal of Labor Economics* 1 (1983):331–44.

135. Miller, Frederick H., Jr. "Wages and Establishment Size." Ph.D. dissertation, University of Chicago, 1982.

136. Mincer, Jacob. "Union Effects: Wages, Turnover, and Job Training." *Research in Labor Economics,* Supplement 2 (1983):217–52.

137. Mincer, Jacob, and Leighton, Linda. "The Effects of Minimum Wages on Human Capital Formation." In *The Economics of Legal Minimum Wages,* edited by Simon Rottenberg. Washington, D.C.: American Enterprise Institute for Public Policy Research, 1981.

138. Mishel, Lawrence R. "The Structural Determinants of Union Bargaining Power." Ph.D. dissertation, University of Wisconsin-Madison, 1982.

139. Mitchell, Daniel J. B. "Some Empirical Observations of Relevance to the Analysis of Union Wage Determination." *Journal of Labor Research* 1 (1980):193–215.

140. Mixon, J. Wilson, Jr. "Earnings Differentials in U.S. Manufacturing, 1972." *Quarterly Review of Economics and Business* 18 (1978):75–82.

141. Moore, William J. "Membership and Wage Impact of Right-to-Work Laws." *Journal of Labor Research* 1 (1980):349–68.

142. Moore, William, J.; Pearce, Douglas K.; and Wilson, R. Mark. "The Regulation of Occupations and Earnings of Women." *Journal of Human Resources* 16 (1981):366–83.

143. Moore, William J., and Raisian, John. "Cyclical Sensitivity of Union/Nonunion Relative Wage Effects." *Journal of Labor Research* 1 (1980):115–32.

144. ______. "Unionism and Wage Rates in the Public and Private Sectors: A Comparative Time Series Analysis." Mimeographed. Washington, D.C.: Bureau of Labor Statistics, October 1981.

145. ______. "The Level and Growth of Union/Nonunion Relative Wage Effects, 1967–77." *Journal of Labor Research* 4 (1983):65–79.

146. Oaxaca, Ronald. "Male-Female Wage Differentials in Urban Labor Markets." *International Economic Review* 14 (1973):693–709.

147. ______. "Estimation of Union/Nonunion Wage Differentials within Occupational/Regional Subgroups." *Journal of Human Resources* 10 (1975):529–37.

148. Olsen, Randall J. "Comment on 'The Effects of Unions on Earnings and Earnings on Unions: A Mixed Logit Approach.'" *International Economic Review* 19 (1978):259–61.

149. ______. "A Least Squares Correction for Selectivity Bias." *Econometrica* 48 (1980):1815–20.

150. Olson, Craig A. "An Analysis of Wage Differentials Received by Workers on Dangerous Jobs." *Journal of Human Resources* 16 (1981):167–85.

151. Pashigian, B. Peter. "Has Occupational Licensing Reduced Geographical Mobility and Raised Earnings?" In *Occupational Licensure and Regulation,* edited by Simon Rottenberg. Washington,

D.C.: American Enterprise Institute for Public Policy Research, 1980.

152. Pearce, James E. "Trade Unionism, Implicit Contracting, and the Response to Demand Variation in U.S. Manufacturing." Research Paper no. 8003. Mimeographed. Dallas: Federal Reserve Bank of Dallas, April 1980.

153. ______. "Unionism and the Cyclical Behavior of the Labor Market in U.S. Manufacturing." *Review of Economics and Statistics* 65 (1983):450–58.

154. Pencavel, John H. *An Analysis of the Quit Rate in American Manufacturing Industry.* Princeton: Princeton University, Industrial Relations Section, 1970.

155. ______. "Wages, Specific Training, and Labor Turnover in U.S. Manufacturing Industries." *International Economic Review* 13 (1972):53–64.

156. Pencavel, John H., and Hartsog, Catherine E. "A Reconsideration of the Effects of Unionism on Relative Wages and Employment in the United States, 1920–80." *Journal of Labor Economics* 2 (1984):193–232.

157. Perloff, Jeffrey M., and Sickles, Robin C. "FIML Estimation of Union Wage, Hours, and Earnings Differentials in the Construction Industry: A Nonlinear Limited Dependent Variable Approach." Mimeographed. Berkeley: University of California; and Philadelphia: University of Pennsylvania, May 1983.

158. Pfeffer, Jeffrey, and Ross, Jerry. "Unionization and Female Wage and Status Achievement." *Industrial Relations* 20 (1981):179–85.

159. Plotnick, Robert D. "Trends in Male Earnings Inequality." *Southern Economic Journal* 48 (1982):724–32.

160. Podgursky, Michael J. "Trade Unions and Income Inequality." Ph.D. dissertation, University of Wisconsin–Madison, 1980.

161. Polachek, Solomon W. "Unionization of the White-Collar Worker." Mimeographed. Chapel Hill: University of North Carolina, Department of Economics, October 1981.

162. Polzin, Paul E. "State and Regional Wage Differences." *Southern Economic Journal* 38 (1972):371–78.

163. Potthoff, Richard F. "A Study of the Determinants of Geographic Earnings Differentials." Mimeographed. Greensboro, N.C.: Burlington Industries, Operations Research Department, August 1977.

164. Raimon, Robert L., and Stoikov, Vladimir. "The Effect of Blue-Collar Unionism on White-Collar Earnings." *Industrial and Labor Relations Review* 22 (1969):358–74.

165. Raisian, John. "Skill Acquisition and Associated Cyclic Variability in Hours, Weeks, and Wages." Mimeographed. Houston: University of Houston, Department of Economics, July 1979.

166. ______. "Cyclic Patterns in Weeks and Wages." *Economic Inquiry* 17 (1979):475–95.

167. ______. "Contracts, Tenure, and Cyclical Variability in Wages and Hours." Mimeographed. Washington, D.C.: Bureau of Labor Statistics, April 1981.

168. ______. "Contracts, Job Experience, and Cyclical Labor Market Adjustments." *Journal of Labor Economics* 1 (1983):152–70.

169. ______. "Union Dues and Wage Premiums." *Journal of Labor Research* 4 (1983):1–18.

170. Raisian, John, and Donovan, Elaine. "Patterns of Real Wage Growth 1967–77: Who Has Prospered?" Working Paper no. 104. Washington, D.C.: Bureau of Labor Statistics, November 1980.

171. Rapping, Leonard A. "Monopoly Rents, Wage Rates, and Union Wage Effectiveness." *Quarterly Review of Economics and Business* 7 (1967):31–47.

172. Roback, Jennifer. "The Value of Local Amenities or the Price of Sunshine." Mimeographed. New Haven: Yale University, Department of Economics, January 1980.

173. ______. "Wages, Rents, and the Quality of Life." *Journal of Political Economy* 90 (1982):1257–78.

174. Rosen, Sherwin. "On the Interindustry Wage and Hours Structure." *Journal of Political Economy* 77 (1969):249–73.

175. ______. "Trade Union Power, Threat Effects, and the Extent of Organization." *Review of Economic Studies* 36 (1969):185–96.

176. ______. "Unionism and the Occupational Wage Structure in the United States." *International Economic Review* 11 (1970):269–86.

177. Ryscavage, Paul M. "Measuring Union-Nonunion Earnings Differences." *Monthly Labor Review* 97 (1974):3–9.

178. Sahling, Leonard G., and Smith, Sharon P. "Regional Wage Differentials: Has the South Risen Again?" *Review of Economics and Statistics* 65 (1983):131–35.

179. Sandell, Steven H., and Shapiro, David. "Work Expectations, Human Capital Accumulation, and the Wages of Young Women." *Journal of Human Resources* 15 (1980):335–53.

180. Schmidt, Peter. "Estimation of a Simultaneous Equations Model with Jointly Dependent Continuous and Qualitative Variables: The Union-Earnings Question Revisited." *International Economic Review* 19 (1978):453–65.

181. Schmidt, Peter, and Strauss, Robert P. "The Effect of Unions on Earnings and Earnings on Unions: A Mixed Logit Approach." *International Economic Review* 17 (1976):204–12.

182. Shapiro, David. "Relative Wage Effects of Unions in the Public and Private Sectors." *Industrial and Labor Relation Review* 31 (1978):193–203.

183. Sloan, Frank A., and Elnicki, Richard A. "Determinants of Professional Nurses Wages." *Research in Health Economics* 1 (1979):217–54.
184. Smith, D. Alton. "Government Employment and Black/White Relative Wages." *Journal of Human Resources* 15 (1980):77–86.
185. Smith, Robert S. "Compensating Wage Differentials and Hazardous Work." Technical Analysis Series Paper no. 5. Washington, D.C.: Department of Labor, Office of Evaluation, 1973.
186. Smith, Sharon P. "Are Postal Workers Over- or Underpaid?" *Industrial Relations* 15 (1976):168–76.
187. ______. "Government Wage Differentials by Sex." *Journal of Human Resources* 11 (1976):185–99.
188. ______. *Equal Pay in the Public Sector: Fact or Fantasy.* Princeton: Princeton University, Industrial Relations Section, 1977.
189. ______. "Government Wage Differentials." *Journal of Urban Economics* 4 (1977):248–71.
190. Smith, V. Kerry. "The Role of Site and Job Characteristics in Hedonic Wage Models." *Journal of Urban Economics* 13 (1983):296–321.
191. Solnick, Loren M. "Unionism and Fringe Benefit Expenditures." *Industrial Relations* 17 (1978):102–7.
192. Stafford, Frank P. "Concentration and Labor Earnings: Comment." *American Economic Review* 58 (1968):174–81.
193. Thaler, Richard, and Rosen, Sherwin. "The Value of Saving a Life: Evidence from the Labor Market." In *Household Production and Consumption,* edited by Nestor E. Terleckyj. New York: National Bureau of Economic Research, 1975.
194. Throop, Adrian W. "The Union-Nonunion Wage Differential and Cost-Push Inflation." *American Economic Review* 58 (1968):79–99.
195. Victor, Richard B. "Municipal Unions, Wages and Employment." Mimeographed. Santa Monica: Rand Corporation, November 1979.
196. Viscusi, W. Kip. "Wealth Effects and Earnings Premiums for Job Hazards." *Review of Economics and Statistics* 60 (1978):408–16.
197. ______. "Union, Labor Market Structure, and the Labor Market Implications of the Quality of Work." *Journal of Labor Research* 1 (1980):175–92.
198. Weiss, Leonard W. "Concentration and Labor Earnings." *American Economic Review* 56 (1966):96–117.
199. Wessels, Walter J. "Economic Effects of Right to Work Laws." *Journal of Labor Research* 2 (1981):55–75.
200. ______. "Wages, Unionization, Strike Frequency, and Union Political Power: A Simultaneous Equations Model." Mimeographed.

Raleigh: North Carolina State University, Department of Economics, 1981.

201. White, Halbert. "Consequences and Detection of Misspecified Nonlinear Regression Models." *Journal of the American Statistical Association* 76 (1981):419–33.

202. Woodbury, Stephen A. "Substitution between Wage and Nonwage Benefits." *American Economic Review* 73 (1983):166–82.

Author [References] Index

Note: Bracketed numbers following author names refer to numbered references beginning at page 203.

Subject Index